CW00926101

Harm Reduction Psychotherapy

Marlatt et al . Harm Reduction: Pragmatic Strategies
1998. for Managing High Risk Behaviour.

Harm Reduction Psychotherapy

A New Treatment for Drug
and Alcohol Problems

With Forward By Alan Marlatt

Edited By

ANDREW TATARSKY

JASON ARONSON INC.
Northvale, New Jersey
London

This book was set in 11 pt. Bookman by Alabama Book Composition of Deatsville, AL and printed and bound by Book-Mart Press, Inc. of North Bergen, NJ.

Library of Congress Cataloging-in-Publication Data

Harm reduction : the new paradigm for treating drug and alcohol problems / edited by Andrew Tatarsky.
     p. cm.
  Includes bibliographial references and index.
  ISBN 0-7657-0352-1
    1. Drug abuse—Treatment. 2. Alcoholism—Treatment. I. Tatarsky, Andrew.
RC564 .H3643 2001
616.86'06—dc21

                                  2001046079

Printed in the United States of America on acid-free paper. For information and catalog, write to Jason Aronson Inc., 230 Livingston Street, Northvale, NJ 07647-1726, or visit our website: www.aronson.com

I dedicate this book to the countless men and women who have been incarcerated for the unjust crime of possessing or using a substance to alter their states of consciousness. It is my hope that this book will contribute to changing attitudes and laws to reflect greater understanding, compassion, respect, and freedom of choice for these and all of our fellow citizens.

Contents

Foreword

It gives me great pleasure to welcome readers to Andrew Tatarsky's excellent new book on harm reduction therapy. As a long-time friend and colleague, I have had many long and interesting conversations with Dr. Tatarsky, often over dinner in one of Manhattan's inviting restaurants. Many of these conversations were about the topic of this book, and I encouraged him to pursue his plans to put his thoughts into writing. All this has been well worth the wait since we first started our discussions about harm reduction in the mid-1990s. We now have the fruits of his efforts in the form of a ground-breaking volume that provides readers with both an overview of harm reduction therapy and a series of ten "stories" or case studies treated by different therapists that vividly illustrate this treatment approach with a wide variety of clients.

In his Introduction, the author describes harm reduction as a "new paradigm" for treating drug and alcohol problems. Some would say that harm reduction embraces a "paradigm shift" in addiction treatment, as it has moved the field beyond the traditional abstinence-only focus typically associated with the disease model and the ideology of the twelve-step approach. Others may conclude that the move toward harm reduction represents an integration of what Dr. Tatarsky describes as the "basic principles of good clinical practice" into the treatment of addictive behaviors. As such, harm reduction therapy represents a kind of "paradigm redux" in which the basic principles of psychotherapy are reintroduced and amalgamated into the treatment of clients with alcohol or substance abuse problems that often co-occur with other behavioral or psychiatric disorders. As such, the paradigm is shifting from the traditional "top-down" approach in which treatment goals are dictated by the program provider, to a more client-centered approach involving the collaborative development of "shared goals" between therapist and client as an integral component of the therapeutic alliance.

I am often asked by colleagues whether or not I would recommend harm reduction as an approach for a particular client, typically a case with the worst possible prognosis in terms of the severity of substance abuse problems. Would I recommend a nonabstinence goal for someone with severe addiction problems? My response, like that of many therapists whose cases are described in this book, is to shift the issue of goal choice back to the client. I am willing to work with clients, whatever their goal may be, from abstinence to moderation. Clients often change their goals as treatment progresses (or fails to progress), from harm reduction to abstinence or the other way around. Changing addictive behavior is often a complex and complicated process for both client and therapist. What seems to work best is the development of a strong therapeutic alliance, the "right fit" between the client and treatment provider. Without the "right fit," clients are more likely to give up and drop out of treatment. Given the ups and downs of the behavior change process, the role of the harm-reduction therapist is closer to that of a guide, someone who can provide support and guidance throughout the difficult journey. A reliable mountain-climbing guide would never desert a client who fails to make it to the peak or who stumbles and falls on the upward climb. The therapist-guide offers validation and respect for each client, along with a willingness to meet the person where he or she "is at" on the journey and to help them achieve the next step toward their goal.

The case studies presented here represent a broad spectrum of therapeutic "schools," ranging from psychoanalytic to cognitive-behavioral therapy. Despite these theoretical differences, all the therapists share a common set of values associated with harm reduction, including a compassionate, client-centered therapeutic relationship that treats each client as a unique individual. Harm-reduction therapists also adopt a holistic and humanistic approach when it comes to treating dual disorders or co-occuring problems, as illustrated in several chapters. Clients often resort to alcohol or other drugs as an attempt to adapt to or cope with other problems in their lives, as stated in the self-medication hypothesis outlined by Edward Khantzian and other authors represented in this volume. One of the main tenets of harm reduction therapy is *not* to attempt to eliminate a client's main adaptive coping response (including alcohol or drug use as self-medication) until other more effective coping mechanisms are in place. This compassionate principle is highlighted in many of the case studies presented here.

Overall, Andrew Tatarsky does a fine job of introducing each chapter and setting the stage for the case study or "story" that follows. Each case is also followed by his insightful commentary and conclusions that tie together and integrate the various themes he raises in the introductory chapter. The overall final product is well worth the reader's time and effort in understanding how harm reduction works in the "nuts and bolts" of clinical practice. I congratulate Andrew Tatarsky for his creative vision in communicating the heart and soul of harm reduction therapy.

Alan Marlatt, Ph.D.
Addictive Behaviors Research Center
University of Washington, Seattle

Acknowledgments

I've learned many things on the adventure that culminated in the completion of this book. Most important is that the ideas expressed through my writing reflect the gifts given me by the many clients, colleagues, teachers, and family members I have had the honor and pleasure to have known over the course of my life.

Most important to this project have been the many clients who had the courage and generosity to invite me into their lives, sharing their stories with me and teaching me about substance use and misuse and how people change and grow. To you whose names may not be mentioned, I am deeply grateful—you have inspired in me a powerful belief in the strength of the human spirit to overcome all obstacles in its quest for freedom and loving connections.

Many thanks to the psychotherapists who contributed stories about their work that reflect a level of honesty, humility, and sensitivity rarely seen in the psychotherapy literature. Their words touched and inspired me deeply.

For their hard work, generosity, and commitment, I also especially want to thank four psychotherapists who contributed important stories that are not appearing as they did not fit within the ultimate focus of the book. Their stories explore important issues in the field and are each important contributions to the treatment of substance use: Richard Yensen and

Donna Dryer ("Addiction Despair and the Soul: Successful Psychedelic Psychotherapy, A Case Study"), Leon Wurmser ("The Analysis of a Case of Alcoholism, Masochistic Character, and Perversion"), and Elizabeth Zelvin ("Carla: A Case Study").

A special thanks are due to my good friend and treasured colleague Alan Marlatt for introducing me to harm reduction, being a trailblazer in the field, and encouraging me to speak the truth and stand up for what I believe.

For their insightful comments and criticisms that propelled the development of my work, I especially want to acknowledge my dear colleagues and friends Julie Barnes, Michler Bishop, Antonio Burr, Patt Denning, Armand DiMele, Lisa Director, Jeannie Little, Mark Goldenthal, Marc Kern, Robert Lichtman, Deborah Liner, Bart Majoor, Michael Morrison, David Ost, Stanton Peele, Stephen Reisner, Debra Rothschild, Gordon Rovins, Jeremy Safran, Mark Sehl, Michael Varga, Ora Yemini, Arnold Washton, and Alexandra Woods.

I owe a debt of gratitude to the harm reduction community for providing me with a large group of thoughtful, socially committed, loving friends and colleagues who have become a spiritual family to me. You have reminded me that the personal is the political, supported me in "coming out" about harm reduction and in my personal and professional development in more ways than you will ever know. Special thanks are due James Cannon, Allan Clear, Donald Grove, Ernie Drucker, Jason Farrell, Mark Gerse, Don McVinney, Ethan Nadelman, Anna Oliveira, Joyce Rivera, Paula Santiago, and Edith Springer.

For their loving, gentle support for my undertaking the challenge to learn to write I have intense affection and gratitude for my writer friends in the Thursday night Write Club who read and commented on sections of the manuscript, gave crucial suggestions to me, and taught me about the process of writing: Jonathanavery Landerz, Peter Rondinone, Stephen Michaels, Errol Selkirk, Chris Ross, and Evan Lerner.

I am grateful to Michael Moskowitz for initially encouraging me to begin this project—he's a rare psychoanalyst with a clear commitment to seeing the intersection of the personal and political dimensions of human functioning.

I am indebted to Liz Rymland for her help down the stretch

with important editorial suggestions, sweet language, an injection of spirit and manuscript preparation; these gifts raised the overall level of the work.

Most importantly, I am forever indebted to my loving family who have sustained my life. To my mother, Sheindi, who gave me life and planted the seeds that flowered in my discovery of harm reduction; to my fathers, Jack and Dick, who inspired me to think large and believe that anything is possible in love, beauty and truth; to my siblings, Laurie, Miles, and Nikolas, who have been wonderful company in the darkness and light; to my amazing children, Alexandra, for reminding me to stay open to the great mystery of spirit and lightness, helping me to believe in magic, and reminding me of the joys of dance and poetry, and Lucas, for helping me to keep my heart soft and open, enjoy the interplay of strength and vulnerability in all that is, and for filling my life with delight; and to my wife, Dr. Wendy Miller, you have made my life possible by your warm sustaining love, brought the joy to my life, and supported me in uncountable ways that made this book possible.

About the Contributors

Gary Dayton, M.A., is completing academic requirements for the doctorate in clinical psychology at Rutgers University, where he has also been a National Institute of Alcoholism and Alcohol Abuse Predoctoral Fellow. He holds master's degrees in clinical psychology and public administration and is keenly interested in addictions treatment and addictions program development. He is currently developing a construction enterprise that hires and provides work skills development and therapy to veterans who are addicted, homeless, and chronically unemployed at the Veteran's Administration New Jersey Health Care System.

Patt Denning, Ph.D., worked in San Francisco Community Mental Health as a clinician and program director for 16 years. She developed specialties in differential diagnosis, psychopharmacology, psychotherapy with seriously disturbed patients, HIV, and substance use disorders. She has been in full-time private practice since 1993 as the founder of Addiction Treatment Alternatives, a comprehensive assessment, treatment, and training program based on harm reduction. In 1997 Dr. Denning completed the Diplomate-Fellow training in Psychopharmacology and also was named to the Drug Policy Resources Directory for the Media in the area of Dual Diagnosis. She is a certified addiction specialist through the APA College of Professional Psychology. Dr. Denning is a locally well-known speaker on issues of drug policy, chemical dependency treatment, dual diagnosis, HIV, and the organizational development of alternative treatment settings to meet the needs of a drug-using population. She and a colleague have just started a nonprofit treatment and training program, The Harm Reduction Therapy Center, which is in the initial funding and start-up stage. She has just finished a book on the subject, *Practicing Harm Reduction Psychotherapy* (Guilford Press, 2000), and is the author of several articles on the subject. She can be contacted through: www.harmreductiontherapy.org

Valerie R. Frankfeldt, Ph.D., is in private practice in New York City. She is faculty, New York University School of Social Work, Riverdale Seminars in Modern Analytic Psychotherapy, Psychoanalytic Psychotherapy Study Center, Mid-Manhattan Institute for Psychoanalysis; Training Analyst: PPSC, Center for Modern Psychoanalytic Studies, and MMI; supervisor: MMI, RSMP and PPSC; and faculty member, Committee on Psychoanalytic Treatment of Alcoholism and Substance Abuse, PPSC. Dr. Frankfeldt has written papers on alcoholism treatment techniques from the disease concept and psychoanalytic perspectives, including "How to Conduct an Alcoholism-Focused Intake: A Verbatim Illustration," *Social Work Treatment of Alcohol Problems*, Monograph #5 of Treatment Series, Rutgers Center for Alcohol Studies, 1984; "The Compatibility of the Disease Concept with a Psychodynamic Approach in the Treatment of Alcoholism," *Alcoholism Treatment Quarterly*, Spring, 1985; and "Becoming Able to Feel Hate: The Treatment of a Psychotic, Somatizing Patient," *Modern Psychoanalysis*, 15: 63–78, 1990. E-mail: vfrankfeldt@cs.com

Gail Hammer, CSW, is Network Manager and psychotherapist at Corporate Family Network, an employee assistance program, and psychotherapist in private practice in New York City. In 1995, upon completion of her MSW degree at Hunter College School of Social Work, she won the Rebecca Donovan Faculty Award for her professional seminar paper on the use of self in a paradigm shift to a constructivist stance. Before that, Ms. Hammer taught English at the University of Salerno in Italy and then at Columbia University's American Language Program. At the same time, she worked as an independent language and cultural consultant. For years she implemented the English language and cultural component of an overseas banking seminar at Chemical Bank headquarters in Manhattan. She has also spoken at various institutes about cultural differences, most recently at the China Institute in New York.

Edward J. Khantzian, M.D., received his medical degree from the Albany (NY) Medical School. He served residencies in psychiatry at the Massachusetts Mental Health Center and The Cambridge Hospital and completed his psychoanalytic training at the Boston Psychoanalytic Society and Institute in 1973. Dr. Khantzian is now Clinical Professor of Psychiatry, Harvard Medical School, and a founding member of the Department of Psychiatry at The Cambridge Hospital, where he is currently Principal Psychiatrist for Substance Abuse Disorders. He is also the Associate Chief of Psychiatry, Tewksbury Hospital, Tewksbury, Massachusetts. From its inception in 1986 to 1991, Dr. Khantzian was a supervising physician for the National Football League Drug Control Program and now serves as a senior consultant to the NFL/NFL Players Association program of substance abuse. Dr. Khantzian has a private practice in psychiatry and psychoanalysis in Haverall, Massachusetts, is a participant in numerous clinical research studies on substance abuse, and a prolific lecturer and writer on psychiatry, psychoanalysis, and substance abuse problems. He has spent more than 20 years studying psychological factors involved in drug and alcohol abuse. His studies, publications, and teaching have gained him international recognition for his introduction of the now widely accepted "self-medication hypothesis" as one primary motivation for using substances and contributions on self-care deficits in substance use disorders, and the importance of modified techniques in group therapy for substance abusers. Dr. Khantzian has authored several book and numerous scientific articles and book chapters, including: *Addiction as a Human Process* (Aronson, 1999), *Addiction and the Vulnerable Self: Modified Dynamic Group Therapy for Substance Abusers* (Guilford, 1990), and "The self-medication hypothesis of substance use disorders: a reconsideration and recent applications," *The Harvard Review of Psychiatry*, 4: 231–244. E-mail: drejk@aol.com

Jerome D. Levin, Ph.D., is Director of the Alcoholism and Substance Abuse Counselor Training Program at the New School University in Manhattan, where he also serves both on the Humanities Department faculty, and as co-director of the joint masters program in psychology and substance abuse treatment. He is editor of the Library of Substance Abuse and Addiction Treatment book series and adjunct Associate Professor of Social Science at New York University. Dr. Levin has authored eleven books dealing with subjects ranging from the history of ideas, (*Theories of the Self*) to narcissism (*Slings and Arrows: Narcissistic Injury and Its Treatment*), to addiction (*Treatment of Alcoholism and Other Addictions, Couple and Family Therapy of Addiction, Recovery from Alcoholism,* and *Primer of Treating Substance Abusers*), to contemporary affairs (*The Clinton Syndrome*). He maintains a psychotherapy practice in Manhattan and Suffolk County, New York. Tel: 212–989–3976.

Jeannie Little, C.S.W., is a Licensed Clinical Social Worker and Certified Group Psychotherapist in private practice and the Executive Director of the Harm Reduction Therapy Center, a nonprofit agency providing harm reduction therapy for drug and alcohol users with other emotional problems. She specializes in dual diagnosis and in individual and group treatment of substance use disorders. Since 1994 Ms. Little has developed harm reduction treatment services for dually diagnosed clients at the Veterans Administration and in private practice. She has trained hundreds of staff in the areas of dual diagnosis and group treatment and provides ongoing consultation to staff groups in outpatient clinics, outreach and drop-in centers, case management programs, and housing facilities for multidiagnosed clients. She also published "Treatment of Dually Diagnosed Clients," in *The Journal of Psychoactive Drugs* 33(1), January–March 2001. She can be contacted through www.harmreductiontherapy.org.

Frederick Rotgers, Psy.D., holds a doctorate in clinical psychology from Rutgers University and is currently in private practice in Manasquan, New Jersey. He was formerly Assistant Chief Psychologist at the Smithers Treatment Center of St. Luke's–Roosevelt Hospital Center in New York, one of the oldest and most well respected centers for the treatment of drug and alcohol problems; and formerly a faculty member of the Rutgers Center of Alcohol Studies and director of the Center's Program for Addictions Consultation and Treatment. Dr. Rotgers has published widely, is a former member of the editorial board of the Journal of Studies on Alcohol, and is currently an Associate Editor of the Journal of Drug Issues. He is senior editor of the book *Treating Substance Abuse: Theory and Technique* (Guilford Press). E-mail: fred_etoh@yahoo.com.

Mark Sehl, Ph.D., C.S.W., is a psychoanalyst in private practice in New York City. He is a graduate of IPTAR, and a member of the IPA. Dr. Sehl is the director of the Alcoholism Counseling Service, co-director of the Psychotherapy Information Center, and faculty member of the Institute for Modern Psychoanalysis and the Metropolitan Institute. Together with Dr. Andrew Tatarsky Dr. Sehl is also co-editor of the Harm Reduction Psychotherapy and Training Associates. Dr. Sehl's interest in countertransference and the client-therapist relationship is the result of years of psychoanalytic study, insight gained from clients, and experiential training with Dr. Gerald Lucas, director of the Institute for Modern Psychoanalysis, New York City. Dr. Sehl has written in depth about the mutual problems encountered in the therapist-patient relationship in a paper entitled "Stalemates in therapy and the notion of gratification," *Psychoanalytic Review*, 81(2), Summer 1994. He has also published a paper, "Erotic countertransference and clinical social work practice: A national survey of psychotherapists' sexual feelings, attitudes, and responses," *Journal of Analytic Social Work*, 5(4), 1998. Email: drsehl@aol.com or www.marksehl.com.

Barbara C. Wallace, Ph.D., is Associate Professor, Department of Health and Behavior Studies at Teachers College, Columbia University. In addition to maintaining a private practice, Dr.

Wallace consults as the staff psychologist at CREATE Inc. Medically Supervised Outpatient Substance Abuse Treatment Program, located in Harlem in New York City. Dr. Wallace delivers international, national, and regional keynote addresses, papers, and intensive skill-building training workshops. Topics include chemical dependency treatment, relapse prevention, sexual abuse, physical abuse, domestic violence, school- and community-based violence prevention, and diversity training. She has published several books and numerous articles and book chapters in the area of substance use treatment including: *Crack Cocaine: A Practical Treatment Approach for the Chemically Dependent* (New York: Brunner/Mazel Inc., 1991), *Adult Children of Dysfunctional Families: Prevention, Intervention and Treatment for Community Mental Health Promotion* (Westport, CT: Praeger Publishers, 1996) and as editor, *The Chemically Dependent: Phases of Treatment and Recovery* (New York: Brunner/Mazel Inc., 1992). E-mail: bcw3@columbia.edu.

Introduction: Harm Reduction

Tom: Harm Reduction to Moderation
—Andrew Tatarsky

Ideas have different meanings at different moments in history. Ideas that once appeared crazy, dangerous, or incomprehensible later become so much a part of accepted truth that society temporarily forgets the time when these ideas were dormant. New ideas arise in response to current conditions as an attempt to make sense of and help guide us in responding to these conditions. Ideas determine our view of reality, both expanding and limiting our possibilities. As history marches on and conditions change, ideas that were once progressive and useful can become stale, empty, regressive barriers to change. When the dinosaurs of outmoded ideas die, the ideas that have been hiding in the hinterlands creep back into the mainstream to repopulate the field. New ideas once again arise that attempt to explain the limitations of those that came before. This is as true for individual psychology as it is for scientific paradigms.

Within the drug and alcohol treatment field, there have been a number of great ideas that have represented new paradigms for understanding problematic substance use. The application of these ideas to clinical treatment led to revolutionary changes in practice that resulted in dramatic improvements in the care available to people with substance use problems. The addiction-as-disease concept (Jellinek, 1962) challenged the moral model of drug misuse, which blamed the problem on the inappropriate values or immoral character of the user. The disease paradigm opened the way to treatment, rather than punishment, for these problems. The self-medication hypothesis (Khantzian, 1985) pointed out that for many, drug use is a form of self-care that reflects an attempt to cope with painful feelings. This idea highlighted the important dimension of the meaningfulness of drug use and the necessity to recognize and address the underlying issues the user is trying to heal through drug use. Relapse prevention (Marlatt and Gordon, 1985) pointed out that, rather than viewing a return to problematic drug use after a period of abstinence or diminished use as failure, relapse should be seen as a common, natural part of the process of changing behavior, which can be an opportunity for learning that might decrease the possibility of future relapses.

Harm reduction is the most recent of these important new ideas in the substance use treatment field. It heralds a paradigm shift in the way we understand and respond to problematic drug and alcohol use. Harm reduction rejects the presumption that abstinence is the best or only acceptable goal for all problem drug and alcohol users. Harm reduction sees substance use varying on a continuum of harmful consequences to the user and the community. In doing so, harm reduction accepts small, incremental steps in the direction of reduced harm with the goal being to facilitate the greatest reduction in harm for a given person at this point in time. Inherent in this change in the treatment focus is a radical redefinition of the relationship between the client and the clinician, a departure from the paternalistic model associated with more traditional substance use treatment. Harm reduction places respect for the client's strengths and capacity to change as the starting point for developing egalitarian relationships in which clients are encouraged to collaborate in setting up the treatment and choosing goals and strategies that they find useful. This shift in basic assumption is actually consistent with psychodynamic and behavioral models of drug misuse and has many beneficial implications for treatment that will be discussed in this book. A growing group of clinicians, researchers, and public policy makers have recognized that the philosophy of harm reduction has a critically important role to play in our efforts as a field and in the larger society to improve the treatment of people struggling with substance use problems.

This book represents what I have learned in my twenty years in the field of substance use treatment as a psychotherapist, psychologist, supervisor, program director, and teacher. I will share with you some of the experiences that led to my coming to embrace harm reduction as a clinical principle essential to effective treatment of substance misuse. This book presents harm reduction psychotherapy as treatment that works psychotherapeutically, and it examines how and why.

The practice of harm reduction is a needed corrective to the limitations of our current professional and public policy response to drug use problems in this country. I will present my perspective on harm reduction psychotherapy and why I think it has great promise for dramatically improving our success at helping people struggling with substance use problems. Each chapter focuses on a specific aspect or application of harm reduction psychotherapy. The stories in this book demonstrate how harm reduction psychotherapy is rooted in the basic principles of good psychotherapy practice and is consistent with psychodynamic and cognitive-behavioral models of substance misuse. I will discuss how harm reduction psychotherapy specifically lends itself to effectively addressing several important emotional dynamics commonly associated with substance use problems.

Additionally, each chapter contains a detailed story describing the psychotherapeutic process with a client experiencing a substance use problem. All but one of these stories were contributed by other psychotherapists in the field. The stories were chosen to illustrate the particular topic of each chapter, but each is like a multifaceted gem containing much more than I am able to address. As a collection, the stories show the range of treatment approaches that fall under the harm reduction umbrella as I understand it. They differ in theoretical bias, psychotherapist style, and outcome; some result in moderation of substance use and others lead to abstinence. I discuss how I see them each falling within the continuum of treatment linked by the harm reduction principle.

Each story can also be read as a window through which to

view the very unique interplay between client and clinician that characterizes all good psychotherapy. We witness how successful therapeutic relationships are established, how goals emerge as problems are clarified. We discover that the general ingredients for the successful psychotherapy of drug use problems are hard to distinguish from those of effective psychotherapy with other kinds of clients.

The following stories humanize the diversity of faces of individuals with unique drug and alcohol problems, a group of people generally stereotyped by their drug use. They reveal the wide range of people who can develop drug and alcohol problems and enable the reader to identify and empathize with their struggles and respect their efforts to change and grow.

The stories also demystify the work of psychotherapy, bringing the reader into the consulting room like a fly on the wall witnessing some of the actual processes. The stories humanize the psychotherapists as they reveal what the therapists thought and felt about their clients as they worked.

To my mind, the basic principles and ingredients of successful psychotherapy with clients with drug and alcohol problems are essentially the same as those used with other groups of people. The argument can be made that the term "harm reduction" really stands for the re-introduction of basic principles of good clinical practice into an area where they have often been absent. I hope this book will contribute to that effort.

WHY HARM REDUCTION?

I got my first job after completing my internship in clinical psychology as a psychotherapist at the Division of Drug Abuse Research and Treatment at New York Medical College in the fall of 1982. This was a research-oriented "multimodality" outpatient substance abuse treatment clinic in East Harlem, New York City. I had no way of knowing at the time that this job would be the start of a twenty-year journey through the world of substance use treatment that would bring me to embrace harm reduction as the most effective approach to helping the broad spectrum of people with substance use problems.

I had worked with several clients with drug and alcohol problems during my training, but I was by no means an expert. In contrast to the bleak and negative stereotypes about substance-using people with which we have all grown up, I found the clients to be a varied group of very interesting people with many strengths, open to working in psychotherapy to change. My initial experiences working with substance users were so gratifying that I decided to complete my dissertation in the area and specialize in the field.

I had been trained in a psychoanalytically oriented graduate program and began to use a psychodynamic approach with my patients. While I felt that this perspective enabled me to thoroughly understand my clients and the meaning and function of their substance use, the psychodynamic approach offered a limited set of specific clinical interventions to actively help people change their substance-using behavior. Patients didn't stop using and, by that criterion, my approach was not effective. I was introduced to the more active, strategic focus of traditional drug counseling, Alcoholics Anonymous, cognitive-behavioral interventions, and a variety of the developing pharmacological interventions. I began to integrate them with my psychodynamic thinking, which emphasized the multiple meanings that drug use can carry and the importance of the therapeutic relationship in treatment. I gradually developed a more effective integrative approach that blended dynamic, cognitive, behavioral, and biological strategies, which combine to target the drug use as well as the broad range of other biological, psychological, and social issues that factor into drug use and misuse.

After leaving my first job, I designed and directed two outpatient programs in which I taught and supervised clinicians in this integrative approach, and I continued to use this approach with clients in my private practice for many years. I have experienced much satisfaction in helping many of my patients to achieve stable long-term sobriety from drugs and alcohol. I have maintained contact with numerous clients through the years, and I am inspired by their continued progress.

However, despite the many successes along the way, I became increasingly concerned about a serious problem that I experienced in my work and saw in the field as a whole. At the last clinic that I directed, I did an informal study that produced evidence that we were not helping most of the patients who came to us initially. Our experience was similar to that of other traditional abstinence-oriented treatment programs; we had a fifty percent rate of no-return patients, who dropped out after the initial evaluation or were discharged because of "slips" or relapses of their habits. Added to the number of patients who returned to drug use after completing the program, the individuals who relapsed represented the majority of visitors to the clinic.

I was astonished and deeply troubled by this information. I studied the literature to see what others were reporting and found that we were doing no more poorly than others. Studies report, at best, a thirty-percent success rate, and most treatments cannot claim outcomes this high. For example, see the summary of drug and alcohol outcome research by Hester and Miller (1995). Yet this was considered the best that could be expected. These statistics don't begin to include the users who never seek help because of the unrealistic expectations that characterize mainstream treatments in this country. It was common for rehabilitation programs to tell their patients that only one out of ten of them were "going to make it," that is, stay sober.

These poor outcomes have generally been explained as reflecting the lack of motivation of substance users or the difficulties inherent in treating people with substance use problems. A popular scapegoat for this poor success rate is the disease itself: "the cunning and baffling nature of the disease of addiction."[1]

I began to rethink the "abstinence-only" requirement that informs traditional substance use treatment. The assumption that abstinence is the only cure for addiction is related to the addiction-as-disease concept. According to this model, people with substance use problems cannot benefit from psychotherapy while they are using, must accept abstinence as a goal

---

1. This is a slogan commonly used in the Alcoholics Anonymous community that is presumably based on the description of alcohol in the "Big Book" of AA (Alcoholics Anonymous, 1939, pp. 58–59) as "cunning, baffling, powerful!"

of substance use treatment to be in treatment, and must achieve and maintain abstinence in order to be allowed to remain in treatment. When clients say that they believe that other issues are more important, they are told that they are in denial about the central, primary nature of their "disease" and that these other issues must be put on the shelf while the substance use is tackled.

Most treatment programs have "high threshold" access, meaning that there are many requirements to which clients must agree to gain access to treatment: for example, urine testing, attending Alcoholics Anonymous meetings every day, breaking contact with other substance users. Clients unable to live up to these requirements are often referred for more intensive treatment, while unwilling clients are routinely discharged from treatment with the statement that they should come back when they are ready.

Two true stories will illustrate how this often plays out in practice. Several years ago, a competent, experienced professional associate who runs a well-respected intensive outpatient program for substance abusers told me about a woman whom he had seen for an evaluation. At the end of the initial interview, he told her he thought she clearly had an addictive disorder and recommended that she enter his program, which, he said, could help her stop using. She reacted with surprise, stating that she had not come to stop using but, instead, thought that she needed to cut down. He replied that his program was only able to help her stop and that he thought she should come back when she was ready to do that; there was nothing else he could offer. The interview was over with no other recommendations made. I wondered about the look on her face and the emotional impact that abrupt conclusion must have had on her.

Another story illustrates the problem from the psychotherapy perspective. Several years ago, a student in a class I was teaching, a social worker, related the story of a recent occurrence. She had seen a new client in a general psychotherapy clinic for five sessions before presenting the case to her supervisor, a senior social worker at the clinic. The client was a woman in her late twenties who had a serious drug problem in the past for which she had completed a drug rehab program. She came for therapy to work on several issues including problems at work, a stormy relationship, self-esteem problems, and a return to occasional drug use. The therapist felt that they were off to a good start in their work together; there was the beginning of a solid treatment alliance, and the client seemed to be settling into working on her issues, apparently feeling good about the therapist's input. The supervisor's response was quick and final; the client had to be terminated from treatment because the clinic had a policy of not providing psychotherapy to active drug users. She added with authority, "You can't trust what drug abusers have to say until they have been clean for at least six months; they cannot effectively make use of therapy until then."

The social worker was nearly in tears as she described to the class her client's reaction to this agency mandate. When she informed her client in the next session of the clinic policy, she quickly tried to express empathy for the client's feelings and discuss making a referral to a good drug program but it was too late; she knew immediately that the client was lost by the pained, withdrawn look in her eyes. The client did not return for her next session.

Unfortunately, these stories are not uncommon. The abstinence-only assumption operates in subtle ways. Another director of a large, well-known substance abuse treatment program said in a panel presentation to a group of employee assistance professionals, "I would work with someone who is actively using drugs for a limited period of time, but I would make my assumptions clear: I do not believe an addict can moderate his use and I would like the patient to prove me wrong if possible." This stance is taken by many clinicians who may or may not verbalize these views to their clients, and it has a different, dangerous impact on the therapeutic encounter. How does a troubled substance user approach a course of healing when the person being paid and consulted for help believes that what he is trying to do is impossible? How does a client enter a therapeutic relationship with a clinician who secretly believes that the client is not capable of being honest or is emotionally unavailable for treatment?

My own limited success left me feeling ashamed and guilty about my inability to help the people that appeared in my office or programs asking me for assistance. The idea that people needed to "hit a lower bottom," that is, to suffer more as a result of their substance use in order to become more motivated to stop using, became unacceptable to me. It seemed as if our field was putting the responsibility for our failure on our clients, rather than taking responsibility for the problem by looking at how our treatment approach might be limited by its own basic assumptions and processes. It seemed to me that this level of failure challenged us to find new, more creative, and inclusive ways of working with people. I began to feel uneasy and unsatisfied with the unmotivated-client explanation for our limited success, and I started to wonder whether the abstinence-only assumption might account for a large measure of our failure. Now, I had been trained in the milieu of abstinence-only treatments, so I felt confounded and in a difficult quandary. Although our work had clearly been helpful, in some cases lifesaving, to many people, it became clear to me that the constraints and limits of an abstinence-only treatment system was both off-putting and damaging to individuals urgently pursuing a quest for help. I uneasily began to look for alternatives.

I had begun a private practice in psychotherapy in 1987 in which I was free to work with my clients in a more flexible way. In the late 1980s I began to experiment working with clients who were not interested in stopping their drinking or drug use completely but wanted help to figure out what they should do. They wanted to see if they could learn to use in less damaging ways. I knew I would be breaking the traditional rules by agreeing to pursue these goals, but I had been trained in a graduate program that aimed to *really* meet people where they are. Some of these clients seemed sufficiently motivated, insightful, and open to make me feel hopeful about undertaking this experiment. It seemed to me that stable moderation would be a great improvement and, if not, our therapeutic process might take them steps toward stopping. Either way, there were possible advantages beyond the available practices of the day.

Over the next several years I began to see significant breakthroughs and gains in both moderation and cessation of drug misuse. Some individuals were able to cut down significantly, while others found moderating their use impossible and instead became motivated to stop using altogether. These successes were not supposed to be possible according to the traditional model. I was concerned that if my colleagues knew what I was doing, my ethics would be seriously questioned.

Sometime in 1994 I was speaking to Alan Marlatt on the telephone about my work. Alan is a psychologist with a long-respected career as a clinician and researcher in the alcohol treatment field who wrote the groundbreaking book, *Relapse Prevention* (1985). I was lucky to have him as a friend and colleague. I told him about my concerns about the limitations in the traditional model and the experimental work I was doing in my private practice. He responded by saying, "You are doing harm reduction." I said, "What is that?" When he introduced me to harm reduction as an alternative to the traditional treatment model, I immediately realized a philosophical and clinical basis for my work.

Since that conversation, I have discovered harm reduction as a philosophy guiding how we meet our clients and ourselves, pragmatically and with compassion; as a clinical theory that can inform treatment across the broad spectrum of substance-using people; as a critique and corrective to the limitations of the existing treatment system; and as a growing movement composed of clinicians, researchers, and policy makers who collectively provide a progressive perspective to the field.

Harm reduction is a framework for helping drug and alcohol users who cannot or will not stop completely—the majority of users—reduce the harmful consequences of use. Harm reduction accepts that abstinence may be the best outcome for many but relaxes the emphasis on abstinence as the only acceptable goal and criterion of success. Instead, smaller incremental changes in the direction of reduced harmfulness of drug use are accepted. This book will show how these simple changes in emphasis and expectation have dramatic implications for improving the effectiveness of psychotherapy in many ways.

This book reflects the path my own work has taken since that conversation with Alan Marlatt to incorporate harm reduction into my approach to psychotherapy. I see harm reduction as an idea that builds upon what has been available before. It challenges and critiques the limitations of existing models of drug and alcohol treatment in an effort to extend the reach of treatment to the majority of problem alcohol and drug users who have not been helped by the traditional approach.

This book also adds to a growing literature on the subject. In 1998, Marlatt and a group of his colleagues published *Harm Reduction: Pragmatic Strategies for Managing High Risk Behaviors*, an innovative book introducing harm reduction and describing its history, supporting research, and applications to different client groups. In 2000, Patt Denning, another friend and colleague who has been a major contributor to the application of harm reduction to psychotherapy, published the first in-depth exploration of the application of harm reduction to psychotherapy, *Practicing Harm Reduction: An Alternative Approach to Addictions*. In it she presents her multidimensional approach to harm reduction psychotherapy.

This book extends these contributions with my own perspective. It is an exploration of the particular value harm reduction psychotherapy has for dealing with a range of emotional issues commonly associated with problem drug use and a collection of stories showing the variety of forms this approach can take.

THE CHAPTERS

In Chapter 1, I provide the clinical rationale for harm reduction psychotherapy and an outline of the integrative approach that I have developed. This approach considers the complex interplay of personal meaning, conditioning, biology, and social context both in the genesis of drug problems and in the development of individually tailored psychotherapy. The illustrative story, my contribution, is about Tom, a depressed problem drinker who achieved stable moderation from alcohol after having failed at a coerced abstinence-oriented treatment.

Chapter 2 explores the contribution that the psychoanalytic tradition has made to harm reduction psychotherapy, particularly in its emphasis on the importance of the multiple meanings of drug use and the centrality of the therapeutic relationship in effective psychotherapy. The accompanying story, the case of Mrs. G. by Mark Sehl, is about a depressed, socially isolated elderly woman with severe alcohol dependency who was helped by a harm reduction approach to achieve abstinence from alcohol in the course of addressing her emotional difficulties. The story shows how a harm reduction approach is consistent with a psychoanalytic understanding of Mrs. G.'s drinking. It also challenges prevailing misconceptions about psychoanalytic treatment in describing an analytic psychotherapy that was very different from the classical approach yet remained true to analytic principles.

Chapter 3 discusses the theoretical support that learning theory provides to harm reduction psychotherapy and the value of blending cognitive and behavioral strategies with a psychoanalytic understanding of the meaning of drug use in helping people change. The case of Archie, by Gary Dayton and Frederick Rotgers, is about a man with a serious drinking problem that was related to depression and obsessive compulsive disorder. Like Tom, Archie had found prior abstinence-oriented treatment to exacerbate his difficulties but was able to dramatically reduce his drinking and address his psychological problems with the harm reduction approach.

Chapter 4 looks at the cornerstone of harm reduction psychotherapy, the right fit between client and treatment as central to the success of the work. It explores the importance of the match between the client and the treatment modality, and the therapeutic relationship and how this is built. The accompanying story by Gail Hammer is about Michael, an alcohol-abusing man with AIDS who successfully moderated his drinking. At the start of the story, we read that the therapeutic alliance was almost derailed by the therapist's supervisor's mandate that the client be referred elsewhere to stop drinking. The therapist quickly realized that she had to shift to a harm reduction approach that accepted his continued drinking in order to form an alliance with him that enabled the therapy to get under way. It ultimately supported him in moderating his drinking and addressing a range of other important emotional issues.

Chapter 5 discusses the complexity of the people and problems that can be associated with problematic drug use, the need for psychotherapies that are correspondingly complex and, sometimes, long, and the relevance of harm reduction psychotherapy to these issues. The psychotherapy story in this chapter by Valerie Frankfeldt is the story of Donnie, a multiple drug user with severe emotional and communication problems who achieved abstinence after a six-year-long psychotherapy. The story reveals how Frankfeldt was pulled to harm reduction despite her prior abstinence-oriented training because of Donnie's needs. She had to work with great uncertainty about what were appropriate goals for him as he continued to use drugs for a long time before he was able to begin to step down his drug use and eventually begin attending Alcoholics Anonymous and stop using drugs and alcohol.

Chapter 6 explores the importance of seeing drug use as carrying or expressing multiple personal meanings for people and the value this has for promoting change. It discusses the value of seeing drug use as an adaptive attempt to cope with painful feelings and personality vulnerabilities and suggests that until this function of drug use has been recognized and addressed in another way, many people are unable to consider modifying their drug use. The accompanying story, the case of Gary by Edward J. Khantzian, is about an opiate-dependent physician who went to a traditional 12-step oriented drug rehabilitation program followed by psychodynamic psychotherapy and 12-step program attendance and achieved stable abstinence. The story particularly shows how treatment can have an impact both on the drug use as well as on many aspects of personality functioning that render people vulnerable to developing drug problems. Unlike previous stories in this book of failed "coerced" abstinence-oriented treatment, in Gary's case, a coerced traditional treatment was the right fit for Gary and had dramatic positive results. It illustrates how the harm reduction umbrella encompasses traditional treatment for drug users who need it; those whose use is out of control, are unable to meaningfully engage in psychotherapy without outside intervention, and seem to need outside pressure to get moving in a positive direction.

Chapter 7 discusses the role of trauma and early experience in general in shaping the vulnerabilities that may lead people to drugs. It further explores how an appreciation of these experiences early in life can be used in psychotherapy. The case of

Sally by Jerome David Levin was chosen to illustrate these issues. Sally came for help with severe anxiety that was the result of early physical and sexual abuse. A dependence on amphetamines was only revealed some time into the therapy after much work had gone on to create a safe space in the treatment. Until this time the treatment had to progress while she used the drug to hold herself together. The story illustrates the need to accept ongoing drug use in many clients for some time into therapy before it is possible to work directly on changing the drug use. In this case the therapy led to an abstinence outcome.

Chapter 8 discusses a common dynamic expressed through drug use: the rebellion against the inner critical voice. It explores how harm reduction psychotherapy is specifically suited to help people find a third solution between the submission-rebellion bind that is often expressed in the cycle of binging, pledging to stop, binging, and on and on. The illustrative story for the chapter, the case of Diana by Patt Denning, is a story of a woman who had a long history of heavy drinking that was related to relationship problems, difficulties feeling and expressing feelings, and depression; all of these in turn related to a severe inner critic that tormented her. The first goal of this psychotherapy—to stop drinking—failed as it was revealed to be a submission to the inner critic. It was only when they shifted to a harm reduction approach that helped her find what was right for her that she achieved a stable moderation of her drinking.

Chapter 9 discusses the long-term residential therapeutic community, one of the oldest approaches to the treatment of people with drug problems. It explores the rationale for the therapeutic community and which clients may be best suited for it. The accompanying story, the case of Ms. E by Barbara Wallace, is the story of a woman with a long addiction to crack cocaine that was related to a childhood history of physical and sexual abuse. Following numerous failed outpatient treatments, Ms. E was mandated to the therapeutic community and, like Gary in Chapter 6, found this to be the push that she needed to get to a treatment context that fit her needs. In this context she began to heal the intense traumatic suffering that underlay her drug use. With the help of ongoing psychotherapy after she left the program, she was able to maintain stable abstinence and become a model for how to heal trauma. The story also reveals how Dr. Wallace was transformed by her work with Ms. E.

Chapter 10 introduces the harm reduction group as an approach to group therapy that can have benefits that more limited abstinence-only groups do not. The accompanying story, "The Sobriety Support Group" by Jeannie Little, is about the development of a harm reduction group she and a colleague ran for homeless dually diagnosed (drug use problems and psychiatric problems) veterans. She describes the evolution of the group's structure and norms in collaboration with the members and shows how the group was able to be helpful to clients who had been failed by traditional treatments. She particularly emphasizes how the diversity in the group members in terms of goals (moderation or abstinence), mental health, and motivation was what made the group effective.

1

Harm Reduction Psychotherapy

THE CURRENT CONTEXT: WHAT IS WRONG WITH THIS PICTURE?

Mainstream abstinence-oriented treatment of alcohol and drug users in the United States today continues to have poor success by anyone's criteria. Clinical observations and empirical studies typically report that a majority of clients seen initially do not successfully complete treatment or maintain their gains after treatment. These poor outcomes are evident in residential and outpatient programs and across different theoretical approaches. The Substance Abuse and Mental Health Services Administration reported that between 1992 and 1997 only 47% of patients completed American drug and alcohol treatment programs with another 12% referred to other programs (SAMHSA, 1999). Several treatment outcome studies suggest that only 20–40% of patients who complete treatment achieve long-term success even when abstinence and moderation are both considered as successful outcomes (Keso & Salaspuro, 1990; Nordstom & Berglund, 1987). For example, Helzer and colleagues (Helzer et al., 1985) looked at three-year outcomes of four abstinence-oriented programs of patients who met D.S.M. III criteria for alcohol dependence. They found only 15.1% reported total abstinence and 18.4% reported some form of problem-free drinking. Ditman et al. (1967) did a one-year follow up of 301 "chronic drunk offenders" who were randomly assigned to no treatment, Alcoholics Anonymous, or clinic treatment as a condition of probation. Using re-arrest for a drinking-related offense as the primary outcome measure, they found that 68% of the clinic group, 69% of the AA group, and 56% of the no treatment group were re-arrested; the differences were not statistically significant. And, more recently, a large scale controlled study, Project MATCH (Project MATCH Research Group [1997]) was funded by the National Institute on Alcohol Abuse and Alcoholism to compare patients' responses to different treatment approaches. 1,726 people with alcohol use problems were randomly assigned at sites across the country to twelve sessions of 12-Step Facilitation Therapy (TSF), Cognitive-Behavioral Therapy (CBT), or Motivational Enhancement Therapy (MET). Using complete abstinence during the year after treatment as the measure of success, 24% of individuals in the TSF group were abstinent, 14% of those in the CBT group, and 15% of those in the MET group.

Standard approaches are not equipped to address serious emotional or socioeconomic problems accompanying substance use problems. These statistics for failure in substance abuse treatment do not include people with drug and alcohol problems who never seek traditional treatment, a group that represents the majority of problem users in this country. The United States Department of Health and Human Services (USDHHS, 1997) estimated in 1997 that about 15 million adult Americans are alcohol dependent or abusing. SAMHSA (1999) estimated that there were 2,207,375 admissions to 15,000 American in- and outpatient treatment facilities in 1997. Assuming that some of these were multiple admissions by some people, it is likely that approximately two million people were treated in that year. These data suggest that close to 85% of individuals with alcohol problems in 1997 were untreated in this country. This is supported by the Institute of Medicine's (1990) estimate that 80% of American alcoholics have never made contact with self-help or professional treatment, and by the National Institute on Alcohol Abuse and Alcoholism's (1999) estimate of 10 million untreated American alcoholics. I think it is safe to assume that the statistics for other drug users are comparable. For example, researchers at SAMHSA (Woodward et al., 1997) estimated that 48% of the need for drug treatment, excluding treatment for alcohol problems, is not being met. If the helping profession of addiction treatment was a Fortune 500 company, it would have gone out of business long ago.

THE "ABSTINENCE-ONLY" ASSUMPTION IN TRADITIONAL SUBSTANCE USE TREATMENT

While these results are related to the complex and challenging nature of substance use problems, I have come to believe that the prevailing assumption that informs most mainstream treatment contributes to this limited effectiveness. Mainstream drug and alcohol treatment has been informed by an "abstinence-only" assumption. According to this model, abstinence from all mood-changing chemicals is the only acceptable goal for compulsive substance users; it must be accepted by the client in order to gain access to treatment and must be quickly achieved and maintained to remain in treatment. Abstinence is the criterion of success for the client and treatment provider and the prerequisite for continued assistance. People who want to address other issues before they address their substance use are generally said to be rationalizing their substance use and denying their "disease."

This model is based on the assumption that unless problem users are willing to accept total abstinence from all drugs and alcohol, they are not suitable for treatment; active users are assumed to have such impaired awareness and judgment that they cannot engage in treatment or psychotherapy in a meaningful way. The consensus belief is that the user must "hit a lower bottom," that is, suffer more from the assumed negative consequences of their use in order for motivation toward abstinence to grow. This mandate results in a Catch-22 for the user that results in the denial of any treatment. Substance users seeking help for issues other than substance use are routinely denied psychotherapy and referred to substance abuse treatment, while substance users unwilling or unable to accept abstinence are denied substance use treatment. Clients in treatment who are unable to stop using are routinely terminated from treatment, often with no other treatment recourse, or with a recommendation that is not suitable for the client. Not only does this approach prevent many people from obtaining the help they are seeking, it frequently demoralizes and damages people who come at the depth of their vulnerability and the peak of their readiness to change.

Assumptions are Based on the Ambiguous Disease Concept

These assumptions are based on an ambiguous "disease concept" that sees compulsive substance use as born from a hypothetical and unsubstantiated "addictive disease." The disease is believed to have a life of its own, separable from the complex of issues that influence the life of the user. The disease is deemed a permanent, lifelong condition, dormantly active even when the client isn't using drugs. The hypothetical addictive disease inevitably causes loss of control over drug use and is generally understood to be lethal if not arrested, that is, if the user doesn't accept total abstinence. In effect this model isolates the drug-using behavior from the rest of the person and claims that it must be dealt with before anything else in the user's life.

Biological and Behavioral Reductionism Denies Personal Meaning

While there are often biological and behavioral conditioning factors involved with excessive drug use, this model reduces problem use completely to biology and conditioning. The prevailing abstinence-only approach is not process or depth oriented and denies the importance of the unique personal meanings that drug use carries for people. This model tends to devalue, dehumanize, and objectify drug users and often alienates the user from seeking help rather than examining the insufficiencies of its own assumptions.

Abstinence is sometimes the ideal approach in terms of risk reduction for many substance misusers; however, it may be argued that the majority of users are not willing nor able to accept this as their goal at the beginning of a treatment process for a wide variety of legitimate reasons. Consequently, they are met with an expectation that keeps them from becoming effectively engaged at the start. This zero-tolerance, "high threshold" approach (the prospective client must jump high to get in the door) simply does not begin where many clients live; rather, it requires that the client come to match a model that is riddled with outmoded assumptions and expectations.

HARM REDUCTION AND THE DIVERSITY OF SUBSTANCE USERS

Substance misusers are a broadly diverse group of people who differ in many important ways, including the severity of their substance use problems, personal goals regarding use (e.g., moderation vs. abstinence), motivation and readiness to change, emotional state, personality strengths and vulnerabilities, and socioeconomic and cultural variables. It is obvious that any one-size-fits-all model is doomed to fail with the majority of clients. This diversity suggests the need for a more flexible, inclusive, and comprehensive model to increase overall effectiveness at helping this broad spectrum of people.

Harm reduction is an alternative paradigm for approaching the treatment of this diverse population that has many advantages over the abstinence-only approach that make it more acceptable and relevant to a greater number of clients and can increase overall treatment effectiveness.

History

Harm reduction first emerged in the Netherlands in the 1970s as a response to the limitations of the traditional abstinence-only treatment approach. It has since become the best available practice informing numerous national policies on drug treament including the Netherlands, Germany, England, Australia, and Canada (Marlatt, 1998). In the United States, harm reduction became accepted in the late 1980s and early1990s as a set of pragmatic public health strategies for reducing the spread of HIV and other risks associated with active substance use (Heather, Wodak, Nadelman, and O'Hare, 1993). These strategies include clean needle exchange, condom distribution, and methadone maintenance.

An Alternative Paradigm

Inherent in these strategies is an alternate philosophical paradigm for helping drug users. Harm reduction is not at odds with abstinence, but includes it as one possible goal for substance users and for many the best possible harm reduction outcome. But it *is* a critique of the abstinence-only model I discussed previously. Whereas abstinence-only limits who can be helped and how, harm reduction turns abstinence-only upside down by giving up the presumption that abstinence is the required goal for all clients with substance use problems. In so doing, it opens the door to the possibility of engaging the whole spectrum of substance users.

Alan Marlatt, in his groundbreaking book *Harm Reduction* (1998), has called harm reduction "compassionate pragmatism." As a pragmatic approach, active substance use is accepted as a fact, and substance users are engaged where they are, not where the provider thinks they should be. In effect, harm reduction follows the client's nature rather than asking the client to match imposed treatment demands. It recognizes that substance use and its consequences vary along a continuum of harmfulness for the user and the community and that behavior generally changes by small incremental steps. Harm reduction seeks to help the client move along the continuum in the direction of decreased harm. Therefore, any reduction in harm is seen as a step in the right direction. For many users, abstinence is considered ideal in terms of reduction of harmful consequences, but alternative goals that "step down" the negative consequences of substance use are also embraced (Marlatt and Tapert, 1993).

As an approach that emphasizes compassion, harm reduction actively challenges the tendency in our society to deal with drug users in stigmatized, disrespectful, coercive, and punitive ways. The disease concept that informs abstinence-only treatments denies the complex personal meaning that drug use can have for drug users, which contributes to failure. We also see this in the country's commitment to the criminalization of drug users. Rather than dedicating monies to treatment reforms, education, and other supportive services to meet the various needs of this group of people, our country spends significantly more on punitive criminal justice measures. This clearly speaks to the hypocrisy of the country's commitment to seeing drug misuse as a disease or related to serious psychological or social issues. In what other areas of health care do we terminate people from treatment for continuing to have a problem and then sentence them to prison for engaging in the behavior in question? Harm reduction challenges us as practitioners and as a society to find more creative and effective means to help drug users.

Harm Reduction Has Treatment Implications

This simple but profoundly important shift in focus has positive treatment implications at two levels. As an umbrella concept, harm reduction suggests the need for an integrated system of treatment with linkages across the full spectrum of treatment modalities that are matched to the needs of the broad diversity of users. Harm reduction also has implications for how treatment is conducted in the moment-to-moment interactions between clients and clinicians at every stage of the treatment process from evaluation and initial engagement through goal setting and working toward change, that is, moderation, abstinence, or other harm reduction goals. This issue of the *right fit* between client and treatment will be explored in more depth in Chapter four.

HARM REDUCTION PSYCHOTHERAPY

A growing number of researchers and clinicians have broadened the application of the harm reduction approach from a public health strategy to psychotherapy and counseling of active drug users (Carey and Carey, 1990; Denning, 2000; Marlatt and Tapert, 1993; Marlatt, 1998; Peele and Brodsky, 1992; Rothschild, 1995; Tatarsky, 1998). I think of harm reduction psychotherapy as a general category of psychological interventions that may vary in theoretical perspective and clinical approach but share in the commitment to the reduction of the harm associated with active substance use without assuming that abstinence is the ideal goal for all drug users.

In the section that follows, I describe what I consider to be the essential features of harm reduction psychotherapy and its clinical rationale.

THE INTEGRATIVE MODEL

I will summarize an approach to harm reduction psychotherapy that I have developed in my own practice with a broad range of substance-using clients over the last fifteen years. My approach is consistent with a bio-psycho-social model of drug use problems in that it recognizes that personal meaning, social learning and conditioning, social-interpersonal and biological factors may all play a role in the genesis of these problems, and that the specific contribution of each for each client must be understood in developing individually tailored treatments that have the most chance of success. This approach begins with the assumption that substance use problems may result from a variety of different psychological, social, and biological factors, the combination of which is unique for each person.

Integrating Strategies for Change

Harm reduction psychotherapy is an integrative approach in that it also recognizes that drug use can be motivated by behavioral, sociocultural, and biological factors that must be understood in formulating effective interventions. A proper understanding of the contribution of all of these factors will inevitably lead to a treatment approach that integrates strategies that target all of the relevant factors for a given client. Given the diversity of drug-using individuals, harm reduction psychotherapies can look very different depending on the particular client. This dictates that harm reduction psychotherapists be attuned to the unique qualities of each client and flexible in blending different kinds of psychological, behavioral, and biological/ pharmacological intervention depending on the client's needs.

People use substances because they work, at least initially, in addressing some psychologically, socially, or biologically based needs. We may define substance use as problematic or excessive when it compromises or interferes with other important needs and values. But, for any substance use treatment to have a chance at being successful, it must begin with an effort to discover the specific reasons or motives that have made the substance so compelling in spite of these problematic consequences. As these factors are identified, strategies and modalities can be combined that specifically target them.

THE PSYCHOANALYTIC CONTRIBUTION

For me, the multiple personal meanings that drug use carries, expresses, and reflects that are unique to each user are pivotal in understanding the motivation to use and misuse. Identifying these meanings is essential for creating lasting positive change in drug use. My thinking on this has been largely influenced by the psychoanalytic/psychodynamic contribution to understanding the myriad personal meanings drug use can have for people.

Contemporary psychodynamic writers on substance problems have generally emphasized the "adaptive" value that substances may fulfill as one possible reason that substance use becomes compelling (Khantzian, Halliday, and McAuliffe, 1990; Wurmser, 1978). According to this perspective, substances may come to serve important psychological functions that help the user cope more effectively. They may be relied on to self-medicate or defend against overwhelming affect states; regulate fragile self-esteem; support interpersonal effectiveness; comfort or soothe oneself; or tranquilize the harsh inner critic ("super-ego") to allow temporary experiences of pleasure unavailable while sober, among other possible functions.

I discuss the importance of the psychoananlytic contribution to harm reduction psychotherapy in Chapter 2 and look at some of the specific meanings drug use can have for people and how they can be addressed in psychotherapy in Chapters 5, 6, 7 and 8.

Personal Meaning and the Vicious Cycle of Excessive "Addictive" Drug Use

Over time, chronic substance use may take on multiple functions for the individual as it becomes increasingly integrated into one's psychological functioning and lifestyle. Chronic use is also often associated with psychological, conditioning, lifestyle, and biological changes that compound and can intensify the original motives for using, thus increasing the pressure to use. The interaction between the initial meanings that drugs have for people that make them appealing and the consequences of chronic drug use is a way of understanding excessive drug use is an alternative that to the disease model. As the expression of a complex interaction of personal and social factors, drug use can be seen as the expression of an interactive process that is more open to change than the more static, reified disease model for which abstinence *now* is the only starting point.

GOALS OF TREATMENT

The goal of this work is to engage clients in a relationship that will support them in clarifying the problematic aspects of their substance use and work toward addressing these problems with goals and strategies that are consistent with who they are as individuals. The ideal outcome of this approach is to support the user in reducing the harmfulness of substance use to the point where it has minimal negative impact on other areas of one's life. Whether the outcome is moderation or abstinence depends on what is practically realistic for the client and emerges out of the treatment process. Ultimately, this is accomplished by identifying the various bio-psycho-social factors that initiated and contribute to ongoing substance use and discovering alternative, more effective drug-free solutions. However, the harm reduction principle places the value of engaging clients in treatment around their own initial goals as the starting point, with the ultimate goal of treatment emerging out of the process of the therapy.

ENGAGEMENT/ASSESSMENT PHASE

The cornerstone of all effective treatment is the therapeutic alliance between client and clinician around shared goals. Thus the focus of therapy must be on the client's definition of the problem and goals. By starting with an attempt to understand the client's reason for coming, an alliance can form around a mutual exploration of the client's concerns and how, if at all, the substance use impacts on them. Without preconceptions about the substance use, we are free to join the client in the exploration, keeping open the question of how the substance impacts on other areas of the client's life. This puts us on the same side as the client, avoids power struggles about what the client "should" do, and conveys a respect and empathy for the client that is conducive to the client feeling safe and supported in our presence.

The nature of the problem is explored through a detailed consideration of the client's reason for coming, the current substance use pattern, history of use, and the impact of the substance on other important areas of life. It is acknowledged that the substance has some positive value to the user and that this must be weighed against the negative consequences of use. Identifying the positive function of the substance opens up the issue of whether other, more effective, and less harmful ways of meeting these needs may be discovered.

Clients are taught a self-observation strategy for developing a clear picture of how substances fit into their lives in relation to situational triggers, thoughts and feelings, and positive or negative consequences of use. The strategy consists of paying close attention to physical sensations, thoughts, and sense perceptions in the present moment and describing them in detailed, nonjudgmental language as fully as possible. Then, clients are asked to use the technique whenever they become aware of thoughts or behavior that are related to using drugs or alcohol in order to identify the thoughts and feelings that immediately precede and follow the substance-related behavior. This may be assisted by having clients keep written records of these observations that can be brought into sessions to be reviewed with the therapist.

GOAL SETTING

As the problematic aspects of substance use and other issues of concern to the client become clear, it becomes possible to establish goals and agree on a treatment plan to work toward them. I take my lead from what is most pressing to the client, whether this is working toward moderation or abstinence, clarifying the motivational obstacles to addressing the substance use directly, or addressing some other non–substance-related issues. Rather than beginning with my assumptions about how realistic these goals are, I state my experience with similar clients, where appropriate, and suggest a pragmatic approach to determining if the client's goals are achievable. We can discover together what is practically possible by working together toward the client's chosen goals. Goals and strategies can be revised as difficulties are encountered along the way.

For many clients whose substance use continues to serve some positive function, the question of whether they can moderate their use must be answered before they will consider stopping. This is more likely answered by a supported, direct attempt that includes learning ways to achieve moderation. If clients are unable to achieve moderation in this context, they are more likely to have a clear recognition of why it has not been possible for them based on their own observations and are more likely to consider stopping altogether.

WORKING TOWARD CHANGE

Out of this process, an "ideal substance use plan" is developed that is designed to maximize the positive value of using substances for the client while minimizing the negative impact of using *to the point where the client is presently ready to go*. Ideal route of administration, amount, and frequency of substance use are arrived at empirically by examining the client's experience with using. As the client attempts to put the plan into effect, how well it achieves the desired goals can be assessed in an ongoing way and the plan can be fine-tuned to more effectively achieve the goals as therapy proceeds.

Difficulties encountered in successfully implementing the plan are "micro-analyzed" to identify the situational and psychological issues that are driving excessive use. These difficulties may be related to conditioned environmental or emotional triggers, social pressures, emotional states that substances are used to cope with, or motives about which the client may be unaware (e.g., the passive, self-destructive expression of anger through substance use that hurts oneself). The identification of these motives leads to the exploration of alternative ways of coping. These may include the full range of coping skills such as relaxation training, anger management, assertiveness training, and identifying and verbalizing feelings in constructive ways. The therapist teaches these coping skills and invites the client to practice them in therapy sessions and out in the client's life. This permission-giving stance may challenge clients' early messages that caring for oneself is unacceptable and help empower them to use their innate capacities to care for themselves effectively. When they become aware of the variety of motives for using substances, the compulsive need to use them may abate somewhat as it now becomes possible to make alternative choices. At this point, a discussion of other ways to manage, express, or resolve these broader emotional or characterological issues becomes possible. The envisioning of alternative possibilities is a prerequisite for many people to feel motivated to consider giving up their familiar, habitual ways of coping. Over the course of therapy, the focus of the work broadens from substance use to a whole set of larger issues related to getting to know oneself better, learning to listen to and accept oneself more deeply, and discovering more effective ways of caring for oneself.

Because this approach does not begin with preconceived goals, it is applicable to a broad variety of people with substance use issues. With some clients, this work is relatively simple and straightforward and may consist of a small number of contacts of evaluation and recommendations resulting in dramatic, long-term positive changes in use. With many others, however, the work is very complicated, uncertain, and difficult for both client and clinician. This is often what is required for the resolution of substance problems that exist in more complex psychological and sociological contexts. This reality, which is avoided by the abstinence-only approaches, is embraced by harm reduction psychotherapy.

Tom: Harm Reduction to Moderation
by Andrew Tatarsky

Tom called me four years ago because he was concerned about "drinking too much and at the wrong times," and he wanted "to get it under control." He called me specifically because he had heard of my reputation as an alcohol treatment specialist who will work with problem drinkers who do not want to stop drinking.

Tom appeared at my office for our first meeting looking scared and shaking. The faint odor of alcohol accompanied him as he entered my office. I found myself feeling somewhat anxious and wondered if this would interfere with our work. As it turned out, this first meeting ended with us feeling optimistic about the possibility of doing some valuable work together, a feeling that has grown and strengthened over the past four years of weekly psychotherapy.

Tom is a somewhat heavy man, at that time looking his 43 years of age, wearing a neatly trimmed mustache and a hoop earring in his right ear. Along with his neat, casual style of dress, he projected the image of a hip, downtown, arty man trying to look younger than he was. His initial wariness and guarded manner melted quickly in response to my interested, accepting stance. He seemed painfully lonely and hungry for contact, and he expressed intense gratitude for my willingness to help him on his terms, that is, while he continued to drink. This also seemed to reflect a desperate need for validation of his adequacy as a person. He was exploring whether I might be able to offer that to him. As Tom talked, I also quickly formed the impression that he was a very bright, honest, emotionally vulnerable, and talented man. I immediately liked him and felt optimistic about embarking on a psychotherapeutic journey together.

Tom described himself as a 43-year-old single Italian-American gay man who lived alone in New York City. He said that he was glad to be gay, although there were certain changes in the gay world that had become increasingly problematic. While he was vague at this point, these problematic changes would become clear over the course of our work together; they were powerfully related to his drinking problem and a number of other emotional and lifestyle problems.

During the next few meetings, Tom revealed himself as sensitively attuned to the nuances of my reactions to him, belying both a keen attention to detail and a particular sensitivity to the emotional responses of others. He expressed a strong need for emotional support and reassurance, frequently asking if I thought he was "doing it right," showing me things that he had done to address his problems and asking for my approval. He didn't actually want my opinion but rather my approval for the decisions that he had already made. These aspects of him revealed a very fragile sense of self and an intense reliance on the approval of others to maintain a positive self-image. I felt as if I was being invited to play the role of mother, applauding and feeling proud of his baby steps toward learning to take better care of himself in the world. Not only did it seem to me that he wanted my approval to maintain a good feeling about himself, but as a kind of mother/father, he wanted me to help him to construct a more firm and more effective self. I wondered if this vulnerability in his sense of self might be directly related to his drinking, a suspicion that was to be supported in several important ways.

Tom said that he indeed saw his drinking as a problem, though the most important factor motivating him to seek treatment was pressure from his job. Tom had a responsible position as curator at an art museum. Prior to his visit, Tom's supervisors had given him an ultimatum: go in for alcohol treatment as the condition for keeping his job. Tom was in a crisis in his workplace. He was extremely disturbed by the way his co-workers had responded to his excessive drinking and felt that he was being misjudged and misunderstood. Our session was Tom's second attempt at seeking help for alcohol use. His first experience was a coercive intervention that occurred nine months prior to our meeting. Tom's colleagues had staged a semi-theatrical intervention to get him into an intensive treatment program, assuming for him that he had no other options. As Tom spoke, he was controlling strong feelings of anger and sadness. Without warning, his colleagues had confronted him publicly, at the start of the workday, and told him that they had made arrangements for him to be evaluated by a well-known alcohol treatment program that morning and that a car was waiting just outside to take him there. At that moment Tom realized that he had no choice but to go, unless he wanted to risk losing his job of twenty-three years.

Tom said that he felt "shell-shocked." He said that he had never been approached by anyone about his drinking or job performance before this and felt utterly humiliated and betrayed. He wondered aloud why no one had spoken to him if they had concerns. He said that he would have willingly gone for an evaluation if he had been consulted and included in the process. Stricken with shock in front of the others, he felt he had no choice but to submit to their thoughtless suggestion and went for the evaluation.

At the evaluation, Tom was told he was an alcoholic. The interviewer said that he believed that Tom was minimizing the nature of his problem and that he believed that Tom needed to stop drinking altogether. He recommended that Tom enter the program's four-night-per-week intensive outpatient program. Thinking that he had no alternative, Tom entered the program under pressure.

During the course of that six-month treatment, Tom did not drink at all. He had had questions that he wanted to raise about whether he could drink safely in the future, but was not able to explore these options because they were taboo in the program. Tom quickly learned from the staff's automatic, seemingly presumptuous responses to his questions with proclamations of his minimizing and denial and "inability to accept his disease." His treatment experience left him feeling traumatized and wary of entering therapy again. Later on in our work together, Tom described that this first treatment experience had contributed to his feeling worse about himself than when he began.

Shortly after completing that treatment program, Tom began to drink again, this time with a vengeance. His drinking quickly came to the attention of his superiors at work after he made some phone calls to co-workers while intoxicated. He appeared at a work function obviously drunk. Tom's supervisors again required Tom to seek treatment or risk losing his job.

Tom now felt nervous on the job, afraid that expressing his feelings might further jeopardize his relationships there. These feelings distracted him; they interfered with his concentration at work and on a book-writing project. As a result of this rupture in his relationships within his workplace, he felt more lonely than ever. He saw his most recent drinking as his way of handling his feelings of anger and loneliness. He said that his "co-workers' attempt to help had not helped at all" and had left him with feelings that compounded the more long-standing problems that contributed to his drinking.

At first I was unclear about the nature of Tom's drinking problem or whether he could successfully achieve his goal of moderation. My initial impression was that his heavy drinking was a meaningful reaction to a number of painful emotions, the emotionally charged present as well as the ongoing, more chronic situations in his life.

Tom felt quite depressed much of the time. As background to the recent betrayal at work, his depression had grown over fifteen years with the gradual loss of several primary sources of support for his fragile sense of self. Tom had managed his vulnerable self-esteem by depending on external sources of positive feedback from others. His relationships were preserved by an overly friendly, nonconfrontational style of relating to others. He had long ago traded away any freedom to express anger or sexual desire in a direct and assertive way.

The harm reduction approach was used to set up a therapeutic context for evaluating Tom's problems and establishing a therapeutic alliance with him while he continued to drink. The integrative aspect of this approach enabled me to explore the various meanings and functions of Tom's drinking while actively supporting the use of specific coping strategies for addressing his needs in more direct, effective, alcohol-free ways.

COURSE OF TREATMENT

Engagement/Assessment Phase

I agreed to work with Tom to explore whether he could successfully moderate his drinking. We planned to meet once weekly for 45-minute sessions. I told him that I did not believe that it was possible to know whether he could successfully make this change in his drinking, and I suggested that we adopt an experimental attitude toward this question. Tom said that he liked this framework as a starting point for our work together. He said that he was aware that it might not be possible for him to learn to control his drinking but that he needed to give it a serious try before he could ever accept that he would need to stop drinking entirely.

Our initial alliance was quickly formed around the shared goal of exploration in the area of moderation management. My initial stance conveyed an understanding and respect for what was important to Tom and contributed to an atmosphere of safety in therapy. Tom quickly developed a very positive feeling about working with me and said that he felt optimistic about being able to get what he needed. My interest in supporting him to discover whether he could achieve his desired drinking goal also had some value in relation to some of the particular aspects of Tom's character problems, vulnerabilities that are often present in clients with substance problems. Tom's compliance with his prior treatment despite feeling that it did not address his needs was characteristic of his relational tendencies generally. His self-esteem was so dependent on the approval of others that he generally went along with their wishes even when it might be in stark contrast to his own. This was shown by his passive acceptance of what he felt to be mistreatment at work as well as a pattern of personal relationships in which he was physically or verbally abused and taken advantage of in one way or another. Rather than change the pattern of relating, he became increasingly isolated in his life. Like many problem drinkers, his drinking expressed his anger passively rather than in words or appropriate assertive actions. His reticence to claim his needs and express his voice eroded his self-esteem. The critical inner voices contributed to depression over a ten-year period, assisted by drinking, which numbed his pain. My willingness to support Tom in investigating what he needed to clarify for himself was a good step in the direction of self-expression. As I helped him to identify what was important to him, he began to find the resources to commit to a program that suited his own emerging nature.

The first phase of the treatment focused on clarifying the nature of his drinking. This assessment was designed to identify the problematic aspects of his drinking, to discover how his drinking was meaningfully related to his emotional and external life issues, and to get a baseline level of drinking to develop clear behavioral drinking goals. To this end, I suggested several behavior therapy strategies. I taught Tom self-observation techniques to identify the relationships between external events, thoughts, feelings, and thoughts or feelings related to alcohol. I describe this to clients alternately as "self-monitoring," "awareness training," or "mindfulness," and think of it as related to the psychoanalytic concept of the "observing ego." I suggested that between sessions, Tom try to practice observing the accompanying thoughts, feelings, and circumstances whenever he noticed the desire for a drink and to keep a mental or written record that we could review together in sessions. I suggested that the initial purpose was to get a clear picture of his current drinking patterns and that he not change anything until he could identify specific goals for himself.

This examination included both written and mental notes over the first several weeks. It revealed that the current pattern of Tom's drinking was between two and six drinks daily and occasionally as many as twelve. His drinking mainly occurred in bars where he met with his bar friends, as well as sexual partners. He said he had been generally drinking in this way for the last ten years. The quantity had slowly increased over this period of time. He said that he did not experience blackouts, alcohol withdrawal, or medical problems as a result of his drinking. He identified negative consequences of drinking, including lapses in judgment leading to engagement in inappropriate and risky behavior such as unsafe sex while drinking. Another lapse was the occasional appearance at work with alcohol still on his breath from the night before, the morning after leaving him in a semi-intoxicated state in which he worked at half his capacity. While intoxicated he had called co-workers from time to time and expressed dissatisfaction with people's work and attitudes. These intoxicated calls made the listeners understandably ill at ease. His assessment of character was impacted by alcohol; he took several strangers home from bars who ended the evening by robbing and beating him.

Tom believed that his drinking was excessive, inappropriate, and self-destructive, but he did not want to see himself as an alcoholic who could never learn to control his drinking. He said that he had never really tried to control his drinking and that he thought there were a number of emotional issues causing him to drink excessively. He said that he wanted to try to learn better control.

We reviewed Tom's drinking history in depth to understand together how drinking fit into the larger context of his life. It became clear that the escalation in Tom's drinking was a response to two major issues that reflected older and deeper emotional and characterological problems. When these were identified, they became the focus of our ongoing and current work together.

Tom had felt a gradual loss of social support that had once given him a sense of belonging, self-esteem, and possibilities for intimate and sexual relationships. In his twenties and thirties, Tom had been a well-respected popular artist in the downtown scene. He was actively involved in the gay community during the 1960s and 1970s when there were many opportunities for social and sexual contact. These communities gave Tom a sense of belonging, pride in his artistic and social accomplishments, and opportunities for intimate relationships of which he had two important, long-term lovers and many brief but exciting sexual encounters.

As Tom grew older and heavier, and as the AIDS crisis hit in the early 1980s, he gradually withdrew from these worlds; he was no longer as desirable and the opportunities for intimacy disappeared with the changing times. Tom began to satisfy his need for social contact with the pseudo-contact available in bars but stopped having casual sex because of his fear of AIDS. He drank more as a way to blot his feelings of sexual frustration and loneliness. Then in the 1980s, Tom's career at the art museum took off and he gained another support system to replace those he had lost. He advanced progressively into responsible positions and developed a highly respected status with co-workers and artists in the art world.

During this period, Tom's social life diminished but he derived great satisfaction from his working relationships. In the several years prior to entering treatment, there were major changes in the administration's support of Tom's interests and the social environment at work. Support staff were let go, the physical plant was allowed to deteriorate, raises became smaller, and his input seemed less valued. The existing staff became more competitive as a result and the earlier sense of community was fractured. These changes left Tom feeling powerless and "unloved." Tom's drinking became more frequent and intense. It was in this context that the intervention was staged, which was temporarily devastating. Tom gained fresh clarity and relief by understanding the link between the change in his social milieu and his escalating depression and self-esteem issues.

Goal Setting

I wondered aloud with Tom if the occasions of his drunken, inappropriate phone calls to colleagues from work had coincided with the intervention or had increased since the intervention had taken place. Tom was realizing that he had long felt unsafe expressing anger in general and particularly now at work after his job had been threatened. I then posited whether he was using alcohol to free himself to express these feelings that he was unable to express when sober as well as to defy other people's efforts to control him by flaunting his drinking at them. Tom felt his feelings confirmed and recognized as we followed these trails. As his feelings were clarified he became more aware of the underlying messages carried by his drinking.

This raised another question in my mind: Why would Tom express anger and defiance in ways that would risk his job which had been so important to him in terms of social life and status? Tom was self-reflective and curious enough to actively engage in this question. Our exploration that followed led to a series of associations taking him back to a sequence of interpersonal conflicts with parents and other loved ones; he was always more prone to blame himself than to criticize others. His fear of losing their affection and acceptance, as well as his guilt about hurting those that he loved, seemed to explain the conflict that led him to feel inhibited about expressing anger and other assertive feelings. The self-destructive aspect of his drinking was self-punishment for guilt provoked by his anger at his colleagues, the most important people currently in his life. Drinking soothed and numbed the pain associated with recent losses. It was also a means to express anger at the worlds that had abandoned him, as well as anger at himself for having let it happen that way.

This interpretation had a dramatic impact on Tom and led to a broadening of the focus of therapy from simply on the drinking behavior and the immediate crisis at work to include his conflicts about expressing anger and other self interests, including sexual and romantic needs, and the character vulnerabilities and relational/interpersonal issues in which these conflicts were rooted.

I suggested that Tom describe his ideal pattern of drinking. This pattern would enable him to enjoy what he defined as the benefits of drinking without the negative consequences. This required that Tom do a cost/benefit analysis of his drinking based on what he found to be the self-affirming benefits of alcohol compared to the ways in which alcohol conflicted with things that were important to him. Tom decided that he wanted to limit his drinking to a level at which he felt somewhat relaxed without impairing his judgment or losing control. He would cease drinking on evenings preceding three morning meetings weekly. He would try not to drink when he was upset and thus more vulnerable to overdoing it.

He wanted to develop other skills for managing these feelings. We agreed to establish drinking limits for the times he would drink and evaluate them over time to see whether they accomplished his stated goals. Based on his experience and some reading that I suggested,

Tom decided on a limit of two drinks per day. For events lasting more than three or four hours, he was allowed four drinks maximum. He also decided to stick with wine rather than vodka, because he could better regulate his intake with wine.

Working Toward Moderation

By the end of the second month of therapy, Tom had dramatically cut down his drinking to his target ideal drinking plan. By examining the external circumstances historically associated with heavy drinking in the past and identifying the internal feeling states and external triggers currently associated with drink thoughts and urges, Tom developed an active plan to support himself in achieving his drinking goals. This plan included lifestyle changes that would support moderate drinking and alternative ways of addressing the painful issues.

Tom lacked opportunities for alcohol-free socializing, and this vacuum needed to be filled with alternative ways of meeting people. As Tom considered this problem, he recognized that his lack of social contact was, in part, avoidance motivated by a fear of being hurt and disappointed as he had been in the past. Tom recognized the value of social support for facilitating the changes he was making as well as giving him a context for tackling these fears. I suggested a group with a harm reduction orientation run by a colleague of mine. The group assisted attempts at moderation, helping members to find out whether this was a viable option for them. Tom joined the group immediately. He was able to use the group effectively as a source of information and learned coping strategies used by other group members. The group served Tom as an interpersonal laboratory for working on the fears that kept him from socializing in his life.

As Tom monitored his drinking and witnessed related thoughts arising spontaneously, he was examining his feelings more now that he was drinking less. He clarified and separated the relationship between drinking and angry, depressed withdrawal at work and in relation to his art career. Tom realized how he had experienced a loss of support, first in the art world and gay community, and later at work, which was translated into withdrawal of support from his sense of self. He witnessed that his passive-aggressive approach expressed by excessive drinking at inappropriate times compounded his deflated self-esteem.

I pointed out that this other-orientation was related to a childlike sense of himself as dependent on the encouragement of others and fearful of risking further loss or retaliation if he expressed himself in a powerful, autonomous way. The strength of our therapeutic alliance that had been built during the course of our work together enabled me to feel that I could risk making such a direct confrontation to Tom, and he accepted it in the helpful spirit in which I meant it. Tom thought about my comments and became interested in exploring the fearful fantasies that had kept him trapped in this powerless state. The museum might fire him for making waves; he decided that if he couldn't get the support that he needed at work that he would never find a better job; if he tried to reinvigorate his career in the art world through writing, teaching, public speaking, and so forth, he would never be accepted by his peers. He was able to see that all of these concerns were unrealistic and more likely based on echoes of past relationships, mainly those with father and mother.

Tom's father had been a hard-working, uninvolved, distant man who died when Tom was in his early twenties. Tom felt like they never really knew one another. Tom said he always wished they had been closer and wondered whether he could have done more to make that happen. He could see how he had actively avoided conflict with his father in the hope that they might be closer. On the other hand, Tom experienced his mother as too involved. She was always criticizing him and was very reactive to his successes and failures. With her, he always tried to perform perfectly to avoid her disapproval, yet he secretly resented the pressure and wished to be free of her. These relational binds set the stage for Tom's fragile self-esteem and later patterns of relating to others. Tom began to recognize how his drinking fit into these issues in several ways.

These insights seemed to reinvigorate Tom. He felt validated in his anger and sadness about his past losses and current difficulties at work yet felt optimistic about expressing himself in an active, assertive way. He made plans to present at a major international conference in his area of expertise, became re-energized in his work on his book, and began to address problems at work. Eventually Tom went to his supervisors and spoke with them about his drinking problem, from his perspective, as he now identified it. He explained to them about his moderation goal and plan for maintaining the changes by addressing the other issues in his life. Over the next few months, Tom was able to get his associates' active support for his plan and began to bring ideas for new projects to them in a way that elicited their encouragement. This helped rebuild a sense of teamwork. Now Tom could see his own contribution to the old patterns of losing, and how his renewed participation could turn that around.

In the fifth month of treatment, Tom decided to attempt thirty days of abstinence from alcohol. This came from him with no direct recommendation from me. He wanted to prove that he could do it, in part as a way to symbolically show the prior treatment program that they had been wrong about him. He had also become deeply interested in what he might learn about himself off alcohol when he was not doing it as a response to pressure from others or fear.

The thirty days went by in a rather uncomplicated way, although some very important work went on around the problem of how he might fill his time and what he might drink as alternatives to alcohol. He discovered several alcohol-free bars and became more active in the art world of gallery openings and other art-related events. After this period, he gradually re-instituted his drinking plan.

He told me about one minor "slip" that occurred a month later, about seven months into the treatment. He had violated his two-drink limit by having four drinks in a two-hour period. As he described the situation, he was not upset because nothing inappropriate or risky had happened. He had internalized the value of examining his drinking to understand what fueled it and was eager to talk about it with me. He had been out at a bar to see the bartender who worked there. He was very attracted to the bartender although he knew nothing would happen between them; the man was in a monogamous relationship. In talking about the slip, it became clear that his drinking helped him entertain a fantasy about something between them and, at the same time, was a response to sadness that was evoked by his awareness that nothing could happen. The slip had been a useful doorway to important issues not yet fully addressed in the therapy. This event brought the issue of Tom's intense wishes for sexual and romantic relationships into the therapy and the conflicting feelings that had kept him frustrated and lonely.

This issue was also revealed in two instances when Tom had come to sessions while somewhat intoxicated, once early on in the therapy and a second time close to the slip described above. In both instances, soon into the sessions, Tom mentioned that he had had two glasses of wine before coming. In the first instance, Tom said that he had wanted me to see him in that state. He was more spontaneous and lively than usual. I stated the obvious, that alcohol seemed to loosen him up, and said that I also wondered whether there were particular aspects of himself that he found easier to discuss after having had something to drink. He giggled and said, "Absolutely! It has to do with sex. I don't think I could have said that if I hadn't been drinking." Our discussion revealed that his drinking had enabled him to bring up a subject that he had otherwise been too inhibited to discuss with me. It also led me to wonder whether he was aware of any conflict or anxiety about his sexual wishes. He denied feeling conflicted and the subject was dropped for a while.

It re-emerged during our discussion on the second occasion that he came to a session after drinking. Now, several months later, he was able to recognize that he had a whole set of uncomfortable concerns about talking about sex with me. Would I become uncomfortable and withdrawn or criticize him? Would we be able to talk about sex and maintain our professional relationship, that is, not act out together sexually? He also began to recognize that he did feel some shame about his sexuality related to self-critical attitudes that he had not acknowledged as his own, instead projecting them onto others. This process had been reflected in his worries about my criticizing him. This exploration of his feelings about discussing his sexuality with me led to our looking at how these issues contributed to his avoidance of close personal relationships in his life that had the possibility of becoming romantic.

In the following months, Tom's drinking stabilized in the ideal pattern that he had envisioned for himself. His relationships at work continued to improve and his career seemed to open up again with opportunities for consulting and the professional acceptance that he had longed for. He began to seek out social opportunities in his professional world as well as through gay organizations that held activities of interest to him. During this period, he began to widen his circle of friends and began to date.

At this point in the therapy, ten months into the

work, Tom's drinking was no longer an active issue, although he was aware that he needed to be ever mindful of his vulnerability to fall back into his earlier patterns of drinking. We discussed a relapse prevention plan that included an identification of the emotional and lifestyle triggers that had been associated with heavy drinking in the past. We discussed specific cognitive and behavioral strategies for managing them in alcohol-free ways. For example, Tom had identified sexual frustration and loneliness as two main precipitants of heavy drinking. However, the more important trigger seemed to be when he began to tell himself that it was hopeless for him to think that he could ever have a healthy, satisfying relationship and that the best he could hope for was whatever contact was available, regardless of how demeaning it was to his sense of self. Excessive alcohol use could then be justified as a necessary way of assuaging the feelings of shame and self-degradation accompanying these pursuits. Anticipating these feelings and depressing thoughts as heavy drinking triggers enabled Tom to come up with an alternative way of thinking about his loneliness and frustration when it arose. He discovered means to tolerate these feelings while he developed the social skills and socializing opportunities necessary for him to meet an appropriate partner. He would also actively affirm to himself the actual steps that he had taken and progress that he had made toward successfully meeting these needs in his life. The plan contained specific goals for continuing to modify his lifestyle in ways that would further support moderate drinking. It continued therapeutic work on the self-esteem and relationship issues that kept him vulnerable to relapsing to his earlier problem drinking.

Outcome

Because the focus on alcohol receded into the background at this point, I will end the detailed description of Tom's treatment here. The treatment is still alive and productive at the time of this writing. During this period, he has generally maintained his moderate drinking with a few minor slips similar to those discussed previously. These occurred around emotionally charged interpersonal situations and were used as opportunities for further learning that deepened Tom's work in therapy. The central focus of therapy has been on strengthening Tom's ability to maintain his self-esteem in more autonomous ways. He thinks differently about these insecurities and is able to take constructive actions in the world that give him direct feedback about his value as a person. A related focus has been on working through the threatening fears and fantasies that have kept Tom from freely expressing his emotional needs in relationships. Therapy has helped Tom to feel more confident about and successful at pursuing satisfying relationships in his life. During this period his depression has not returned.

Tom has demonstrated an ability to cope without alcohol with many challenging situations that had been triggers for excessive drinking in the past. These strategies have become familiar tools in his repertoire of coping skills. This, in conjunction with his awareness of his emotional vulnerabilities and continuing commitment to his emotional growth, suggest a very good prognosis for the future.

Commentary by Andrew Tatarsky

Tom's case is representative of the experience of many problem drinkers in several important ways. Many are coerced into unnecessary, expensive, and inappropriate abstinence-oriented treatments. Tom's experience of being unnecessarily "intervened" at work and coerced into treatment are unfortunately very common. These dangerous tendencies reflect society's attitudes toward problem drinkers and other drug users. These attitudes inform typical treatment approaches available for these clients. This often results in a jump to the kind of drastic intervention that Tom experienced, which may actually increase a potential client's unwillingness to work on the substance problem.

Secondly, his experience reflects a tendency to lump all excessive substance use in the category of addiction with the generally accompanying assumption that abstinence is the only acceptable goal. Tom's first treatment experience did not allow for an open discussion of moderation of his drinking as an alternative goal to be considered. As a result, he had no way to explore in depth whether this might be possible for him and to learn the necessary skills to seriously attempt this change in drinking behavior. The overwhelming majority of all forms of substance use treatment and training programs in this country require that participants begin with a willingness to work toward complete abstinence as the only acceptable goal. These limitations in thinking and treatment options prevent many people, like Tom, who wish to explore the moderation option, from getting the support that they need to see whether this is possible for them. This lack of appropriate treatment may set people up to intensify their substance use because the actual problems do not get addressed. They become compounded by feelings of resentment, frustration, and anxiety caused by the negative messages given to them. That experience, as in Tom's case, can exacerbate the issues related to the problem drinking, contribute to intensified drinking, and set up both client and clinician to fail. This problem may explain much of the failure reported by the substance use treatment field.

By beginning with an attempt to join with the client around his or her view of the problem and desired goals, the harm reduction approach has a better chance of creating a therapeutic atmosphere of safety in which the client can begin to meaningfully address the drinking *where the client is ready to begin.*

With Tom, this approach did lead to a strong alliance early on in the treatment, which supported him in achieving his goal of moderating his drinking while successfully addressing the depression, self-esteem problems, conflicts about constructively expressing anger, and other relational needs, as well as the lifestyle deficits that needed to be modified to support continued moderate drinking.

Tom is representative of many problem drinkers whose drinking is secondary to powerful emotional issues driving the heavy use of alcohol. Many, like Tom, have the motivation and psychological-mindedness necessary for making good use of psychotherapy while successfully moderating their drinking. Many others recognize through their attempt at moderating their drinking that this is a practical impossibility and become more willing to accept abstinence as the most reasonable goal for themselves. The context created by this approach allows this awareness to arise from an examination by the client of his own direct experience rather than from the judgment of someone else.

The approach described and illustrated here is an example of harm reduction psychotherapy for active substance users that is based on an integration of psychodynamic and social learning theories in its understanding of substance use problems and in the combining of cognitive and behavioral self-management strategies with psychodynamic interventions in the treatment process. The case illustration demonstrated its effectiveness in helping a client whose excessive drinking was secondary to depression achieve stable moderation of drinking while addressing a range of other emotional and lifestyle issues related to the drinking problem. This approach is also effective with clients whose ultimate goal is abstinence, as both the initial choice of goals and the outcome of the therapy emerge out of a therapeutic process that clarifies what is ideal for each individual rather than being prescribed in advance by the clinician.

References

Carey, K.B. and Carey, M.P. (1990). Enhancing the treatment attendance of mentally ill chemical abusers. *Journal of Behavior Therapy and Experimental Psychiatry*, 21, 205–209.

Heather, N., Wodak, A., Nadelman, E. and O'Hare, P. (Eds.)

(1993). *Psychoactive Drugs and Harm Reduction: From Faith to Science.* London: Whurr Publishers.

Khantzian, E.J., Halliday, K.S. and McAuliffe, W.E. (1990). *Addiction and the Vulnerable Self.* New York: Guilford Press.

Marlatt, G.A. and Gordon, J. (1985). *Relapse Prevention.* New York: Guilford Press.

Marlatt, G.A. and Tapert, S.F. (1993). Harm reduction: Reducing the risks of addictive behaviors. In J.S. Baer, G.A. Marlatt and R.J. McMahon (Eds.). *Addictive Behaviors Across the Life Span: Prevention, Treatment and Policy Issues* (pp. 243–273). Newbury Park, CA: Sage.

Peele, S. and Brodsky, A. (1992). *The Truth about Addiction and Recovery.* New York: Fireside.

Rothschild, D. (1995). Working with addicts in private practice: Overcoming initial resistance. In A. Washton (Ed.). *Psychotherapy and Substance Abuse: A Practitioner's Handbook* (pp. 192–203). New York: Guilford Press.

Rotgers, F. (1998). Using harm reduction in treating problem drinkers. In L. Van DeCreek (Ed.). Innovations in Clinical Practice, 16. Odessa, FL: Professional Resource Exchange.

Woodward, A., Epstein, J., Goerer, J., Melnick, D., Thoreson, R. and Wilson, D. (1997). The Drug Abuse Treatment Gap: Recent Estimates. Health Care Financing Review, 18(3).

Wurmser, L. (1978). *The Hidden Dimension: Psychodynamics in Compulsive Drug Use.* New York: Jason Aronson Inc.

2

The Psychoanalytic Contribution

Mrs. G.: One Woman's Struggle for Dignity
                                    —Mark Sehl

During the twenty years that I have worked with people with drug problems, my conviction has grown that psychoanalytic thinking about these issues offers the most powerful framework for helping people address them. A psychoanalytic perspective sees an understanding of the total person as relevant to one's personal difficulties and the treatment process: needs, feelings, self-image, expectations of others, ideals, strengths, vulnerabilities, interpersonal skills, judgments, coping skills, and environmental factors. Based on this, psychoanalytic treatments are thoroughly individualized treatments. Thus, psychoanalytically informed treatments can vary widely in their appearance from the classical four- to five-times-per-week psychoanalysis to once weekly, behaviorally oriented therapy, and everything in between, depending on the needs of the client. This individualizing of the treatment process, the emphasis in matching the treatment to the needs of the client, and the primacy placed on the therapeutic relationship as anchor in the process and area for exploration of the issues are all in accordance with the framework of harm reduction.

The treatments described in the stories in this book all have psychoanalytic elements. The variety in the stories reveals the diversity of forms that psychoanalytic psychotherapy can take. Yet all share the commitment to the central psychoanalytic idea that problematic drug use reflects personal meanings that are not fully in the user's awareness and that the process of bringing these meanings more fully into awareness opens up possibilities for positive change.

BRIEF OVERVIEW OF PSYCHOANALYSIS

Since Freud established psychoanalysis at the turn of the twentieth century, many different schools of psychoanalytic thought have evolved, each emphasizing different elements in its theories of human functioning or therapy. The thread that runs through the variety of psychoanalytic approaches that currently exist is the idea that human behavior is shaped and driven by a number of different elements within each individual that are personally meaningful and that a conscious awareness of these meaningful elements increases our possibilities for greater choice and freedom in our lives.

This perspective begins in the late 1890s with what is to me the most important of Sigmund Freud's (1895) contributions to understanding of human suffering: his discovery of what he called the "dynamic unconscious." Simply put, he proposed that there are forces—dynamics—partially outside of our awareness, that motivate our behavior. By forces he meant needs, wishes, judgments, and beliefs. In short, he discovered a hidden dimension of personal meaning within human behavior. Further, he suggested that these forces are kept out of our awareness by another part of the mind, another force called "ego defenses," because they are threatening to us and cause anxiety, guilt, or shame. The anxiety-provoking threat leads to various defensive ways of keeping these aspects of ourselves out of awareness. The defenses also operate out of awareness. As long as these dynamics remain outside of awareness we are relatively powerless over them. Their ability to push us into compulsive or impulsive behavior gives rise to intense inner pressures and creates painful feelings of anxiety, guilt, shame, and despair, all for no apparent reason. Following this idea, psychoanalytic treatments then generally have the goal of helping people to become more consciously aware of these inner motivations and defenses against them, to understand more fully how their minds operate, so they can see new possibilities for addressing or expressing what has been outside awareness.

While this idea remains at the core of all psychoanalytic or psychodynamic schools of psychotherapy, a variety of schools of psychoanalysis have proliferated that differ in almost every other aspect of psychoanalytic theory: what are the important dynamics, how they come into being, how the human psyche is constructed, how to understand human suffering, how to conduct the treatment, and even what to call psychoanalysis (Mitchell and Black, 1995). Psychoanalysis has evolved as a field of study and treatment since being founded by Sigmund Freud more than 100 years ago. Many of Freud's original ideas continue to inform the field of psychoanalysis as well as the world at large and the substance use treatment field, often unbeknownst to practitioners. But it has also proliferated into many different schools with different theories of normal development, emotional and personality problems, and treatment. Many of these developments within the field have led to ideas that have very specific powerful value for understanding and addressing the needs of people with drug problems. In fact, a look at Levin and Weiss's (1994) collection of psychoanalytic papers on drug addiction reveals that each new development within psychoanalytic theory was also reflected in its application to understanding and treating people with drug problems.

In terms of forms of treatment, in classical thinking there is a distinction between a classical full psychoanalysis that I described above and psychoanalytically oriented or psychodynamic psychotherapy (these terms are generally interchangeable). The former had as its goal as complete an understanding of the psyche as possible with a thorough resolution of early traumas believed to be at the core of current emotional problems. In this approach, the ideal was traditionally held to be a treatment in which the patient lay on the couch four to five times a week saying everything that came to mind. It was assumed that the patient would run into conflicts that would cause the person to stop and interrupt the flow of associations because the symbolic conflict caused anxiety. These conflicts were held to be related to the problems for which the person sought help.

The analyst's job was to listen for these moments and try to help the patient recognize and understand the conflict causing the anxiety. The latter, psychoanalytic psychotherapy, entailed the application of psychoanalytic understanding to therapy with more limited goals targeting specific problems only. This approach could be conducted in a once- or twice-weekly format.

However, in the current proliferation of schools of thought, the traditional distinctions between analysis and psychotherapy are being questioned by many prominent contributors, as are ideas about required frequency of sessions and most other hallmarks of the traditional distinctions between what is and what is not psychoanalysis. For a good discussion of these issues see Stephen Mitchell and Margaret Black's book, *Freud and Beyond.*

PSYCHOANALYSIS AND PSYCHOTHERAPY OF DRUG PROBLEMS

Psychoanalysis has gotten a bad rap regarding the treatment of people with drug and alcohol problems. Many people who have heard something about the role of psychoanalysis in the history of the treatment of these problems have heard that psychoanalytic approaches failed in the 1940s and 1950s and are no longer considered as viable treatments for these problems. The idea is that psychoanalysts put drug- and alcohol-dependent people on the psychoanalytic couch four times a week doing no more than listening to their rambling thoughts (free associations), occasionally muttering an analytic "uh huh" in response. The myth continues that while the analytic intention was often sincere, that is, to get at the underlying reasons for the drug use as a way to cure it, the result was usually continued or intensified drug use.

These "historical facts" are often used to justify the mistaken claim that Alcoholics Anonymous or coercive behavioral treatments are the only approaches that are helpful to drug users, as well as the related claim that drug users cannot benefit from insight-oriented therapy (i.e., therapy geared toward discovering the meaningful aspect of drug use) until their drug use is stopped. These ideas are commonly held by laypeople, substance abuse treatment specialists, and psychoanalysts alike. These claims are versions of the one problem/one solution model that I discuss in Chapter 4.

In fact, the psychoanalytic therapies advocated for people with drug problems have never been of the sort characterized above. The stereotype of the silent, uninvolved analyst letting the patient ramble on incessantly with little positive result while life-threatening drug use rages on unaddressed is simply bad psychoanalysis or psychotherapy done by poorly trained professionals. The psychoanalytic approach caricatured in the popular claim is based on the classical approach to psychoanalysis I discussed above.

The claim that psychoanalysis failed drug users because of this approach can be easily put to rest. Classical psychoanalysis has never generally been advocated for people with serious behavioral impulse control problems or in severe life crises (Eisler, 1958). Classical technique was seen as an ideal to be deviated from as the particular client required. The deviations were geared toward greater activity, personal involvement, and direction by the therapist. The caveat was that the client's need for these things from the therapist would also be explored and understood when appropriate. The goal of all this was to maximize clients' sense of self-mastery and of being in charge of themselves, including how to use the therapy.

Since the early 1900s, shortly after the birth of psychoanalysis, this idea is expressed in a thread that runs through the major psychoanalytic writings on the treatment of people with drug problems: namely, that these people need something other than "classical technique." It was generally recommended that effective therapy with this group of people needed to be a more active therapeutic approach that included giving information and advice, emotional support, specific techniques for helping people change their drug using behavior, and the use of larger support systems in conjunction with the ongoing effort to help patients become aware of the meanings of their drug use and how it related to other issues in their lives.

These basic sentiments live on in the work of many psychoanalysts and psychoanalytically oriented therapists who have both a psychoanalytic understanding of problem drug use and how to apply these ideas in the service of actively helping drug users make changes in their drug use and other troubling life issues.

Given the proliferation of psychoanalytic schools of thought, it is risky to describe the basic features of a psychoanalytic approach to psychotherapy for people with drug problems. I do think, based on my own clinical experience and my own reading of psychoanalysis, that the following are some defining features that most psychoanalytically minded practitioners would agree characterize psychoanalytic approaches.

The Inquiry into the Personal Meanings Expressed by Drug Use

This approach is committed to the idea that the more aware one is of the meanings expressed by drug use, the more possible change is. It seeks to discover or create alternative ways of addressing these meaningful elements. Psychoanalytic theory provides many different ideas about how we might understand the personal meaning that drug use has for people. Ideas that I discussed in Chapter 1 of this book all derive from psychoanalytic theories. The idea of the dynamic unconscious helps to point the way to developing curiosity about what these hidden meanings might be. It helps us to have understanding and compassion for why people may continue to use drugs despite increasing negative consequences.

An alternative model, the disease concept of addiction, suggests that this denial is a hallmark of the "disease." But it stops with the idea of the disease as a mysterious, unfathomable entity that can only be controlled.

Psychoanalytic thinking offers a more ambitious model. It suggests that we can get inside this "disease," decode the meanings it carries, and discover a deeper and more constructive resolution of them. I talk with my clients of the importance of us unwrapping their desire to use in order to unravel the multiple personal meanings it carries. It alerts us to question why these hidden meanings may be difficult to keep in awareness and how they might be emotionally or psychologically threatening. How might they create inner conflict? What might be the payoff of staying in the dark about themselves? How might it be painful or scary to see the truth about themselves?

Integrating Active Cognitive and Behavioral Strategies

When drug use feels out of control to the user or is clearly causing suffering and negative consequences in his or her life, the inquiry into the meaning of his or her use is usually not sufficient. The myth of the failure of psychoanalysis to be helpful to drug users that I challenged earlier is based on a view of psychoanalytic treatment that only focused on the inquiry and not the problematic behavior. There is no doubt that there are practitioners who work in this way. However, therapists like this are working to uphold doctrine and not to respond to the needs of their clients.

An analogy that makes the point well would be a therapist working with an actively suicidal person who only focuses on the meaning of the suicidal feelings and does not address potentially life-threatening behavior.

Psychotherapy for people with drug problems does generally need to contain active strategies that address the drug-using behavior and the process of changing behavior directly. This is not at odds with psychoanalytic thinking; psychoanalysis has a framework for understanding why some people may need the therapist to offer more active help in this area. In Chapter 3 I tell the story of the experiences that led me to appreciate the essential value of using behavioral and cognitive strategies with drug-using clients. Here I will say a few words about how I see these two approaches working together in an integrative fashion.

Psychoanalysis contains important ideas relevant to under-standing and helping people with excessive and compulsive drug use. One important idea that I explore in greater depth in

Chapter 6 is viewing drug use as an attempt to cope, to adapt to painful circumstances, or as an attempt to self-medicate. If a drug helps to quell anxiety or other painful feelings, these feelings may come to trigger the intense desire, urge, or craving to use when they arise. In addition, the person may lack the ability to manage, tolerate, sit with, or soothe these feelings. In this event, the feeling triggers for the urge to use may be experienced as overwhelming. So drugs supply, fortify, or compensate for certain emotional management skills that are deficient or lacking. Psychoanalysis calls these "ego functions."

Ego functions (Freud, A., 1936) refers to a set of cognitive skills that are involved in self-managing our feelings and behavior. This includes self-awareness, or observing oneself moment to moment so that sequences of perception, feeling, thought, and behavior can be identified; judgment or thinking things through to see possible consequences of our actions; and emotional management skills like working with breathing, learning to relax, learning to express feelings in words, being able to identify and put feelings into words, and others. This is the area in which cognitive-behavioral strategies are very helpful.

So we can think of the psychoanalytic rationale for using active cognitive and behavioral techniques as helping the client learn or develop the functions that are lacking. As these functions are developed by the client in therapy, the pressure to use drugs will diminish as emotional pressure decreases.

The Importance of the Therapeutic Relationship

Psychodynamic approaches also place great importance on the therapeutic relationship. There are several reasons for this.

A good therapeutic relationship, part of the "right fit" that I discuss in Chapter 4, provides support and creates a feeling of safety that functions as a foundation for doing the often hard work involved with making important changes in oneself.

Today, most psychodynamic practitioners see this relationship as a collaborative effort at discovering the meaning of the client's problematic drug use and suffering and finding new and better solutions. This collaborative quality is also inherently empowering to the client.

The therapeutic relationship can also be a kind of laboratory in which the client's typical ways of relating to important others can be identified and new ways of relating can be explored and practiced. As this relates to our subject, the connections between drug use (or the desire to use) and interpersonal relationship factors may be explored by observing how the client's using relates to the feelings, fantasies, wishes, and fears that appear in the relationship with the therapist. This can work in two ways. How the client imagines or expects the therapist will react to drug use or the desire to use provides important information about how significant others in the client's life have reacted both to drug use but also, maybe more importantly, to what the drug use symbolically expresses, such as anger, fear, the wish to comfort oneself, a wish to be free from the perceived control of the other, and so on. On the other hand, drug use and wishes to use may come up as reactions to what is happening in therapy and to the therapist. Exploring this connection can help unwrap the way in which drug use is a meaningful response to the feelings evoked in the relationship with the therapist.

HARM REDUCTION IS CONSISTENT WITH PSYCHOANALYTIC APPROACHES

The central goals of harm reduction—meeting the client as an individual, starting from where the client is, assuming the client has strengths that can be supported, accepting small incremental changes as steps in the right direction, not holding abstinence (or any preconceived notions) as a necessary precondition of the therapy before really getting to know the individual, and developing a collaborative, empowering relationship with the client—are all consistent with psychoanalytic thinking.

The psychodynamic assumption that drug use holds important personal meanings suggests why some drug users may not be able to give up or otherwise modify drug use until other alternative ways of expressing these needs are found. This provides theoretical support for the harm reduction assumption that many users need to continue to use drugs while in therapy until these alternatives are found. In speaking of the importance of defenses, a psychoanalytic tenet is that you don't take something away unless you have something with which to replace it. The safety and support of a strong therapeutic alliance can be a prerequisite within which clients can begin to develop the courage and skills necessary to make changes in their drug use.

I selected Mark Sehl's story of Mrs. G. to illustrate the topic of this chapter because it describes a psychoanalytic treatment that breaks many of the traditional ideas about what psychoanalysis is and challenges the myth of the passive uninvolved analyst. Yet it remains true to the psychoanalytic project of uncovering the hidden meanings of the patient's alcohol problems and, in this case, leads to a stable abstinence.

It is the story of an elderly woman who suffered from severe "alcoholic" drinking and depression. Using a psychoanalytic harm reduction approach that initially accepted Mrs. G.'s drinking, the treatment led to her stopping drinking, a lifting of her depression, and a general improvement in her health and quality of life. Sehl used an approach informed by the school of modern psychoanalysis, founded by Hyman Spotnitz (1985).

Mrs. G.: One Woman's Struggle for Dignity
by Mark Sehl

When I first met Mrs. G. she was literally lying in her urine, saying she didn't want to go on living any longer. She wasn't eating, the apartment smelled, and neighbors were complaining of the odor. Mrs. G. told me that she couldn't walk because she had fallen and broken a hip while she was intoxicated. The patient said she was just a social drinker and complained that the home attendants were refusing to let her have any more to drink. Mrs. G. said that she had two cocktails a day, while, to make sure I understood the point, the home attendant was shaking the empty quart of scotch behind the patient's back. I said to Mrs. G. that on the one hand she seemed not to be concerned about her drinking, but on the other hand she was telling me she hurt herself badly due to drinking. I was hoping she could grasp the contradictions in her statements.

It is important to understand some of the events that led up to Mrs. G.'s deterioration. This 83-year-old woman came to the attention of the agency several years before I began my employment there. A concerned friend referred Mrs. G. for help. At that time, Mrs. G. required home care assistance due to her inability to care for herself after a hip operation. There was a passing mention of alcohol consumption on the intake form.

Several months later Mrs. G. was hospitalized for severe depression. The precipitating event was the loss of her dog. The evaluating psychiatrist diagnosed the situation as severe reactive depression with alcohol habituation and suicidal ideas. He recommended treatment for the depression, control of alcoholism, psychotherapy and antidepressant drugs, and coordination of health care and social rehabilitation. Mrs. G. was assigned shopping and home attendant services by the agency, but as far as I could ascertain, neither psychotherapy nor consultation regarding alcoholism treatment was ever mentioned in the record.

Not long after her return home Mrs. G. was ambulating badly, had swollen legs, refused to leave her home, and was combining high doses of aspirin with alcohol. By the following year, the patient had completely deteriorated. In other words, within one year the client was almost non-ambulatory. The agency terminated shopping and home care services because the patient was now on Medicaid, which provided daily home attendant care.

Three years later the same family friend contacted the agency again complaining that home attendants were going home early. In addition, she was concerned that Mrs. G.'s Medicaid coverage might be terminated due to the discovery of a cash surplus not allowed by Medicaid. It was at this point that I met Mrs. G.

As I began working with Mrs. G., she gradually told me of her drinking habits and history. Mrs. G. mentioned that she was embarrassed about her loss of bladder control. I suggested that drinking might be affecting her bladder control, loss of appetite, and depression. I said I was convinced that if she could stop drinking, her incontinence and her life in general could improve. She was interested in the fact that her incontinence might improve if she stopped drinking.

In the meantime, her friend told the liquor store owner not to sell her any more liquor. Mrs. G. told me she wished her friend would mind her own business. It seems that many people were telling Mrs. G. what to do—the home attendants, her friend, and the agency. I said maybe she was also telling me to mind my own business. She said no. I noticed in the first months of working with her that this patient had a very defiant attitude, although she couldn't express this defiance directly. It seemed more important for her to be defiant than to take better care of herself.

I was wondering whether my approach might be wrong for her. I was trying to encourage her to stop drinking. She was defiant, but in a passive-aggressive way. She couldn't tell her best friend, or the agency, to leave her alone. Mrs. G. was defeating herself and everyone around her. I was concerned that if she followed my suggestion to stop drinking, she might be inclined to sabotage her own efforts.

On several occasions I asked Mrs. G. again if she didn't feel like telling me to mind my own business. After all, I was trying to get her to do things just like everyone else. First there were many denials. I was different, she said. She didn't feel that way about me. However, at one point Mrs. G. revealed that she was afraid that if she told me to mind my own business I would go away and not come back. She admitted that she did get angry when I was trying to get her to stop drinking, even though she knew it was for her own good.

I used every opportunity I had to elicit some feelings of dissatisfaction with what I was doing. Mrs. G. told me to mind my own business. Because Mrs. G. was discharging angry feelings, the depression lifted. The self-attacks ("I'm no good") associated with the depression can be seen as a way of avoiding attacking the person upon whom one feels dependent. Although the self is attacked, the recriminations belong to someone else. This pattern often stems from early childhood experiences when children are overly reprimanded, punished, and/or abandoned if they misbehave or criticize adults. Ironically, those same adults, unaware of the emotional impact of their upbringing, use methods that were once used on them to exert control over their children.

The school of modern psychoanalysis advocates "joining the resistance," which eventually lays the path for the client's expression of unacceptable aggressive impulses. Instead of suggesting that Mrs. G. stop drinking, I joined the resistance. At times I would say that she might need to drink because it made her feel better. I said I could see her point in wanting a few cocktails to relax her. Other people did that, why shouldn't she? At times I noticed she was surprised at my reactions, but she said nothing. By joining the resistance, Mrs. G. did not have to fight me. Resistance can be viewed as a person's strength until he becomes more aware of his conflicts. It is often difficult to say yes without the capacity to say no. I did not bring up the drinking again.

With the exception of medical emergencies, this patient had not been out of the apartment in two years. I ordered a wheelchair. Mrs. G. was terrified of falling. However, she managed to tolerate these feelings and ventured outside. She greeted Joe, the doorman, who was very happy to see her. She wanted me to come back the next day to take her out again. She enjoyed sitting in the sun and watching people.

Some months later, Mrs. G. told me that lately, when thinking about having a drink, she remembered that I said her life could change if she stopped drinking. She said that thought made an impact on her. She told me she wanted to try to stop drinking. About that time the home attendants noticed that Mrs. G. had been unusually groggy. I asked if she had been taking any medication. The attendants showed me a bottle of Percocet on the dresser. Percocet was known to produce drug dependence of the morphine type; it was dangerous when mixed with alcohol because the patient could exhibit an additive central nervous system depression. It should be given with caution to the elderly and those with liver or kidney impairment. I called her doctor and asked him about the prescription. After our talk, the physician visited Mrs. G. and took the medication with him.

I discovered that the home attendants were indeed leaving Mrs. G.'s home early. This was partially in response to Mrs. G.'s hostility and belligerence when she was inebriated. I think Mrs. G. told the attendants to go home so she could drink. Furthermore, she had a rather snobbish attitude toward "help" and had a self-pitying personality that invited attack, especially when drinking. I talked with the home attendants, explaining that alcoholism was a disease. Mrs. G. really wasn't in control as long as she continued to drink. As a consequence, they didn't feel so angry, alone, and helpless with this problem. They no longer showed up late and they did not leave early.

Mrs. G. struggled with her desire to drink. She felt overwhelmed with the idea of never drinking again. She was often tearful and frustrated. I said it was important to try to tolerate getting through a minute or an hour a day without drinking. She was winning the battle as long as she resisted the impulse in the moment. I tried to enlist the help of Alcoholics Anonymous to see if counselors would visit, but at that time they were not receptive to making home visits. As Mrs. G. drank less, she became more motivated and less irritable, and the home attendants were more interested in working as a team. One home attendant appeared for work in a starched uniform. She made milkshakes for Mrs. G., which I suggested might help fight the urge to drink. Mrs. G. was also eating better, because her appetite improved once she stopped drinking.

During this time, Mrs. G. talked to me at length about the death of her dog, which in turn brought up the loss of her husbands. In her more sober moments, she was intelligible. She was a strong, independent woman, tall and striking in appearance. She had a strong handshake, which she said she got from riding horses. I learned more about her background. She used to get up at 6:00 A.M., go riding with her husband, and then go to work with him. She survived three husbands, all physicians, and she worked with all three, managing the day-to-day details of their offices.

Talking relieved much of Mrs. G.'s depression. I could see that throughout her life, her husbands were the focal point of her existence. I believe the relationship with her therapist, another man, stimulated her and countered the loneliness in her life, particularly while she was giving up her reliance on alcohol, which is often felt to be a "friend."

She began to dream of her sisters. Three sisters died within a short period of each other, but the facts were not available to Mrs. G. because she had a difficult time remembering any details. However, the facts were not important. She had someone who listened; someone who liked her and cared about her life story.

During this period, Mrs. G. had one relapse and started drinking again. I used to visit her on Saturday mornings, and it was on one of those mornings that I discovered her asleep with a bottle of liquor next to her chair. I became irritated, and Mrs. G., after my lecture, asked me to pour the bottle down the drain. After I left the house, I felt uncomfortable with my behavior. Perhaps Mrs. G. needed to drink. After all, alcohol was a way of self-medicating and managing intolerable feelings of helplessness, anger, and low self-esteem. I felt I had made a mistake and returned to Mrs. G.'s home. I said that I didn't have the right to tell her what to do. She might need to drink, and she had a right to make that choice. I offered to get her another bottle. She said she didn't want one. She was just worried that she lost a friend when I got upset and left.

The therapist's feelings (technically called counter-transference reactions) guide the therapist's interventions and provide clues to the dynamic interactions involving *both* client and therapist. Mrs. G. could have been testing me to see how I would react if she drank again. It is likely that Mrs. G. was unconsciously seeking to provoke a negative reaction (my anger), which would prove to her I could not be trusted. Also, she was hoping for a different reaction from me. Her drinking could be seen as an attempt to liberate herself from an internal feeling of being controlled, with the consequent guilt feelings and physical deterioration as punishment for her wish. Admitting I was wrong (what I call a "countertransference slip") gave Mrs. G. the assurance that even if she did rebel (drinking) I would not leave her. In this instance *both* the client and therapist created a different ending to an old but familiar pattern of relationships.

Mrs. G. was on the wagon again. She became friendly with a neighbor whom she hadn't seen in a long time. The smells going through the vents to another neighbor's apartment stopped. Mrs. G. had difficulty remembering the day of the week, an obvious source of frustration. Together we developed a method to help her memory. Mrs. G. began to practice regaining her ability to remember things by organizing herself around a calendar we kept. She put ND for no drinking on each day she refrained from taking a drink. This helped her remember what day it was. I was attempting to stop smoking, so I also put NS on each day I managed to win the battle. I have fond memories of those times sitting with Mrs. G. by her window overlooking Manhattan. She talked about whatever came to her mind. These moments together were calm, unlike the times spent with Mrs. G. when she was drinking.

Mrs. G. gradually regained an interest in food, purchasing fruits on our walks together. "There are two melons, let's buy them," she would exclaim. One night she had a significant dream in which she was at a dinner where there was lobster served and twelve people appeared. If this was a reference to the Last Supper, neither the savior nor the apostles actually came. However, on several occasions the home attendants and I did have dinner with Mrs. G. These were enjoyable visits, far removed from the hostility that once existed between Mrs. G. and the home attendants.

Mrs. G. finally allowed the attendants to wheel her outside, whereas before she only trusted me to do this. One day she proudly called me into her room and with great enthusiasm said, "See, I can walk on my own!" She was now able to maneuver in her apartment with her walker. This made it possible for Mrs. G. to go to the bathroom without the assistance of the home attendants, alleviating some feelings of humiliation. The incontinence improved considerably, and so in turn did Mrs. G.'s sense of self-respect. Her loss of bladder control was what originally motivated her to consider giving up alcohol.

Psychotherapy managed to stabilize this client's life. She did not have a drink in fourteen months. Instead of a thirst for liquor, she became in her words "people hungry." She progressed from a state of self-absorption to having a desire to be more connected to people. In her words, "it's not so good to be so used to being alone."

Mrs. G. was able to walk on her own, had a nutritious balanced diet, and developed a more satisfying relationship with the home attendants. In many ways she regained her sense of pride and self-worth.

Countertransference is a very useful tool in understanding ourselves and our clients. The therapist needs to be aware of attitudes and reactions that can interfere with the treatment—reactions such as having too much invested in the success of the treatment. Also, there is a tendency to infantilize older adults because of their more helpless and dependent state. I have experienced professionals who, on their first meeting, automatically address older adults by their first names when they would not normally do this with a younger adult population.

This treatment was successful because I accepted the patient's expression of angry feelings. If I needed only to feel successful or was threatened by negative, critical feelings, I might not have been able to tolerate Mrs. G.'s angry feelings. Mrs. G.'s ability to be angry at me, the one she depended upon, served to lift her depression, and it helped to foster a sense of identity and inner strength. It is important to remember that Mrs. G. had experienced a number of losses in her life—three husbands, her sisters, and her dog. It was the loss of her dog that triggered one hospitalization for depression. She felt vulnerable to the expectation of losing me if she did something she felt I wouldn't like. Mrs. G. did mention that her parents were very strict, controlling, and impatient with her. One might hypothesize that as a child Mrs. G.'s expression of negative feelings or misbehavior was met with punishment and/or abandonment. Framed in the context of fear of punishment and vulnerability to loss, it was essential that Mrs. G. find a place to experience being able to be angry at someone upon whom she felt dependent and survive. When this capacity is not achieved within the safety of the client–therapist relationship, the self-attacks and self-depreciation related to depression and low self-esteem may remain unchanged.

Mrs. G. benefited from professional therapeutic intervention because the funds and professional expertise were in place at that time in that agency. As a result, Mrs. G.'s condition improved remarkably. She stopped drinking. As a consequence, her incontinence diminished and she was able to regain her appetite. She could walk again, freeing her up to leave her apartment for the first time in two years. She became people hungry. Above all, instead of feeling ashamed and hopeless, Mrs. G. regained her dignity and self-respect.

Commentary by Andrew Tatarsky

The story of Mrs. G. is another example of how powerful harm reduction psychotherapy can be in helping to bring about dramatic positive change for people with serious drug problems who may be simultaneously depressed, withdrawn, socially isolated, and experiencing numerous medical problems. In this case, an elderly, isolated, depressed, alcohol-dependent woman was able to use therapy to ultimately stop drinking, resolve her depression, become more physically healthy, and improve her social life and interpersonal relationships.

While the broad outlines of the psychotherapy described in this story do not fit that of the classical psychoanalytic model, it is clearly psychodynamic in its commitment to discovering the multiple meanings and functions of Mrs. G.'s drinking and the importance placed on the therapeutic relationship. The story also illustrates how a harm reduction approach naturally flows from a psychodynamic point of view.

Mrs. G.'s drinking was both a way of comforting herself in her depression and isolation and a way of expressing her defiance of other people's attempts to tell her what to do. Her need to be defiant may have been a way of sustaining a feeling of personal power and control over herself and her life in the face of the loss of power and control connected to aging and a series of significant personal losses. Yet, Mrs. G. felt unable to express her defiant feelings directly because of her fear of alienating others, and she discovered drinking as an indirect way of expressing them.

In recognizing these meanings of her drinking, Sehl knew that he could not also try to "*get her*" to stop drinking, as other people in her life were, because she would likely have to defy him by continuing to drink. He needed to address her depression before she would likely be motivated to give up alcohol. Sehl's pyschodynamic understanding of Mrs. G's depression, a turning in of anger on herself, led him to actively encourage her to express her anger toward him. When she did so, her depression lifted. In the process, she was simultaneously encouraged to express her defiant feelings directly in words. This took the juice out of defiant drinking, so to speak.

Because Sehl did not try to get her to stop drinking but, instead, encouraged her to express her defiant wishes to keep drinking and empathized with her reasons—that drinking helped her—she was freed from a struggle with him and could explore the problematic aspects of her drinking. In this process, Mrs. G. discovered better alternatives to drinking and became more motivated from within to stop. Talking about the reason for her depression—losses—in therapy and the relationship of Sehl were more effective antidepressants than alcohol; she became people hungry. Sehl helped her work on developing strong emotional management skills to tolerate periods of time feeling her feelings rather than drinking.

Here we see the collaborative discovery of the meaning of Mrs. G.'s drinking leading to a particular response from Sehl that helped create the therapeutic relationship. This in turn made it possible to relieve her depression and increase her motivation to stop drinking.

We can also see how this psychodynamic understanding of the reasons for Mrs. G.'s drinking made it necessary for Sehl to take a harm reduction approach with her. Namely, he had to accept her in therapy while she was drinking and with no expectation that she would stop. An expectation that she stop would likely have triggered her defiance and continued drinking.

This issue is a common reason why many people are not

successful in treatments that require that they stop. Harm reduction approaches do not trigger this defiance and lend themselves, as in Mrs. G.'s case, to positive alliances on the side of exploring all sides of a person's feelings about using drugs.

Another psychodynamic harm reduction strategy was evident here. Sehl helped Mrs. G. to gradually reduce her drinking by supporting her in learning to tolerate increasing periods of time without alcohol. This stepping down of the intensity of drug use is a hallmark of harm reduction approaches. As Mrs. G.'s drinking decreased she became less irritable, her relationships with her attendants improved, she was more emotionally available in the therapy, and she became motivated to stop drinking. Small positive changes led to further positive changes.

This story is also about the power of the therapeutic relationship to heal as a context for working on the issues and as a source of support, caring, and a positive experience of oneself and others.

Mrs. G.'s return to drinking after she stopped illustrates another important meaning that drug use can carry. Mrs. G. seemed to be testing Sehl's sincerity; was he really on her side, genuinely concerned about why she drank and how it related to her suffering, even if she resumed drinking? It was also a way to find out if he would stick around even if she abandoned her stated goals and "rebelled." His acceptance and openness to the meaning of her drinking enabled her to have a powerful positive experience that she could use to build a more hopeful sense of herself and relationships in general.

Sehl's empathy, acceptance, flexibility, willingness to examine and not just react from his own feelings, and ability to be spontaneous and try new things are all reflective of the psychoanalytic tradition and hallmarks of harm reduction psychotherapy.

References

Eisler, K. R. (1958). Remarks on some variations in Psychoanalytical technique. *International Journal of Psycho-Analysis*: 39: 222–229.

Freud, A. (1936). *The Ego and the Mechanisms of Defense.* London: The Hogarth Press.

Levinson, V. and Straussner, S. L. A. (1978). Social workers as "enablers" in the treatment of alcoholics. *Social Casework,* 59: 14–20.

Mitchell, S. A. and Black, M. J. (1995). *Freud and Beyond: A History of Modern Psychoanalytic Thought.* New York: Basic Books.

3

The Value of Cognitive–Behavioral Strategies

Archie: When the Client Says "No" to Abstinence
—Gary Dayton and Frederick Rotgers

I treated my first alcohol-using client at the psychotherapy clinic at the City College of New York, where I received my Ph.D. The training program oriented its students in a theoretical approach based in psychoanalysis. In keeping with that tradition, I worked with this man by exploring the meaning of his drinking and its relationship to his painful emotional and personality issues. The psychotherapy was somewhat helpful in promoting an increased awareness of the sources of his anxiety and related difficulties, as well as the connection between these issues and his drinking. While this greater awareness contributed to a decrease in his anxiety and a lessening of feelings of intense internal pressure, it did not help him to stop drinking. For that he found Alcoholics Anonymous.

This outcome seemed to describe the limitations of using a completely exploratory approach to psychotherapy for people struggling with excessive substance use and other related kinds of problems. After having several similar experiences with substance-using clients during my training, I found a clinical position that introduced me to a broad spectrum of more active interventions. These techniques, combined with psychoanalytic approaches, gave rise to a more well-rounded and effective way of working. I'd been hired by the Division of Drug Abuse Research and Treatment of the New York Medical College. In this research-oriented clinic, I managed groups and saw clients in individual psychotherapy. In remembering my experiences of failure with substance-abusing clients I had treated in the past, I realized that I needed to become open to learning and incorporating more active behaviorally oriented modalities into my work. While I did not want to abandon the psychoanalytic perspective that perceives suffering as a meaningful process in human development, I knew that this alone was insufficient. This research-oriented clinic was an exciting incubator for training because it offered different modalities for treating the full spectrum of drug and alcohol problems among an impressive group of experienced and competent counselors. The staff combined techniques from Alcoholics Anonymous with an educative cognitive–behavioral counseling approach. As I began to integrate these approaches into my work with clients, I immediately began to achieve greater success in stopping or modifying their use of substances.

During the years since those first experiences, I have come to believe in the necessity of integrating cognitive and behavioral elements into psychotherapy with clients who have problems with substance use. I have also come to understand the use of these techniques as consistent with harm reduction.

The cognitive-behavioral approach emerged from the seminal work of behavioral theorists such as Pavlov, Skinner, and Bandura, and the fathers of the school of cognitive therapy, Albert Ellis and Aaron Beck. From the classical behavioral point of view, habitual behavior can be understood in terms of stimuli or triggers that have acquired the power to stimulate the specific behavior and by the consequences that have rewarded or reinforced the behavior. Bandura's social-learning contribution was that an individual didn't actually have to have direct experience of the behavior being rewarded to make it part of his or her repertoire. At certain moments in cognitive development, a child may observe a compelling behavior performed by a respected figure, the rewards for the behavior may be attractive, and therefore the behaviors are copied and learned as the child witnesses the experiences of an elder. The cognitive perspective also suggested that thinking could be viewed as a behavior following the same rules of conditioning that more pure behaviorists have described for other behaviors. Our behaviors in action are guided by our conditioned thoughts. So it is not simply the actual events that prompt and reinforce our actions but our interpretive thoughts about these events. "As we think, so shall we be."

Because excessive substance use is a problem of behavior, it seems self-evident that the cognitive-behavioral point of view would be relevant to it. And there have, in fact, been roughly thirty years of developing applications in these approaches to drug and alcohol problems. From this perspective, excessive substance use is generally seen as use that initially had some positive, rewarding value, often because it was helpful as a form of coping with some emotional or functional difficulty. For example, a teenager discovers that alcohol helps quell the nervousness that most teenagers feel when they begin to date. Over time with repeated reinforcements, the behavior becomes powerfully linked to these feelings and situations such that it becomes compelling to use or want to use (craving), even if use becomes increasingly problematic.

In cognitive–behavioral treatment there is a focus on modifying problematic behavior directly through the learning of behavior-changing, self-management skills. One also works to identify and modify the thoughts and core beliefs that guide behavior. In changing excessive substance use, behavioral goals aim toward the acquisition of skills required to use substances in new, less harmful ways or to learn alternative substance-free ways of coping with situations or feelings that prompt a desire to use. Cognitive goals include identifying and challenging unrealistic and self-defeating beliefs and expectations associated with problem use, and identifying and reworking the beliefs connected to problematic feelings that contribute to substance use.

This emphasis on teaching and skill development appeals to many people because it liberates the view of self as ill or damaged. It also provides theoretical support for harm reduction in that new alternative coping behaviors may need to be learned before chemical coping can be given up. People may need to learn certain cognitive skills in order to prepare the capacity for change. Finally, from the behavioral perspective, behavior changes incrementally, by small steps.

The case of Archie, the illustrative story for this chapter, is an example of a pure cognitive-behavioral harm reduction approach to the treatment of excessive drinking. Archie was treated at the Program for Addictions Consultation and Treatment, the training clinic of the Rutgers Center of Alcohol Studies in New Brunswick, New Jersey. The therapist was Gary Dayton, a Ph.D. candidate in clinical psychology at Rutgers, working under the supervision of Dr. Fred Rotgers. Fred is a psychologist with a long, very active involvement in the cognitive-behavioral treatment of people with substance use problems. Archie's story describes a man with a serious drinking problem that was related to accompanying psychiatric problems. After his life condition worsened due to an abstinence-only approach, this cognitive-behavioral harm reduction treatment was successful in helping Archie to achieve stable moderation of his drinking as well as in helping him with depression and an obsessive compulsive disorder. This treatment particularly illustrates the harm reduction and cognitive-behavioral synthesis and the specific value that cognitive-behavioral techniques can have for helping people change their behavior.

Archie: When the Client Says "No" to Abstinence
by Gary Dayton and Frederick Rotgers

Archie was an alcohol-dependent client with serious accompanying psychiatric problems who sought treatment with the goal of moderating his drinking. He was treated by Gary Dayton under the supervision of Frederick Rotgers at the Program for Addictions Consultation and Treatment (PACT), a training clinic of the Rutgers Center of Alcohol Studies in New Brunswick, New Jersey.

For many readers, Archie's treatment will not be

seen as successful. We disagree. Prior to seeking help with Gary, Archie had been in a near-constant battle with his psychiatrist and other treatment professionals about his drinking. This battle left him even more anxious, depressed, and discouraged than he was when he first sought treatment for social anxiety and depression as well as obsessive-compulsive habits of hand washing and ordering of objects. During this period, Archie's drinking had been increasing, and his anxiety and depression weren't responding to either pharmacological or psychotherapeutic interventions. Although Archie was by no means completely free of psychiatric symptoms at the end of the treatment period described here, those symptoms had substantially reduced, despite the fact that Archie continued to use alcohol. We view this as a successful outcome, although Archie is by no means "cured."

Archie is a 37-year-old, single Korean American who immigrated to the United States approximately twenty years ago after first living in Japan for nine years. He lives with his brother and his brother's family in a home located above the family business in a suburban New Jersey community. He was referred by his psychiatrist to PACT for assessment and treatment of alcohol addiction.

Archie was appropriately dressed, neat and well groomed for our first meeting. He was alert and well oriented. His speech was normal, with a moderate pace. He spoke articulately with no impediments, but with a distinct accent (Archie is multilingual, speaking fluent Korean, Japanese, and English). Archie was attentive during the initial interview and cooperative, quietly deferring to the interviewer. Archie expressed a full range of emotions, but with a dominant depressive tone. His reasoning and problem-solving abilities seemed intact with no apparent difficulties in concentration or higher-order thinking during therapy sessions. It is clear, however, that obsessive compulsive disorder symptoms interfere with Archie's ability to concentrate and to remain on track and complete tasks expeditiously. His memory appears sound with no difficulty in recall.

Archie reported no current medical problems, complaints, or symptoms. He is under the care of a psychiatrist and gets periodic medical check-ups by a primary care physician. In 1983, Archie was hospitalized for ten days resulting from a motor vehicle accident. There are no ongoing problems as a result of this accident. Archie is physically fit and trim, at 5 feet 6 inches and about 140 pounds.

Archie was an anxious, painfully shy young man who had great difficulty interacting with others. Archie fully understood English, but his ability to express himself in English was much less developed than his comprehension. At the time of the referral, Archie was being treated pharmacologically for obsessive compulsive disorder (OCD) by a psychiatrist. Archie is a college graduate in computer science from an eastern university, but because of chronic OCD, bouts of major depression, and alcohol problems, he has been chronically underemployed. He is currently unemployed. He had worked as a partner in the family-run convenience and grocery store until nine months ago when his partnership with his brother was dissolved. Although Archie has significant difficulties with OCD, depression, and alcohol, his motivation for treatment was high.

The early sessions with Archie were mainly focused on assessing the nature and extent of his problems with alcohol, gathering a personal history, and exploring the relationship between Archie's emotional problems and his drinking.

Archie sampled his first beer at the age of 12. "It tasted bad," he recalls. At 16 years old, Archie began to drink with regularity, but without any negative consequences. He reports drinking two or three beers once or twice a week at this age, mostly on weekends with friends and at family gatherings. Alcohol did not become a problem for Archie until he was 23 years old. He had just transferred to a new university after failing to achieve appropriate academic progress at another college. Troubled by the challenges of a new social environment and feeling pressured to attain academic acceptance, Archie turned to alcohol to alleviate feelings of depression and anxiety. He soon developed a pattern of alcohol abuse in which he continued to drink despite having a number of bad experiences as a result of becoming intoxicated. He drank six to twelve standard drinks of beer, whiskey, or Korean rice wine two or three times a week with friends and classmates.

Three years earlier, at 20 years old, the client suffered from his first of two major depressive episodes. The first depressive episode was preceded by the death of his father, which occurred within a few years after the family had immigrated to the United States. Although Archie did not increase his consumption of alcohol while depressed, he did experience melancholic depressive symptoms, including anhedonia, fatigue, insomnia, and a decrease in appetite resulting in weight loss. He also experienced anxiety and tended to avoid social situations. Antidepressant and antianxiety medications were prescribed for his depression and anxiety.

While attending the new university, Archie frequently missed classes because of continuing depression or drinking, or because he felt too anxious. Despite these problems, he continued to attend college part time, and at 31 years old graduated with a bachelor's degree. At 32 years old, Archie experienced his second major depressive episode after a sister's sudden death in an automobile accident. This loss took the client into another bout of depression during which he fantasized about suicide and was bedridden for about one month.

After this second depressive episode, Archie increased his drinking, although this was erratic. Sometimes Archie would drink ten to twelve standard drinks and become quite drunk. At other times, he drank two or three beers. The increase in quantity of drinks typically was contingent on the social relationship. If Archie was alone in a bar or with a drinking buddy, he would consume more; if he were with a nondrinking friend, he was content with one or two beers, or none at all.

At 33 years old, Archie began drinking nearly every day. Approximately one-half of the days were "heavy days" when the client would consume between six and twelve standard drinks; the other days were "light days" when the client would consume three or four beers. This pattern of drinking continued until the patient was 36 years old. After being terminated from partnership in the family store, light drinking days became more rare and daily drinking of six to twelve standard drinks (beer, whiskey, or rice wine) became the norm. He experienced many symptoms of depression including feelings of sadness, loss of interest in pleasant activities, sleeping more than he wanted to, and feelings of hopelessness about the future. Archie's hand washing and ordering of the objects in his room and house increased by hours. During the three months immediately prior to treatment, Archie noted that he had "lost control" and was drinking six to twelve standard drinks daily, with occasional days of eighteen standard drinks.

Archie described mild symptoms of obsessive and compulsive tendencies from about age 7 or 8. He recalls being concerned with orderliness and symmetry of his personal belongings at this time. After he emigrated to Japan at 9 years old, these symptoms gradually worsened. As the only Korean boy in a rural Japanese village, Archie was taunted and teased as an outsider by the Japanese children. He did not speak Japanese and had no real friends. He recalls receiving little support from his family. "My parents, brothers, and sisters were all much older and concerned with their own lives. They just expected me to adapt." Archie said that his father demanded that Archie do well in school and suggested that he learn to "swallow" his emotions.

Archie emigrated again at 16 years old, this time to the United States. He does not admit to any major difficulties when coming to the United States. He had learned to speak English while in Japan, and he was quite happy to be leaving Japanese soil. Because the family retains a traditional Korean household within a Korean community, however, Archie has made few American friends. Even while attending college in New York City, his social network consisted almost exclusively of Koreans.

It was in college that his obsessive-compulsive symptoms began to cause him serious problems. He developed obsessions about completing schoolwork perfectly. He describes endlessly going over and over parts of his homework to such an extent that it was completed very late, and often not at all. This caused him such difficulties that he was placed on academic probation and then finally dismissed from the college for lack of academic progress. It was also during this period that Archie experienced his first major depressive episode.

Archie currently lives with his family in a Korean community. He has several Korean friends, and no American friends. A major concern for Archie is his lack of a girlfriend. He has been to the community's informal "matchmaker" and has had several dates, but no long-lasting relationship has come from these efforts. Archie has had relations with women in the past, including a Korean girlfriend whom he dated until about one year ago when she departed the United States to return to Korea. He has had no girlfriend since that time and fears that he has become too old, and too unaccomplished to attract a worthy female.

Family history information is less than what might ordinarily be developed through early clinical interviewing. Family members and especially those who have died are treated with respect and honor in the

Korean culture. Family matters are considered very private, and it takes time for clients to feel sufficiently comfortable to discuss other than rudimentary family issues (Bok-Lim, 1996). Archie's ethnic heritage thus precluded in-depth discussions about family members and histories. He did, however, complete a Multimodal Life History Inventory (Lazarus and Lazarus, 1991), and much of the following information is derived from the Inventory and discussions about his family background. The Multimodal Life History Inventory is a comprehensive questionnaire that asks questions related to seven categories of functioning: Behavior, Affect (emotion), Sensation (physical feelings), Imagery (fantasy), Cognition (thought), Interpersonal relationship, and Medical problems.

Archie is the youngest son of seven children. He has three older brothers and three older sisters. He is distant in age to his siblings. The closest sibling is a brother who is 7 years older. The eldest sibling is a sister who is 23 years older than Archie. Two sisters have died. One sister was severely depressed and committed suicide when Archie was an adolescent. Another sister who suffered from schizophrenia died from an automobile accident when Archie was 32 years old. He was close to this sister and, as noted earlier, her death was one of the factors that contributed to his second major depressive episode.

Archie's father died suddenly from cardiac arrest at 67 years old when Archie was 20 years old. The father was a physician. Although Archie describes his father as "intelligent, patriotic," and a "far-sighted humanitarian," it is clear that Archie also experienced stern discipline from a father he also describes as "depressive, neurotic, asocial, and lonely."

Archie describes his mother, 79 years old, as "caring," but also stern with discipline, and "possessive." Archie feels that his mother has been disappointed in him because of his psychological problems and his failure to make accomplishments in school and work.

His mother as well as his older sister and brothers tend to criticize him and prod him to return to work full time and become more successful in business and financial matters.

Archie's alcohol use has increased steadily since he first began regular drinking (once a month or more). Both the quantity of alcohol consumed and the frequency with which it has been consumed have accelerated over time. During the nine months before beginning this therapy, Archie was drinking nearly every day, although the quantity of alcohol consumed was somewhat erratic. On half of the days Archie drank, he drank to intoxication. On the other days, he drank in moderation. Despite this irregular pattern, Archie had developed tolerance to alcohol—a cardinal symptom of physiological alcohol dependence. Tolerance refers to the phenomenon that ever-increasing amounts of alcohol are required to achieve the same intoxicating effect experienced at earlier lower levels.

In addition to tolerance, Archie reported occasional drinking bouts when he would drink to such an extent that he would experience blackouts. In a typical blackout, Archie was unable to recall some of the events of the previous night of drinking after reaching a highly intoxicated state. He was unable to remember, for example, how he had made it from the bar to his home. Although Archie was physiologically tolerant to alcohol and occasionally would drink so much that short-term memory was temporarily impaired, he had not experienced alcohol withdrawal when he stopped drinking.

Archie met other accepted criteria for alcohol dependence. Archie drank larger amounts of alcohol over longer periods than intended. He also spent substantial time drinking and recovering from hangovers; he was unsuccessful in several attempts to control his drinking; he curtailed social, recreational, and occupational pursuits for drinking; and he continued to drink despite the advice and feedback of his psychiatrist that his symptoms of depression and anxiety were worsened by alcohol.

Archie completed a modified version of the Time Line Follow-Back (TLFB; Sobell and Sobell, 1992). This version of the TLFB asks the client to complete a blank calendar of the past thirty days with alcohol and drug use information. For each day on the blank calendar, the client indicates how many standard drinks he or she has had, as well as any substances used. Archie's TLFB showed that he had cut back substantially on his drinking from recent higher levels. In fact, for most of the three weeks prior to the assessment interview, Archie had been abstinent. However, as in previous unsuccessful attempts to quit drinking, Archie quickly lapsed back into a near-daily drinking pattern, although he did manage to reduce his quantity of alcohol.

The Short-Form Alcohol Dependence Data Questionnaire (SADD) (Raistrick, Dunbar, and Davidson, 1983) was administered. The fifteen-item SADD measures the full range of alcohol dependence, and is especially sensitive to early signs of dependence (Heather, 1995). Clients identify the extent to which dependence-related drinking habits have most recently occurred using a four-point Likert scale ("never," "sometimes," "often," and "nearly always"). Scores are scaled according to Low, Moderate, and High Dependence. Archie's SADD score indicates that at the time of the initial assessment, he was moderately dependent on alcohol. Items identified by Archie as occurring "often" include: difficulty getting the thought of drinking out of his mind; getting drunk is more important than the next meal; days are planned with drinking in mind; drinking too much despite having many problems that might be caused by alcohol; and, attempts at controlling drinking by giving it up for days or weeks at a time. The SADD data suggest that this client was experiencing early signs of alcohol dependence.

Archie experienced significant adverse consequences

as a result of his drinking. In 1993, he was arrested for driving while intoxicated. During the past year as his alcohol use intensified, family conflict became more frequent, and Archie's siblings cast him as a liability. His brother forced Archie to relinquish his share of the family business because of his alcohol-related lack of reliability. This action soon caused Archie significant financial distress. Archie's mental health had deteriorated as he drank more. His depressive symptoms worsened, and OCD symptoms, especially checking behaviors, became uncontrollable.

The Michigan Alcoholism Screening Test (MAST; Seltzer, 1971) was completed by the client as an objective measure of the cumulative consequences of drinking across the client's life span. Archie's score indicated that he had suffered severe consequences as a result of his drinking. Archie also completed the Problem Checklist. This is an 18-item instrument extracted from the Comprehensive Drinker Profile (Miller and Marlatt, 1984). The Problem Checklist measures current alcohol-related problems. Archie identified eleven current problems related to alcohol.

A history of alcoholism in first-degree relatives (parents and siblings) is often seen in clients with alcohol problems. Archie characterized three of his siblings as having serious problems with alcohol. He described his father as an alcoholic. Members of Archie's family also have suffered from depression, and one sibling was schizophrenic.

Archie reported no other substance abuse, with the exception of nicotine. Archie began smoking cigarettes at 16 years old. He had stopped smoking two times for brief periods, but currently smokes between one-and-one-half and two packs of cigarettes daily.

Archie was suffering from alcohol dependence. His drinking pattern over time reflected increasing consumption and frequency resulting in tolerance. He had experienced several blackouts, and drinking had adversely affected his work, his family, and his physical and mental well-being. Further, his limited finances were being wasted on alcohol, and he had been arrested for minor alcohol-related offenses.

Although this client suffered extensive consequences from alcohol use, he has a likely genetic predisposition to problems with alcohol based on family history, and his case is complicated by the presence of emotional problems, there was reason to be optimistic about Archie's potential for successful controlled drinking. The onset of his drinking problems occurred later in life compared to many who develop severe alcohol dependence. His pattern of use was variable; he had as many light drinking days as he had heavy drinking days. His average weekly consumption of alcohol before treatment (approximately fifty-two standard drinks per week) was similar to the initial average weekly alcohol consumption of subjects who later became successful controlled drinkers described in empirical studies of controlled drinking (Rosenberg, 1993). Objective measures indicated that Archie was still in the early stages of dependence. Also, Archie's addiction was not complicated by the use of other substances with the exception of nicotine. Unlike many severe alcoholics seen at PACT, where the goal of abstinence is likely to be more appropriate, Archie had not suffered liver or other organ damage as a result of his drinking. Finally, Archie seemed highly motivated to make behavioral changes with respect to his drinking.

Archie presented us with a complex set of difficulties, including depression, OCD, and alcohol dependence. Archie's problems included feelings of excessive guilt and despair over lack of accomplishments in school and business. His erratic, uncontrolled drinking worsened when Archie felt depressed or anxious. He was easily depressed by criticism from family; he engaged in excessive self-condemnation and criticism, and he tended to undervalue accomplishments. Obsessions and rituals kept him from functioning at work; for example, repeatedly checking the coffee area of the family grocery kept him from performing more important duties. He spent a lot of time home alone, often sleeping late and engaging in repeated ruminations about events that happened in the recent past.

He also had a poor social life, limited to a few friends (drinking buddies) and family members. He lacked a romantic relationship, with the belief that he is "too old, unaccomplished, and unappealing" to attract a woman. Also, sexual dysfunction was a side effect of the medication he took.

Archie had two primary core sets of beliefs that underlay his problems. These core beliefs were: "I am defective and unlovable" and "I am incompetent and a failure." A secondary core schema involving unrelenting standards also tends to operate and influence Archie's perceptions, thoughts, feelings, and behavior.

In an early session, after the therapist explained the interrelationship of thoughts, emotion, and behavior, and after Archie had had an opportunity to identify negative thoughts and understand their effect on his mood and behavior through a thought record, Archie and the therapist jointly developed a "cognitive conceptualization" of Archie's core beliefs and how these affected him in his day-to-day life. We used Beck's (1995) Cognitive Conceptualization Diagram to outline and understand how the underlying core beliefs produced the problems on the problem list.

At work, Archie failed on several occasions to complete some accounting paperwork because of his repeated obsessing and checking over the figures. This situation led him to repeat the words "I cannot do anything," leading to feelings of shame and anxiety. Archie identified the meaning behind his automatic thought as "I'm an invalid," representing the core beliefs of being defective and incompetent. Archie punished himself with critical self-talk and later drank beer to alleviate his depressed state.

In another situation, Archie made a request of his brother for money to attend a college course. His brother refused and criticized Archie for failing to work. Archie thought, "I'm penniless, and this will not change." The meaning behind this thought Archie identified as "worthlessness" and "incompetence." He felt shameful for his failures, guilty at not having accomplished more, embarrassed at being chastised to work harder by his brother, and anxious about the future. He withdrew, obsessed, and worried about the future, and later he drank.

In a situation in which the local matchmaker had told him she had not yet found a date for him, Archie immediately thought, "No decent girl wants me because I'm ten to fifteen years behind in my life. I'm a failure." The meaning behind this automatic thought was a highly self-critical "I'm a man of less caliber than I thought." Guilt and shameful humility over these perceptions led to self-blaming behavior and what Archie calls "self-abandonment," or a lack of caring and giving up on the self.

Archie often experiences situations and events negatively, triggering self-deprecating negative thoughts of failure and deficiency. These were understood to arise from core schemas of incompetence and defectiveness/unlovability and failure to live up to high and unrelenting standards. He believes in the statement, "I have to perform and achieve to be a successful human being." He attempts to compensate for his beliefs of deficiency and incompetence by overplanning, worrying, obsessing, and performing rituals. The OCD behaviors (e.g., relentless review of events, endlessly checking work, and performance of rituals) were understood as compensatory strategies for his believed defectiveness.

Archie's alcohol use is related to his depressive core beliefs in that as obsessive strategies fail, and affect becomes intolerable, Archie self-medicates through drinking. Because Archie's drinking alleviates his symptoms of anxiety and depression, at least temporarily, and generates subjective, relaxing feelings and euphoria associated with alcohol, alcohol can be viewed as very rewarding and compelling compared to the punishment that may occur later when others or Archie himself are critical of his drinking.

The reinforcing quality of alcohol affects not just overt behaviors, but thoughts, as well as expectancies. Social learning theory emphasizes the role of cognition in coping and behavior. The extent to which a person has effective coping skills or views his or her ability to execute those skills as being adequate contributes to the person's expectations for coping in a given situation (Rotgers, 1996). Archie lacks adequate coping strategies for dealing with negative emotions and thoughts. Further, because of his depressive core beliefs, Archie has low expectations in being able to cope in a healthy manner. Automatic thoughts signaling the urge to drink as a means to cope with negative emotions appeared to be operating in Archie.

Archie describes his father as having been demanding and unrelenting in his expectations of Archie. Archie's father wanted him to follow in his footsteps and become a physician. His father could not accept mediocrity from Archie. Less-than-perfect school grades or performance in athletic activities drew parental disapproval and scorn. Archie describes his mother as also being demanding and unable or unwilling to modulate her husband's demandingness. It is also likely that because of the large age gap between Archie and his siblings (and parents), Archie may have been expected to behave more adult-like within the context of his family. Child-like behaviors "were not really tolerated" in his family. These experiences probably helped to create and sustain core beliefs of defectiveness/unlovability, incompetence/failure, and unrelenting standards. Emigrating to different cultures where Archie was ostracized and ridiculed for being a foreigner also contributed to his difficulties and reinforced core beliefs.

We predicted two main obstacles to his treatment. The first involved his OCD. PACT does not have the resources to appropriately treat OCD. It was clear that Archie's medication was not sufficiently curtailing his OCD symptoms, despite high dosage. Although the depressive core schemas were conceptualized as being the locus of Archie's difficulties, and the OCD more of a secondary, compensating nature, it was clear that he needed treatment for this disorder. Finding behavioral treatment for Archie within his limited budget was expected to be difficult. The lack of behavior treatment for OCD would affect the planned treatment for alcoholism and depression and was identified as a potential obstacle.

Archie's choice of treatment goal was also a potential obstacle. He was disinterested in abstinence; he did not feel that he could succeed if treatment involved no drinking. Archie was committed to moderation as a treatment goal. Given, however, his family history of alcoholism and psychopathology, and his psychiatric problems, we were not optimistic about his chances for controlled drinking and expected this to become an obstacle.

There were four main treatment goals for Archie:

1. **Reduce abusive drinking to controlled, moderate drinking.** It was agreed to attempt this goal for a thirty-day period. If it became clear at the end of thirty days that moderate drinking seemed too difficult an objective, then a reevaluation of this goal would take place.

   For target goals, Archie agreed to drinking limits based on Sanchez-Craig's (1993) controlled drinking program and the Moderation Management program (Kishline, 1994). Drinking was reduced to no more than five drinking days per week (two abstinent days), and no more than four standard drinks per day. Moderation management techniques of pacing drinks, estimating and monitoring blood alcohol level, and expanding one's range of friends and activities that do not involve drinking were employed.

Coping skills training is an effective therapy for alcoholism. Portions of the coping skills training program developed by Monti, Abrams, Kadden, and Cooney (1989) were used to assist Archie in coping with urges and craving for alcohol, in managing thoughts about drinking, in drink refusal skills, in receiving criticism about drinking and criticism in general, in developing sober supports, and in high-risk situation planning and dealing with emergencies. For example, Archie was helped to develop a plan for how he would handle situations with his friends in which he was tempted to drink too much. He and the therapist then role-played how he would carry out those plans.

Finally, rational disputation of positive thoughts about drinking and rational disputation about thoughts linking drinking to the alleviation of negative emotion were conducted. In this cognitive-behavioral therapeutic procedure, the client is taught how to identify irrational core beliefs and dispute them with rational, objective counterarguments. Thus, Archie was taught to remind himself that there were consequences awaiting him later if he drank too much now.

2. **Identifying and disputing negatively biased irrational thoughts and depressive beliefs.** We conceptualized Archie's primary problem as negative core beliefs about his worthiness and the competency of his behavior. Young, Beck, and Weinberger (1993) have developed a two-phase treatment for depression that is applicable to Archie's case. In the first phase, training in the cognition-emotion-behavior relationship is conducted. Irrational thoughts are identified as triggered by activating events. Emotions linked to

irrational thoughts are identified and rated (0–100% scale). These are labeled (e.g., dichotomous thinking, fortune-telling, magnification, minimization, and so on) and then disputed with more rational thoughts. A rating is again given to the belief of the new, rational thought. Burns's (1989) thought record from the *Feeling Good Handbook* was utilized because of its user-friendly nature. We used chapters from the *Feeling Good Handbook* to address how to identify and dispute irrational beliefs.

The second phase of the Young and colleagues (1993) treatment concentrates on schemas (i.e., core beliefs). Explanation of how schemas are used to organize, remember, recall, and filter information were made. Beck's (1995) Cognitive Conceptualization Diagram was used as an aid for conceptualization of schemas as well as an aid for Archie to understand his core beliefs and how they influence his behavior and mood. After core beliefs were conceptualized, Archie developed the "old plan-new plan" described by Persons (1989) to illustrate for himself his existing cognitive-emotional-behavior pattern, as well as a guidepost for the future.

3. **Increasing sober activities.** Archie was encouraged to seek out and participate in new activities that would be pleasurable and that could be pursued without alcohol. Archie developed a list of activities, including several that involved meeting new people and women.

4. **Treatment for OCD.** This goal involved two components. The first was to determine whether or not it would be appropriate to change Archie's medication to another, more recently developed antidepressant. The main reason for this was that Archie was experiencing erectile difficulties associated with the medication. Also, Archie was

taking the maximum dose, and his OCD was still quite active.

The second component to this goal was to refer Archie for behavioral therapy specifically for OCD, because it is not available at PACT. Concurrent use of medication plus behavioral therapy is nearly always recommended for the majority of OCD patients because medication, on average, is effective in reducing the severity of only about 67% of symptoms (Janicak, Davis, Preskorn, and Ayd, 1993).

TREATMENT OUTCOME AND FUTURE CONCERNS

Archie monitored his alcohol use on a daily basis. He kept excellent records, noting consumption by type of drink (typically beer or Korean rice wine, occasionally whiskey). His base line prior to treatment was fifty-two standard drinks per week with daily drinking for at least the previous nine months. Archie was able to cut his consumption level in half, with at least two to three nondrinking days during the week. Throughout the course of treatment thus far, however, he has continued to experience one "excessive" drinking day about every ten days. ("Excessive" is Archie's term, and it means five drinks in one day.) It is noteworthy that he would frequently come to therapy severely criticizing himself for failing to meet his goal. His self-condemnations were used to highlight his schemas of incompetence and relentless standards. It was truly difficult for Archie to allow himself time to learn the new skills of moderation management and to allow himself to experience errors. He also has tended to impose a new, more restrictive target (usually fewer drinks per day) when he exceeded his goal, which, again, has been grist for exposing and disputing his unhealthy beliefs.

Typical situations in which Archie finds himself drinking excessively involve going to dinner or a bar with a drinking buddy or cousins. Drink refusal skills training and planning for this risky situation have helped Archie to limit his excessive drinking to one more drink than the recommended daily amount (only once in nearly three months has he exceeded five drinks). When in the company of others who might be talking about work, school, or other activities that seem to reflect achievement to Archie, Archie tends to think private thoughts of his own lack of accomplishments, feel ashamed, and drink to combat the anxiety. In addition to disputing negative thoughts and illuminating the linkage to his incompetence and defectiveness schemas, we have also employed role-playing of feared social situations based on a hierarchy of anxiety-provoking situations that Archie developed.

Archie's depression has been monitored by the administration of the Beck Depression Index (BDI). Archie's BDI at intake was 26, representing moderately severe depression. As with the recording of his drinking, Archie has complied with keeping thought records and mood logs as homework assignments. Archie has become skilled at identifying and disputing his irrational thoughts. His BDI scores steadily dropped over a period of several months to scores within normal limits of non–clinically depressed persons (BDI scores of 7 and 8).

Arranging treatment for Archie's OCD was more difficult than originally anticipated. Archie's psychiatrist was against any drinking whatsoever. When the therapist consulted with the psychiatrist, he simply did not agree that moderate drinking was a reasonable goal for Archie. The psychiatrist also did not want to consider changing Archie's medication to a new SSRI despite Archie's continued OCD symptoms and sexual dysfunction. In the sixth week of treatment, Archie arrived for therapy clearly despondent. He had seen the psychiatrist the day before. He was told by the psychiatrist that he would not continue to treat Archie if he continued drinking at any level! Archie left the psychiatrist's office, sought out a drinking friend and got drunk. He drank more on that afternoon than at any other time while in treatment. Archie experienced what Alan Marlatt (1985) has called abstinence violation effect, which refers to a giving up on sobriety (or, in Archie's case, controlled drinking) if he drank at all. In addition, Archie reported that the psychiatrist would refuse to refer him for behavioral therapy as long as he continued drinking.

This event was a clear triggering of Archie's core beliefs. Authority figures like psychiatrists are held in high esteem by Koreans and others from Asian countries (Bok-Lim, 1996). In processing this activating event, Archie revealed that the psychiatrist reminded him of his father and his father's stern manner. The event triggered the "incompetent" and "defective" beliefs. It took some time, but Archie eventually sought out another psychiatrist who was amenable to Archie's goal of moderate drinking. The new psychiatrist also changed Archie's medication to Luvox, which has been of benefit to Archie in relieving him of the severity of his OCD and returning sexual functioning. A psychologist-in-training at Rutgers who is specializing in anxiety disorders has begun behavioral OCD treatment with Archie.

Archie also has increased his activity level. He has reconnected with a few nondrinking friends. He has also joined a Moderation Management self-help group, which meets weekly at the PACT offices. In addition, he has joined an OCD group at Rutgers.

Although several goals are in the process of being met, therapy is likely to continue for some time. He has made progress, but Archie's negative core beliefs remain relatively ingrained and additional time will be needed to liberate them. Also, although Archie has reduced his drinking consumption, increased his days of abstinence, and is exercising greater control over his drinking when he does drink, the excessive drinking days continue to occur. We have begun steps to correct this with a closer monitoring of estimated blood alcohol level (BAL). Archie has been supplied with a BAL chart for his gender and weight. BAL changes as a function of alcoholic drinks over time. Archie's goal is to maintain a BAL of no greater than .055. Legal intoxication in New Jersey and most states is a BAL of 1.00. Maintaining a BAL of no more than .055 is a safe and relatively healthy guideline adopted by the Moderation Management program (Kishline, 1994). For Archie, keeping within the Moderation Management guidelines will require him to manage his upper limit of four drinks per day over a four-and-a-half- to five-hour period.

Although his therapist was skeptical at first about Archie's ability to manage his drinking and change from being alcohol dependent to a moderate drinker, Archie has made substantial progress toward this goal, as well as toward other goals of reducing depression and anxiety symptoms. He has not quite "perfected" controlled drinking, yet it is clear that he has come a long way toward reaching it. As he continues in treatment and adds additional support for his goal by joining, for example, the Moderation Management group, we expect he will be able to achieve his goals.

Archie was explicit in his desire to control his drinking. Importantly for Archie, achieving stable moderation as opposed to abstinence reflected a tacit acknowledgement of his unrelenting standards schema: "Quitting drinking for me is like quitting a favorite food. If I know I can have a little, I can do this. I feel I am under control with moderate drinking. If I set too high a standard and can't reach it, well, I feel very bad." Attempting to achieve sobriety and failing increases the risk of feeling weak, incompetent, and worthless.

"If I can't quit alcohol, then what can I accomplish? I blame myself."

Had the treatment goal been abstinence, it is likely that Archie would have initially met it and any subsequent failure to achieve perfect abstinence would have been another confirmation that he was incompetent and worthless. Requiring abstinence would have been a barrier for effective treatment with Archie, and it is likely that he would have dropped out of treatment altogether.

Sobell and Sobell (1995) have concluded that goal choice may matter in consumer appeal. Moderation approaches may be a key to encouraging problem drinkers to access services, as well as a means of reducing the harmful consequences of problem drinking.

Self-selection of treatment goals may better enable clients to achieve their own goals because they may be better motivated, better able to assume responsibility for their behavior, and, importantly, they may understand themselves better than their therapist (Sobell, Sobell, Bogardis, Leo, and Skinner, 1992). Requiring abstinence may magnify the drinker's problems with alcohol and pose a barrier to treatment (Cunningham, Sobell, Sobell, Agrawal, and Toneatto, 1993). Archie's psychiatrist told him that he could resolve his alcohol problem only by admitting to alcoholism and by embracing the goal of abstinence. Had that been his only option, it is likely that Archie would have continued drinking and possibly have progressed into a severely dependent alcoholic.

In summary, Archie has made significant progress in coping with a variety of debilitating psychiatric problems. During the course of his treatment it was clear that some of his problems (or at least the exacerbation of them) arose directly from the stance his psychiatrist took toward Archie's drinking. Archie is a man whose core belief about himself is that he is ineffective and incompetent. By working with Archie, allowing and supporting his own goal choice with respect to his drinking, and providing a setting in which he could develop increased self-efficacy with respect to his drinking, the stage was set for Archie to also experience an alleviation of many of his depressive symptoms. Although Archie is by no means problem-free, he has been able to make significant progress as a result of a therapeutic approach that respected him as a human being who was capable of making decisions for himself and setting reasonable treatment goals.

Commentary by Andrew Tatarsky

Archie's story again illustrates how a harm reduction approach that respects the client's goal of moderating his drinking and his capacity to make use of the therapy while continuing to drink led to a successful outcome that prior abstinence-oriented approaches did not. This is a moving story about a man who became increasingly reliant on alcohol as a way of dealing with lifelong struggles with depression, anxiety, and obsessive compulsive disorder. As he moved into early adulthood, a series of serious social problems and important losses are each followed by a worsening of his depression and increased drinking. As his story unfolds, we see clear links between these current problems and a childhood that included a move from his native Korea to Japan, where he didn't speak the language, had no friends, and was teased by his peers and family. His family, his father in particular, instructed him to swallow his feelings and do well in school. This is common to people who develop problems with substances and may contribute to a vulnerability to these problems. When parents fall short in teaching the child effective ways to manage tough feelings and challenging situations, these feelings may eventually appear as threatening or overwhelming and unmanageable. In Archie's experience, he received the message early on that one's feelings are invalid or indicative of inadequacy. The result is that feelings are experienced as overwhelming, unclear, and therefore shameful and inimical to survival. In the face of this mix of feelings, the individual seeks mechanisms to cope, to solve the problem. For this, Archie first relied on his obsessive and compulsive behaviors to manage the intensity and when these failed him, he found alcohol as a tool for managing his anxiety and depression.

Archie was suffering from both a high level of alcohol dependence and a set of serious psychiatric problems when he came for help. The story reveals how Archie was able to dramatically reduce his daily drinking from a very high level with increasingly severe negative consequences to a rather low level of drinking with minimal impact on his daily responsibilities and structures. Therapy helped Archie to significantly reduce the severity of the psychiatric issues that he brought to treatment while he continued to drink.

This story illustrates how cognitive-behavioral techniques can be very useful in helping people develop tools for changing substance-using behavior. It also challenges two traditionally held beliefs about the treatment of problem substance users. The traditional view is that alcohol-dependent individuals cannot learn to control their drinking and any effort to do so is simply a denial of the true nature of alcoholism; namely, that any drinking will inevitably lead to loss of control and the problems resulting from it. In fact, Archie's experience was the opposite of this. Before Archie found this treatment, his psychiatrist's insistence on abstinence only led to an escalation of his drinking and an exacerbation of his psychiatric problems. It was only when he found the harm reduction approach that he was able to enter into treatment in a meaningful way and begin to make significant headway in dealing with his drinking problem.

Archie's case contradicts the traditionally held view that people with drinking problems cannot address their psychiatric issues until they have stopped drinking. This is based on the assumption that active substance use interferes with one's receptivity to psychotherapy and pharmacotherapy. This case powerfully shows something I have seen countless times in my own practice: Many people make good use of psychotherapy to deal with a whole range of emotional and lifestyle issues not only while they continue to use substances but often as a prerequisite to modifying their substance use. Given the wide diversity of people with substance use problems, the answer to who can and who cannot benefit from treatment while actively using must be answered individually with each client based on the collaborative work between client and clinician. If it becomes clear through the client's actual experience in the therapy that the substance use is interfering with the process, it is more likely to be accepted by the client than if this was simply an opinion offered by the clinician at the beginning of the treatment.

References

Alcoholics Anonymous (1976). Alcoholics Anonymous. 3rd ed. New York: Alcoholics Anonymous World Services.

Alcoholics Anonymous (n.d., presumably 1990). Comments on AA's triennial surveys. New York: Alcoholics Anonymous World Services.

American Psychiatric Association (1994). *Diagnostic and Statistical Manual* (4th ed.). Washington, D.C.: American Psychiatric Association.

Babor, T. F., Hofmann, M., DelBoca, F. K., Hesselbrock, V., Meyer, R. E., Dolinsky, Z. S., and Rounsaville, B. (1992). Types of alcoholics, I. Evidence for an empirically derived typology based on indicators of vulnerability and severity. *Archives of General Psychiatry*, 49: 599–608.

Beck, J. S. (1995). *Cognitive Therapy: Basics and Beyond.* New York: Guilford Press.

Bok-Lim, C. K. (1996). Korean families. In M. McGoldrick, J. Giordano, and J. K. Pearce (Eds.). *Ethnicity and Family Therapy.* 2nd ed. (pp. 281–294). New York: Guilford Press.

Booth, P. G., Dale, B. and Ansari, J. (1984). Problem drinkers' goal choice and treatment outcome: A preliminary study. *Addictive Behaviors*, 9: 357–364.

Booth, P. G., Dale, B., Slade, P. D., and Dewey, M. E. (1992). A follow-up study of problem drinkers offered a goal choice option. *Journal of Studies on Alcohol*, 53: 594–600.

Burns, D. D. (1989). *The Feeling Good Handbook.* New York: Plume.

Burwell, L. (1995). *Handbook of Psychiatric Drugs.* Fountain Valley, CA: Current Clinical Strategies Publishing.

Caddy, G. R., Addington, H. J., and Perkins, D. (1978). Individualized behavior therapy for alcoholics: A third year independent double-blind follow-up. *Behavior Research and Therapy,* 16: 345–362.

Carey, K.B., and Carey, M.P. (1990). Enhancing the treatment attendance of mentally ill chemical abusers. *Journal of Behavior Therapy and Experimental Psychiatry,* 21: 205–209.

Cloninger, C. R. (1987). Neurogenetic mechanisms in alcoholism. *Science,* 236: 410–416.

Cunningham, J. A., Sobell, L. C., Sobell, M. B., Agrawal, S., and Toneatto, T. (1993). Barriers to treatment: Why alcohol and drug abusers delay or never seek treatment. *Addictive Behaviors,* 18: 347–353.

Davies, D. L. (1962). Normal drinking in recovered alcoholic addicts. *Quarterly Journal of Studies on Alcohol,* 23: 94–104.

Ditman, K. S., Crawford, G. C., Forgy, E. W., Moskowitz, H., and MacAndrew, C. (1967). A controlled experiment on the use of court probation for drunk arrests. *American Journal of Psychiatry,* 124(2): 64–67.

Foy, D. W., Nunn, L. B., and Rychtarik, R. G. (1984). Broad-spectrum treatment for chronic alcoholics: Effects of training controlled drinking skills. *Journal of Consulting and Clinical Psychology,* 52: 218–230.

Glatt, M. M. (1995). Comments on Sobell and Sobell's editorial "Controlled drinking after 25 years: how important was the great debate?" Controlled drinking after a third of a century. *Addiction,* 90: 1157–1160.

Glover, Edward G. (1928). The Aetiology of Alcoholics in Proceedings of the Royal Society of Medicine, vol. 27, pp. 1351–1355.

Graber, R. A., and Miller, W. R. (1988). Abstinence or controlled drinking goals for problem drinkers: A randomized clinical trail. *Psychology of Addictive Behaviors,* 2: 20–33.

Heather, N., and Robertson, I. (1983). *Controlled Drinking.* Rev. ed. Cambridge: Cambridge University Press.

Heather, N. (1995). Brief intervention strategies. In R. K. Hester and W. R. Miller (Eds.). *Handbook of Alcoholism Treatment Approaches: Effective Alternatives.* 2nd ed. (pp. 105–122). Boston: Allyn and Bacon.

Heather, N., Wodak, A., Nadelman, E., and O'Hare, P. (Eds.). (1993). *Psychoactive Drugs and Harm Reduction: From Faith to Science.* London: Whurr Publishers.

Helzer, J. E., Robins, L. N., Taylor, J. R., Carey, K., Miller, R. H., Combs-Orme, T., and Farmer, A. (1985). The extent of long-term moderate drinking among alcoholics discharged from medical and psychiatric treatment facilities. *New England Journal of Medicine,* 312: 1678–1682.

Hester, R. K. and Miller, W. R. (Eds.) (1995). *Handbook of Alcoholism Treatment Approaches: Effective Alternatives.* 2nd ed. Boston: Allyn and Bacon.

Institute of Medicine (1990). *Broadening the Base of Treatment for Alcoholic Problems.* Washington, DC: National Academy Press.

Janicak, P. G., Davis, J. M., Preskorn, S. H., and Ayd, F. J. (1993). *Principles and Practice of Psychopharmacotherapy.* Baltimore, MD: Williams and Wilkins.

Jellinek, Emil M. (1946). Phases in the drinking history of alcoholics. Analysis of a survey conducted by the official organ of Alcoholics Anonymous. *Quarterly Journal of Studies on Alcohol,* 7: 1–88.

Kernberg, O. (1998). *Severe Personality Disorders: Psychotherapeutic Strategies.* New Haven: Yale University Press.

Keso, L., and Salaspuro, M. (1990). Inpatient treatment of employed alcoholics: A randomized critical trial of Hazelden-type traditional treatment. *Alcoholism: Clinical and Experimental Research,* 14: 584–589.

Khantzian, E. J. (1975). Self-selection and progressions in drug dependence. *Psychiatry Digest,* 10: 19–22.

Khantzian, E. J. (1985). The self medication hypothesis of addictive disorders. *American Journal of Psychiatry,* 142 (11): 1259–1264.

Khantzian, E. J. (1995). Alcoholics Anonymous—cult or corrective: A case study. *Journal of Substance Abuse Treatment,* 12: 157–165.

Khantzian, E. J., and Mack, J. E. (1994). How AA works and why it is important for clinicians to understand. *Journal of Substance Abuse Treatment*, 11, 77-92.

Kishline, A. (1994). *Moderate Drinking: The Moderation Management Guide for People Who Want to Reduce Their Drinking.* New York: Three Rivers Press.

Lazarus, A. A., and Lazarus, C. N. (1991). *Multi Modal Life History Inventory.* Champaign, IL: Research Press.

Marlatt, G. A., and Tapert, S. F. (1993). *Harm Reduction: Reducing the Risks of Addictive Behaviors.* In J.S. Baer, G.A. Marlatt, and R.J. McMahon (Eds.). *Addictive Behaviors Across the Life Span: Prevention, Treatment and Policy Issues* (pp. 243–273). Newbury Park, CA: Sage.

Marlatt, G. A., and Gordon, J. R. (Eds.). (1985). *Relapse Prevention: Maintenance Strategies in the Treatment of Addictive Behaviors.* New York: Guilford Press.

Marlatt, G. A. (1985). Relapse prevention: Theoretical rational and overview of the model. In G. A. Marlatt and J. R. Gordon (Eds.). *Relapse Prevention.* New York: Guilford.

Miller, W. R., and Marlatt, G. A. (1984). *Manual for the Comprehensive Drinker Profile.* Odessa, FL: Psychological Assessment Resources.

Monti, P. M., Abrams, D. B., Kadden, R. M., and Cooney, N. (1989). *Treating Alcohol Dependence.* New York: Guilford.

Monti, P. M., Rohsenow, D. J., Colby, S. M., and Abrams, D. B. (1995). Coping and social skills training. In R. K. Hester and W. R. Miller (Eds.), *Handbook of Alcoholism Treatment Approaches: Effective Alternatives.* 2nd ed. (pp. 221–241). Boston: Allyn and Bacon.

National Institute on Alcohol Abuse and Alcoholism (1999). [On-Line] Available: http//silk.nih.gov/silk/niaaa1/database/abdep1.txt.

Nordstrom, G., and Berglund, M. (1987). Aging and recovery from alcoholism. *British Journal of Psychiatry*, 151: 382–388.

Nordstrom, G., and Berglund, M. (1987). A prospective study of successful long-term adjustment in alcohol dependence: Social drinking versus abstinence. *Journal of Studies on Alcohol*, 48: 95–103.

Pendery, M. L., Maltzman, I. M., and West, L. J. (1982). Controlled drinking by alcoholics? New findings and a reevaluation of a major affirmative study. *Science*, 217: 169–175.

Persons, J. B. (1989). *Cognitive Therapy in Practice: A Case Formulation Approach*. New York: Norton.

Project MATCH Research Group (1997). Matching alcoholism treatments to client heterogeneity: Project MATCH posttreatment drinking outcomes. *Journal of Studies on Alcohol*, 58: 7–29.

Raistrick, D., Dunbar, G., and Davidson, R. (1983). Development of a questionnaire to measure alcohol dependence. *British Journal of Addiction*, 78: 89–95.

Roizen, R. (1987). The great controlled drinking controversy. In M. Galanter (Ed.). *Recent Developments in Alcoholism*, vol. 5 (pp. 246–279). New York: Plenum.

Rosenberg, H., and Davis, L.-A. (1994). Acceptance of moderate drinking by alcohol treatment services in the United States. *Journal of Studies on Alcohol*, 55: 167–172.

Rosenberg, H., Melville, J., Levell, D., and Hodge, J. E. (1992). A 10-year follow-up survey of acceptability of controlled drinking in Britain. *Journal of Studies on Alcohol*, 53: 441–446.

Rosenberg, H. (1993). Prediction of controlled drinking by alcoholics and problem drinkers. *Psychological Bulletin*, 113: 129–139.

Rotgers, R. (1998). Using harm reduction in treating problem drinkers. In L. Van DeCreek (Ed.). *Innovations in Clinical Practice* (p. 16). Odessa Fla: Professional Resource Exchange.

Rotgers, F. (1996). Behavioral theory of substance abuse treatment: Bringing science to bear on practice. In F. Rotgers, D. S. Keller, and J. Morgenstern (Eds.). *Treating Substance Abuse: Theory and Technique* (pp. 174–201). New York: Guilford Press.

Rothschild, D. (1995). Working with addicts in private practice: Overcoming initial resistance. In A. Washton (Ed.). *Psychotherapy and Substance Abuse: A Practitioner's Handbook* (pp. 192–203). New York: Guilford Press.

Rounsaville, B. (1992). Types of alcoholics, I. Evidence for an empirically derived typology based on indicators of vulnerability and severity. *Archives of General Psychiatry*, 49: 599–608.

Rychtarik, R. G., Foy, D. W., Scott, T., Lokey, L., and Prue, D. M. (1987). Five–six year follow-up of broad-spectrum behavioral treatment for alcoholism: Effects of training controlled drinking skills. *Journal of Consulting and Clinical Psychology*, 55: 106–108.

Sanchez-Craig, M. (1993). *Saying When: How to Quit Drinking or Cut Down*. 2nd ed. Toronto: Addiction Research Foundation.

Sanchez-Craig, M., Annis, H. M., Bornet, A. R., and MacDonald, K. R. (1984). Random assignment to abstinence and controlled drinking: Evaluation of a cognitive behavioral program for problem drinkers. *Journal of Consulting and Clinical Psychology*, 52: 390–403.

Sanchez-Craig, M., and Lei, H. (1986). Disadvantages to imposing the goal of abstinence on problem drinkers: An empirical study. *British Journal of Addiction*, 81: 505–512.

Seltzer, M. L. (1971). The Michigan Alcoholism Screening Test: The quest for a new diagnostic instrument. *American Journal of Psychiatry*, 127: 1653–1658.

Sobell, M. B., and Sobell, L. C. (1995). Controlled drinking after 25 years: How important was the great debate? *Addiction*, 90: 1149–1153.

Sobell, M. B., Sobell, L. C., Bogardis, J., Leo, G. I., and Skinner, W. (1992). Problem drinkers' perceptions of whether treatment goals should be self-selected or therapist-selected. *Behavior Therapy*, 23: 43–52.

Sobell, M. B., and Sobell, L. C. (1973). Alcoholics treated by individualized behavior therapy: One year treatment outcome. *Behavior Research and Therapy*, 11: 599–618.

Sobell, M. B., and Sobell, L. C. (1976). Second-year treatment outcome of alcoholics treated by individualized behavior therapy: Results. *Behavior Research and Therapy*, 14: 195–215.

Sobell, L. C., and Sobell, M. B. (1992). Time line follow back: A technique for assessing self-reported alcohol consumption. In R. Z. Litten and J. P. Allen (Eds.). *Measuring Alcohol*

Consumption: Psychological and Biochemical Methods (pp. 41–72). Totowa, NJ: Humana Press.

Substance Abuse and Mental Health Services Administration (1999). The treatment episode data set (TEDS): 1992–1997 national admissions to substance abuse treatment services. Rockville, MD: SAMHSA.

Tatarsky, A. (1998). An integrative approach to harm reduction psychotherapy: A case of problem drinking secondary to depression. *In Session: Psychotherapy in Practice*, 4: 9–24.

United States Department of Health and Human Services. (1997). Ninth special report to the U.S. congress on alcohol and health. National Institute of Health No. 97-4107.

Wallace, B. C. (Ed.). (1992). *The Chemically Dependent: Phases of Treatment and Recovery*. New York: Brunner/Mazel.

Young, J. E., Beck, A.T., and Weinberger, A. (1993). Depression. In D. Barlow (Ed.). *Clinical Handbook of Psychological Disorders*. 2nd ed. (pp. 240–277). New York: Guilford Press.

Young, J. E. (1990). *Cognitive Therapy for Personality Disorders: A Schema-Focused Approach*. Sarasota, FL: Professional Resource Exchange.

4

Trust and Relationship As Cornerstones of Successful Psychotherapy

Michael: A Delicate Balance
—Gail Hammer

Until recently, the prevailing view in traditional drug and alcohol treatment was an emphasis on the commonalities among drug users as the central focus in treatment. The dominating theme was the excessive or self-defeating use of drugs. Differences between drug users were seen as unimportant or worse, as undermining distractions to the task at hand, which was to help people stop using drugs. The fact that one person might say he used drugs to relieve his depression about being HIV-positive and another said drugs might curb homicidal or suicidal tendencies would be considered beside the point. Individual considerations were interpreted as justifications of drug use and not relevant to the challenge of stopping. They were seen as evidence of the drug user's wish to see himself as unlike other addicts rather than accepting that all addicts have a common disorder or disease that requires the same treatment. The wish to be seen as special or unique was understood to be symptomatic of justification for continued use rather than a serious wish to address some important, relevant issues.

We often hear of the addict's grandiosity, with an unrealistic or inflated sense of self, a sense of being entitled to special treatment. This idea is popularized in a widely used slogan in the recovery community: "Addicts suffer from the disease of terminal uniqueness."

While these ideas certainly have validity for some drug users, serious problems arise when assuming that they, or any generalizations, are true for all people with drug problems. Making assumptions about clients' drug use before getting to know them may enhance the authoritative stance, because it is accurate in some cases. In many instances, it leads to misunderstanding, with the client feeling misunderstood or prematurely judged.

The "one-size-fits-all" treatment approach led to years of factional fighting among different camps within the substance use treatment field about the question of which treatment approach is the most effective: inpatient versus outpatient, intensive outpatient versus psychotherapy, individual versus group, drug-free versus methadone maintenance, abstinence-only versus moderation training, or peer self-help support groups like AA versus professional treatment.

This paradigm of one-size-fits-all treatment is out of step with extensive clinical experience and empirical research (Peele, Bufe, and Brodsky, 2000; Wallace, 1992). While each of these treatments is helpful to some people, as the research cited in Chapter one demonstrates, each does not help the majority of drug and alcohol users. For example, an internal AA document (Alcoholics Anonymous, n.d.) found that one out of twenty people who attend an AA meeting stick with the program and achieve results. Intensive outpatient treatment became popular as the treatment of choice in the mid-1980s because the previously highly esteemed inpatient treatment programs were not showing enough success to justify the high cost of treatment to insurance companies and other payers (Tatarsky and Washton, 1987). Moderation and other harm reduction strategies have become more widely used and explored since the 1990s because the traditional abstinence-only approaches have shown poor success rates overall.

The poor success rates of drug and alcohol treatment were used as evidence for the popular belief that drug and alcohol users are a generally hard-to-treat group of people. They are considered poor candidates for treatment or other strategies for change. The finger of blame was placed on the user and the assumption was that the patient was generally treatment resistant, unmotivated, selfish, manipulative, and deceptive. The conclusion drawn from these blaming diagnoses was that the client needed to suffer more or, in the jargon, "hit bottom," before achieving the authenticity required to get real help.

During the last twenty years, an increasing number of people in the drug use treatment community as well as astute individuals in the general public have begun to challenge these ideas. We began to realize that the treatment community was blaming the consumer of services and not taking responsibility for its own contribution to failure. We began to examine the assumptions and limitations of the treatments being offered.

The basic assumptions in the traditional approach are ideologically biased and not supported by good research, theory, clinical experience, or common sense. A number of fresh hopeful ideas, generally well-grounded in research and theory, have emerged from this reevaluation that, together, support a more comprehensive model for understanding and addressing the full spectrum of problem drug use. These new ideas generally turn the generalizations upside down. Just this step leads to enhanced sensitivity to the unique needs of the client, and the possibilities for positive change increase dramatically.

This alternative model hinges on the fact that drug users are a broadly diverse group of people who need a variety of treatment options from which to choose to maximize overall success (Marlatt, 1998). As people find their way to treatment approaches and therapists that meet them where they are, that is, address their particular, unique needs, the greater overall success we see. This is the "right fit" that is the key to increasing success.

As we have seen in previous chapters, people with drug and alcohol problems vary widely in all of the relevant dimensions: frequency, intensity, and severity of drug use; the personal meanings drug use carries; goals regarding drug use and other areas of life; motivation to change; emotional and personality vulnerabilities and strengths and social context. So we might think of the alternate guiding assumption as something like many problems=many treatments or unique people need unique solutions that are individually tailored to their specific needs, strengths, goals, and preferences (Miller and Rollnick, 1987; Prochaska and DiClemente, 1992).

From this point of view, which treatment is the best is the wrong question to ask. A better question might be: What constitutes the "right fit" for each person? This question suggests how the diversity of treatments and other change strategies currently available are all helpful to some people; we just have to figure out how to best match people with the treatment best for them. What goes into the right fit? Why is the right fit so important? How does a person wanting help go about finding that good match? How can treatment providers help people find the right fit?

WHAT GOES INTO THE RIGHT FIT?

The right fit begins with the client's experience of being met by a concerned person who is open to fully understanding who he is in order to co-create a plan for change that speaks to where the individual lives. This emphasizes both the personal qualities of the therapist and the treatment approach.

We aim for an experience in which the client feels they are in the right place with the right person suited to collaborate with the individual in the often painful, difficult, and uncertain process of making important personal changes.

Really Meeting Consumers Where They Are

Meeting the client where he/she lives has always been a central tenet of drug and all other treatment. However, many traditionally trained clinicians have not met the client where he lives because they begin with a whole set of prior assumptions about the nature of that person's drug problem and what that person needs in the way of goals and treatment strategies. This often clouds that clinician's eyes, prevents him/her from meeting that person cleanly, and contributes to the failure of the endeavor from the outset.

The challenge for therapists is to get their prior assumptions about the client out of the way so that they can embark on a discovery process in order to get to know the client and themselves through the eyes of a new individual. This requires courage on the part of therapists in that they must drop a reflex to seek security in an authoritative stance. They must come to the meeting empty-handed and with a beginner's mind. This attitude includes assumptions about drug use, drug use goals, race, gender, socioeconomic status, personality, needs, and treatment recommendations. Then a collaborative assessment of what the client needs can set the stage for a positive working alliance between them. This collaboration makes it possible for both client and therapist to discover together the problems that need to be addressed and can lead to a joined exploratory process and co-creative discussion of goals and possible strategies for achieving those goals.

This attitude alone opens a new world for clients entering their sessions, as they suddenly enter into a kind of threshold space conducive to transformation. In this space, surface tensions between self and other fall away. In the outside world these surface tensions are reinforced by judgments and hierarchical ranking. With a decrease in surface tension between self and other, the illusion of separation that lives in the outside world is temporarily suspended, making the therapist's room a safe space conducive to transformation. This attitude is also conducive to progress; the therapist comes as a beginner each time, staying open to changes in the client's needs that can lead to changes in the focus, direction, goals, and therapeutic approach.

TREATMENT MATCHING

In terms of the therapeutic approach, the right fit refers to a match between the approach and the client around as many variables as possible.

Personal Goals Regarding Drug Use and Other Life Issues

It is important to discover why the client is coming to therapy. It may take time to discern the deep needs and motives of the client for coming to therapy, but this must be ascertained for the client to sense that he or she is being met in a radical and profound way. If an individual comes to therapy saying she is worried about her drug use and the treatment provider says "I will help you to stop," the individual is likely to feel misunderstood and not helped; she had never mentioned stopping, only her concern about her drug use. The client often wants help in clarifying the nature of the problem and needs an approach that recognizes that goal. On the other hand, if an individual feels in great danger from continued drug use and wants help to stop and the provider says "Let's talk about it," the individual may feel unsafe, misunderstood, and not helped, because it seems the urgency of his life crisis goes unrecognized by the provider. The challenge for both is to try to see if a lack of fit can be made right by talking about what doesn't feel right. When goals regarding drug use are clarified, whether it is a goal to stop, to moderate use, to use more safely, or to abstain completely, a treatment oriented toward helping the client achieve his chosen goal can evaluate how realistic the goal is. With an attitude of flexibility and respect for process, the therapist and client can change the focus or refer to a different treatment if other goals emerge as more appropriate.

I suggest here an experimental attitude between client and treatment provider that evolves as goals are pursued. As difficulties arise around achieving the agreed-upon goals, client and therapist can explore whether these difficulties point to additional issues that need to be addressed in the pursuit of the goal or if they mean that the goal is unrealistic and a new goal needs to be considered. Patt Denning's story about Diana in Chapter 8 illustrates how the need to change goals in the course of therapy can emerge from difficulties that arise in the pursuit of the initial goal. In Diana's case, she was not able to maintain her own initial goal of abstinence despite early success. In exploring the nature of her return to problematic drinking, Diana recognized that her desire to stop drinking reflected her wish to be a "good girl" submitting to an inner critic that partially represented her critical mother. This submission inevitably provoked a rebellious reaction that Diana expressed through excessive drinking. As the meaning of submissive abstinence and rebellious over-drinking became clear to her, Diana was able to successfully pursue moderate drinking as a goal for herself and as a way out of the submission/rebellion bind in which she had been caught.

Readiness to Change, an Important Subset of Goals

One of the most important new constructs to emerge in this recent period of reevaluation in the drug use treatment field is the "motivational stages of change," a model developed by Prochaska and DiClemente (1992). There have been constructs related to this model in the behavior change field; however, this model identifies stages in the behavior change process that include an area traditionally neglected, namely, "preparing to change."

Preparing to change begins with the precontemplation stage. This is the point before making change has been considered, before difficulties with the present behavior or pattern of drug use have been identified, before there is any reason to think about making a change. At this stage an individual begins to identify and focus on the negative consequences of drug use or ways in which the drug use impacts or causes other problems.

Once problematic aspects of drug use have been identified, a person becomes motivated to consider what is wrong and what they want to do about it. The person now moves into the contemplation stage.

When the problem has been well identified and a goal or new direction has been chosen, it becomes possible to make a plan. This is known as the preparation stage, when people prepare to make the change. What approach? With which therapist? What else needs to be cleared out of the way before the individual feels ready to commit to taking action?

Once the person is well prepared to make the change, he moves into the action stage; he puts a plan into action.

The maintenance stage is focused on addressing the things that will make it possible to successfully maintain the new behavior. In this model a relapse, or return to the earlier behavior, is seen as a learning opportunity. What didn't work? What led to the relapse? The answers to these questions create a new focus on the deeper issues involved.

To find the right fit also means identifying the care provider who is able to meet the stage of preparation with awareness and sensitivity to the evolving needs of the unique individual.

LENGTH AND INTENSITY OF TREATMENT

I have seen some clients once for an evaluation and made treatment recommendations that led to dramatic and enduring positive changes. I have seen some clients several times weekly over many years before they were able to begin making noticeable behavioral changes in their drug use. Some have done extremely well with a once-weekly psychotherapy that lasted for several months. Others lapsed at varied and numerous treatments, as in the case of one individual who eventually accepted residential treatment, followed by five-times-weekly intensive outpatient treatment with long-term psychotherapy during and after, continuously lapsing for seven years before finally turning around a severe drug problem.

These experiences have convinced me that there is no one way regarding length and intensity of treatment. A general rule of thumb is at best vague but worth considering. The intensity of treatment should correspond to the following factors: the severity of the drug problem in terms of intensity and risk; the individual's personal support structure for making changes; and the severity of emotional, personality, social, and economic problems that impact the individual process of change.

However, another factor that may be the most important to consider at the outset is what the client feels is the right amount. This will increase that person's openness to the process. If problems arise in the pursuit of change, these can lead to a consideration of whether the intensity of treatment should be increased or whether they can be addressed within the current set-up.

PERSONAL, SOCIAL, AND DEMOGRAPHIC VARIABLES

Regarding factors such as race, gender, sexual orientation, economic status, and so on, the client's preferences and feeling of safety seem most important. The importance of these issues to the consumer should be part of the planning in determining the right fit. For some people, commonality in one or many of these factors is very important, while for others they are less so.

The story I have selected to illustrate this chapter is "Michael: A Delicate Balance," by Gail Hammer. Hammer used a psychodynamic harm reduction approach in her work with Michael.

Michael: A Delicate Balance
by Gail Hammer

Michael was transferred to me after meeting briefly with a social work intern. He had come to our agency, a professional organization for those in the entertainment field, for financial assistance. The intern had begun his assistance a month before but he needed to see me in order to continue the aid, because I was to be his new case worker. Michael was a 38-year-old, light-skinned African American, who wore flamboyant and provocative clothes, suggestive of his homosexual orientation. Although there was an artistic bent to his appearance, the overall look was one of poverty. He had been HIV-positive for almost a decade before being diagnosed with AIDS. It was a couple of years after that that he sought our help.

At the time of his request for assistance, Michael had

not yet suffered from an opportunistic illness, but he was extremely frail. He was so easily fatigued that he could no longer work, and because his T-cell count was below 200, he received monthly Social Security Insurance payments. His medical care was covered by Medicaid and his housing subsidized and managed by an AIDS-related agency. Michael's appearance, economic dependence, and lack of higher education belied an unusual intelligence and exquisite sensitivity, immediately discernible from his speech if one suspended judgment.

Michael had been a talented artist. He had earned enough money in the entertainment industry to be eligible for our agency's assistance, but performing in struggling companies downtown had left him without any savings. Our financial aid, while meager, enabled him to take an extra subway, see a movie, install cable TV, or buy something other than the bare essentials. Already living with the indignity of AIDS, these funds protected him from some of the humiliation of poverty. Unfortunately, this assistance soon became leverage for the agency.

Shortly after Michael came to the agency, a problem with alcohol use was identified. Michael's social work intern had inadvertently run into Michael at our agency, where he also volunteered, sending out mailings and organizing social events for the AIDS clients. His behavior and slurred speech indicated that he had been drinking. That same day, the director of the volunteer program had smelled the odor of alcohol on Michael and had also noticed altered behavior. Neither the intern nor the program director had mentioned their impressions to Michael.

As Michael was to be transferred to me the following day, the agency wanted me to address his drinking immediately. I was told to inform him that his assistance was in jeopardy and that he would have to be evaluated for chemical dependency. The goal was to use our assistance to coerce Michael into a structured rehabilitation program. Sobriety was the rule, but fortunately, flexibility in the structure of the agency allowed for some maneuvering.

Michael did not appear for his appointment the next day, nor did he call. I realized that I was relieved because I was uncomfortable focusing on his drinking before I had a chance to know him and assess his situation. I was equally uncomfortable insisting on a policy of immediate sobriety when I didn't know if it was the appropriate treatment for this client. I was clearly resistant to doing what I had been advised to do. With more time to ponder the situation, I began to question my own clinical judgment and wondered whether my discomfort wasn't indicative of my own fear or a need to be liked.

It was several days later when Michael finally came to the office; his visit was unannounced. As previously planned in supervision, the former worker met with him alone and mentioned his drinking. Then she brought me into the room, and in front of Michael said that they had talked about the drinking and that he had agreed to be evaluated. Then she left the room. What had been a fairly congenial atmosphere between me and Michael suddenly changed. The intern was also African American and had long maintained a friendly (and lucrative) relationship with Michael. The tone of her announcement had put me in the position of punitive authority and her sudden departure left a void, filled only by my difference and perceived cruelty.

Michael was polite, but I felt he was somewhat disingenuous. There was an edge to his voice and a faint smell of alcohol on his body. He answered my questions but didn't initiate any conversation of his own. His face was almost expressionless except for a faint glimmer of hostility. We talked about his relationship with the agency, and without being obsequious, he praised the agency for giving him assistance. He said it helped him to do many things he had never been able to. He also apologized for having missed his previous appointment. He spoke with assurance but seemed angry. Although we had not talked about his drinking, his reference and praise of the agency's assistance indicated his awareness that the assistance might be in jeopardy.

What was he feeling? He was dying; there was no combination of drugs then to prolong health and inhibit the disease from worsening. AIDS was more or less a death sentence. There was a permeating sense of hopeless failure, familiar to Michael, as he had probably often failed to get his needs fulfilled in life. In retrospect, that first session must have been extremely difficult for Michael as feelings of vulnerability, fear, failure, self-hatred, and anger flooded his body and mind.

Of course, Michael tried his best not to let me see any of this. However, it was not his skill at deception that hid his feelings from me but my preoccupation with the agency's mandate. It influenced how I moved the session along according to my needs rather than his. I missed how devalued he must have felt. In our culture, where alcohol is alluring yet condemned, the exposure of his drinking was perceived as a disgrace. As I later learned, Michael had been subjected to ridicule and contempt throughout his life and was angry at his own failure as well as at those who had failed him. He felt devalued by a critical father, who then died; he was invisible to a society that was white and prejudiced; he was despised by the openly homophobic African American culture, and his kin, who demanded a manliness he did not have; and he was further stigmatized by the skittish, anti-AIDS sentiment of the 1980s.

Glossing over all of this, our conversation turned to his involvement in our volunteer program and that of another AIDS-related agency. When we talked about ways in which we could work together in the future, I said it might be useful if I contacted his other workers. At that point Michael became slightly more animated.

He said he would like that and added that I might be able to have the worker who managed his apartment fix his front door. Responding to my puzzled look, he explained that the door was broken and that repeated requests to have it repaired had failed. He said that a friend had finally boarded up the door so that he would be safe, adding that there had been three locks and now there was only one. Still confused, I questioned him further.

A more complete story unfolded: The smoke detector in his apartment, which Michael said went off all the time, particularly when there was heat, had begun to sound in the middle of the night. Michael had gone to sleep, forgetting to turn off the oven and the heat had triggered the alarm. Firefighters arrived on the scene. They rang the bell and banged on the door. Receiving no response, they broke the door down. It was only then that Michael awakened, with several men in cumbersome black rubberized jackets standing in the middle of his studio apartment. He told the story with more detail this time, but it was still sketchy. There was no affect or verbal expression of feelings. The agency, which subsidized and managed his housing, had apparently refused to pay for repairs because it had not been responsible for the damage.

Michael had probably been drinking, I thought. He had probably forgotten to turn off the oven before falling into an alcohol-induced slumber from which the firefighters could not awaken him. More importantly, I wondered if he was trying to alert me to the danger of his situation, a danger far greater than the loss of two of the locks on his door. Given what I already knew, it seemed likely that Michael had been drinking and that another time he might not be as lucky. It added pressure for me to focus on his drinking, but I left those thoughts for a moment and told him I would look into the situation.

Now, I was a beginning social worker at this time and inexperienced in the treatment of substance use.

So with little time remaining in the session and a feeling of obligation to my supervisor and agency, I confronted his drinking. The faint cry for help I had perceived from his story was now followed by the tough stance: "Don't tell me what to do." He acknowledged that he drank too much and said he wanted to change all that, but added that it would be impossible to do because of the holidays: Thanksgiving, Christmas, New Year's Eve, and his birthday were soon approaching. Then becoming more assertive, Michael claimed that his drinking did not affect his health anyway. Unexpectedly, he pulled out a pack of cigarettes and placed it on the table in front of us. He had never smoked until he was 28, he said in a somewhat agitated manner. A quick calculation told me that 28 was the age when he was diagnosed with HIV. I imagined he needed a cigarette now.

He was visibly upset. His body tensed and his face flushed red with anger. He said he did not want anybody to tell him what to do. He did not want any part of Alcoholics Anonymous or any other program, he insisted, as his eyes filled with tears, held back with determination. I told him that it was his choice, but he countered this, saying that he knew I could take his assistance away. I said that I hoped it would not come to that but I could not promise. My words rang as hollow as those of a ventriloquist's puppet, and Michael clearly needed to escape our small, windowless space. He asked to go to the men's room.

While he was gone I reflected on my own feelings and behavior. I had not recognized his fear or distrust, only anger. This was something I would have felt if it had not been for the omnipresent drinking *problem* and my own preoccupation with the agency mandate. When I began to work with someone my goal was to build a warm, trusting relationship, but I had not done that this time. Although it would have been difficult with such a well-guarded man, I would have followed his lead and listened to what was important to him. I felt that our relationship was dishonest. I was extremely uncomfortable with his anger and questioned my own opposition to enforcing agency policy. Did I oppose it to protect myself from his rage? I knew that I had not tried to elicit how Michael felt at any point during our session, and I had certainly not provided a safe environment for him.

I felt as if we had begun our work at cross-purposes and needed to start all over again. I had been preoccupied with my assigned task and had been as insincere as he had been disingenuous. I had not focused on his concerns, and he must have felt scared and unprotected. He had been transferred from one novice to another at the very moment his drinking was discovered, and this time to a white woman, who held his welfare in her hands. I could understand his sense of impotence and fury.

Given Michael's history and strong opposition to sobriety, I felt that to insist that he enter a rehabilitation program would be futile. I might lose him if I did. We would end up in a power struggle with no positive outcome. More importantly, although I knew little about my client at this time, I did know that he had a terminal illness and that both the physical and emotional implications of his illness would have to be considered when formulating a treatment plan. How could I demand that he stop drinking when this demand might prove to be harmful? I felt there had to be a better way to help him.

Michael was more calm when he came back to the interview room. As his appointment had been unscheduled and brief, we scheduled another one for later that week. He said he could come at the end of the week but could not stay long because he had to serve a meal for an important function at the other agency where he volunteered. He proudly joked that he might have to come in a tuxedo, but anger still showed on his face. Michael needed to set his own rules. He seemed to be rebelling against my authority and protecting himself at the same time. It was clear he did not want to leave time for any evaluation of his drinking.

In supervision I confronted my conflicted feelings in regard to agency policy and treatment of Michael. I was told that Michael was a very astute manipulator and that anger was his tool. Did that mean that I should not try to understand what was behind his anger? In addition, my supervisor dismissed my argument that there was something punitive about a rigid policy of abstinence in Michael's case. He said he couldn't understand how I could entertain such a thought. I was frustrated after our meeting, but not nearly as much as I would be after my meeting with our chemical-dependency expert.

With this staff member I reviewed a very cut-and-dried evaluation and mandate, which I was to administer. It questioned a client about all aspects of his or her life and alcohol use. I thought of the very sensitive and private Michael and how difficult this would be. I was told to run through all the items on the three-page form and was warned for a second time not to be manipulated. Moreover, I was indirectly told that if I could not confront the issue head on that it would bely my own weakness, and this failure would ultimately fail my client. The message was that I had to be tough; I had to break through his resistance and denial. Neither the chemical-dependency expert nor my supervisor seemed interested in what Michael was like. It appeared to me that the person with the *problem* was invisible, and that there was a one-size-fits-all model that I was to apply. I later presented Michael's case in group supervision, where there was just as little support and where I managed to earn myself a reputation for weakness and incompetence.

After these meetings, I knew I was diametrically opposed to agency policy and that I would have to circumvent this policy in order to help Michael. I would have to use my clinical training and instincts. I would have to consider Michael's natural distrust for authority, his devalued status as a gay, African American male with AIDS, his negative self-image, and the emotional implications of his illness. I told myself Michael would not die that day from alcohol use and tried to dismiss the agency's urgent mandate to pressure him. I was quite sure he would never enter a 12-step program, and as far as I could determine, I was the only person around who could give him the support he needed; I wanted to be able to do that.

Although Michael expected to be evaluated when he arrived for his next session, I began all over again, this time trying to build a relationship. I assessed his situation as if he were a new client. I took as much of a history as I felt was appropriate, leaving some questions for later sessions. I encouraged Michael to talk about what was important to him. I felt that if I were to help him, I had to gain his trust and begin to work with him on his own terms. I also needed to question Michael specifically about his illness—even that had been neglected because of the alcohol issue—but under the circumstances I felt that the medical history could wait a week or so.

The session was difficult. Michael was reticent but did reveal a little about himself, although nothing about his feelings. At a certain point, I brought up our first meeting and asked him if he had any thoughts about it. He did not. I suggested that he might have had some feelings about having come for financial assistance and being confronted with his drinking instead. He was very careful, and although I noticed the same anger cross his face, he just reiterated his objection to alcohol treatment programs. I told him that I understood and that this time I thought we could work together without that being necessary. He seemed to absorb that silently, but offered nothing more.

I tried again to address the feelings that might have come up in our first session. I asked if anything else had been difficult for him. Whether, perhaps, my being white had been a problem. I reminded him that he had been transferred to me from an African American social worker, with whom he had had a warm relationship. He said he had absolutely no problem with whites and had many white friends, but then he expanded on the ways in which whites could be deceptive. He was not going to make this easy, I thought. I didn't feel he was ready to explore whether he felt I was deceptive, so I let it go. Neither he nor I had gained much insight, but I hoped that some of my genuine interest in how he felt had come through and that our shared space had become a little safer.

In one of the following sessions, I assessed his medical situation. We talked about his health, his care, and the progression of his illness. I discovered that he was being treated for a liver-related problem, although Michael had said that the drinking had not had any physical consequences. Not wanting to determine the focus of his narrative, I stored the information. Our talk turned to everyday life. He said he lived in a neighborhood that was controlled by Dominican drug dealers, which scared him. However, more than the usual fear of drive-by shootings or muggings, Michael feared the *machismo*. It was a difficult world to be gay in, he explained. When he first moved into the area, he did not make any accommodation in his dress; perhaps he had even provoked the situation. Because of his flashy, almost costume-like clothes, which immediately identified him as gay, he often had derogatory names and rocks hurled at him as he walked down the street. He was unable or unwilling to talk about his feelings when this happened, but he expressed his anger.

My supervisor had been right to some extent. Anger was a tool, but one that he used to protect himself from his painful feelings, rather than to manipulate me. He also protected himself in a more tangible way. Though he carried his rebellion with him in the form of a bandanna or foulard with which to adorn himself when he emerged from the subway in a friendlier environment, he modified his dress. I was encouraged that he was able to find a way to avoid harm yet maintain his self-respect, and I hoped he could do the same with his drinking.

Our discussion then moved to his support network. Despite claims to the contrary, I realized that Michael was isolated. The people in his life were limited to the doctors who saw him in the hospital as a Medicaid patient, and it was unlikely that they had enough time to listen to him or understand his needs. He had limited contact at his two support agencies and perhaps an occasional encounter with a friend. He said he had friends, but his stories never included other people. He never mentioned friends visiting him or vice versa. He had no present lover or intimate relationship. His days appeared to be filled with medical appointments, volunteer work, and most likely, drinking.

He did not have much family to speak of either; his mother, father, and one brother had died, and he did not see his sister often because she still lived in the South. Michael's remaining brother was a born-again Christian who did not approve of his lifestyle or sexual preference. They hardly spoke. He spoke mostly with his sister's daughter, with whom he had the closest relationship. When I asked if he would see any of his family during the holidays, he simply said no.

Talk of the holidays gave me the chance to bring up the drinking in a more gentle way and to try to understand what it meant to him. I reminded him that he had said that it would be difficult to drink less during holidays and asked him why. He said there would be many parties with a bountiful supply of liquor and that it would be hard to resist in those social circumstances. Because Michael could not be specific about any of these parties or about where he would spend Thanksgiving and Christmas, I suspected that he might actually spend most of the holidays at home by himself, and that he would drink. He did not mention it, but I sensed drinking erased the loneliness, especially intense at that time of the year. I finally asked him what purpose he felt alcohol served for him. Still a bit distrustful, he offered that it gave him comfort. I asked him how often he needed it, and as I had imagined, he described drinking a few glasses of vodka at night when he was home alone.

Returning to the subject of the holidays, I said that I understood how difficult it would be to control his drinking then, but that because he had expressed a desire to do so, I wondered whether he thought he could drink a little less. As if he had already given it some thought, he said he planned to limit himself to beer and wine and eliminate the "hard liquor." Choosing drinks with lower alcohol content seemed like a sensible start and certainly better than drinking straight vodka, but would he be able to carry out his plan? He appeared content and self-assured. I told him that it sounded like a good idea and expressed that I sincerely hoped it would work.

I knew I needed to see Michael weekly, which was not procedure at this agency. In general, we saw clients on a need-to-see basis. In cases of monthly assistance, the process was often so automatic that there was no need to see the client at all; a check was left at the reception desk. But I managed to schedule weekly appointments with Michael, ostensibly to work with him toward entering a rehabilitation program. I began treatment with him the way I would have with any client in therapy, while I monitored his drinking at the same time.

It was a bumpy road initially. Michael vacillated between openness and open hostility. In one early session, just when I had begun to feel good about our progress—Michael had actually begun to moderate his drinking and was more forthcoming—he arrived in a dingy undershirt, smelling of alcohol. His clothes were often old, but never dirty, tattered, or inappropriate. It was unclear whether he had relapsed into past drinking patterns or whether he needed to test me. Maybe both. Would I judge him? Would I try to change him? I did neither. He had been told what to do too often, and deviating seemed to be something else that comforted him. I just assessed for any danger and waited to see what subsequent meetings would bring.

Surprisingly, there was no more testing or deviating. Michael came clean and sober to all of our subsequent sessions. In one session he even read me some poems he had written. Like the Michael I met with each week, the poems were a mixture of quiet reflection and anger. The feelings he was unable to express in our sessions were in his poetry, many of which had themes of racism. The poems, written throughout most of his adult life, were beautifully handwritten and compiled in a notebook. He never gave me any poems to take home or to keep for myself. Michael said he never gave his poems to anyone because he was afraid they would steal them. He talked as if he expected to publish them, even though I think he knew he never would. It was more that giving something so intimate was too dangerous.

Sharing Michael's inner world through his poetry was a turning point in our work. From that time on, the progress was more consistent, albeit slow. Michael came regularly to sessions and was always on time. Our sessions varied from talk about the week's events—a doctor's visit, his volunteer work, or his involvement with some performance—to his health, less frequently to carefully guarded memories of his childhood, and even less frequently to how he felt about something. I tried to keep our sessions genuine, to be where he was, and to be there for him.

I had to be careful in my work with Michael. I felt any slip on my part could destroy the delicate balance we had achieved. There was finally the requisite mutual trust and respect to allow him enough authority to make decisions about his own life that allowed me to treat him. If this were jeopardized, it would be seriously injurious to his fragile sense of self. This was hard work for me but even harder for Michael. Just coming to the sessions showed a great deal of strength, as did moderation of his own drinking.

Michael proved that a person with a drinking problem can limit his alcoholic intake, in spite of the consensus professional view to the contrary. He drank less and substituted beer and wine for vodka. With a thinly veiled sense of pride, he would give me the count for that week in each session. He was able to moderate his drinking so well that it was no longer an issue. I never had reason to suspect that he had relapsed, and I never smelled alcohol on him again. Unlike the session in which he appeared in a dirty undershirt, he began to put more attention into his dress. He even dressed more conventionally. Because there was no longer the threat of his losing financial aid—I think at that point he trusted me in that regard—the change in his appearance was probably a sign that he felt safe enough to let down his defenses. He seemed not to need to be so defiant anymore. And by conforming a little, he obtained the respect, the community through his volunteer work, and support for his illness that he really craved.

Simultaneously, with Michael's consent, I had contacted two other workers. I discovered that the man he worked with at the agency that subsidized his housing was in recovery himself and knew all about Michael's drinking. We shared our suspicions about the night of the smoke alarm and our general concern for Michael. When I began to talk about Michael's treatment I was sure I would encounter criticism, but I was wrong. Although this case worker had been "saved" by a 12-step program, he was not a strict advocate of sobriety as the immediate or sole goal of treatment. Nor did he necessarily believe that it was the appropriate way to work with Michael. Although his contact with Michael was limited, he was working with him in much the same way that I was; he monitored his drinking as best he could, trying to reduce the harm. My work with this case worker became one of comparing notes.

What I discovered at the other agency where Michael volunteered was even more interesting and helpful. That agency had also discovered his drinking. In fact, as a result of being intoxicated one evening while he was serving meals, they had suspended his volunteer privileges. This had happened just before my first meeting with Michael, but he had never mentioned it. I communicated my fear to his case worker, who was also in recovery, that Michael would become more isolated if he could not continue his work and that this would probably lead to more drinking. I told him about the progress Michael had made in reducing his alcohol intake. He said that he, too, had seen a change for the better in him.

Fortunately, at that time this particular agency was undergoing a change of its own. It was moving away from sobriety as the only acceptable goal in treating compulsive substance use. I later learned the term for this was "harm reduction." Michael's worker and I devised a plan, which we hoped would allow Michael to regain his privileges. A group of people with AIDS and substance problems had just been formed. The mandate was attendance not abstinence, and the group was time-limited. Both of us began to encourage Michael to attend the group, dangling the carrot of his volunteer work in front of him. After he attended a number of sessions, he would be able to serve meals again. Although he could not admit it, Michael was scared to join the group. He was a private person with trust issues and low self-esteem. He might have to share some events and feelings with others and expose himself. He would also have to follow the rules, something he did not do willingly. Moreover, he would have to believe he could do something to help himself. Because I had seen him do that before—in his neighborhood and with his drinking—I was optimistic.

I helped Michael to become aware of the importance

of his volunteer work, the devastation that came from its loss, and the necessity to get it back. I also helped him talk about his fears related to the group. After not too long, Michael decided to take the risk and join the group. In the same way he was able to alter his appearance so that he could walk safely down the streets of his neighborhood, he was able to act in his best self-interest in his new group.

Up until this time, I had needed, but could not find, confirmation for the work I was doing with Michael. I had researched the literature and spoken with colleagues, but the message was always the same: sobriety before clinical treatment. Nowhere did I read that anyone was struggling with the problems as I was. I proceeded anyway. I followed my instincts and tried to believe in the progress I saw with Michael, but now my contacts with his workers finally gave me the support that I needed.

When Michael was secure that I would not force him into any treatment and that I would protect his monthly payments, he began to tell me something about his life. In the first half of our treatment he appeared as a person with no past and a sketchy present. Shortly after the halfway mark of our treatment process, a picture began to emerge of a sensitive, unusually bright boy of color growing up in the South, struggling against feelings of inferiority.

Michael described childhood in a small segregated southern town. His father died when he was young and his mother worked as a domestic. Although he must have been poor, the picture he painted of his neighborhood was one of modest homes with small, well-groomed lawns and children playing outside. He had some happy memories and some painful ones. But what was most present in his narratives, even though he could not verbalize it, was a feeling of loneliness and sadness. All of his stories showed a little boy who often felt different and out of place, a little boy who probably had an inner life that was more rich and full than his outer life.

Michael began his education at an all-black school in his neighborhood, but because of his intelligence, he and soon transferred to a gifted program in a white school. There Michael was intellectually stimulated but completely isolated. He was the only black child who talked about feeling alone, friendless, and different. He remembered feeling that way especially during adolescence. He did not talk much about his sexual orientation but shared memories of very early sexual experiences with boys in the neighborhood, experiences he had never shared with anyone.

Life at home had been difficult, too. Michael's father, an alcoholic who often stumbled home drunk for all to see, was very critical of Michael and often emotionally abusive. Michael described loving his father but not receiving much in return. He also remembered feeling embarrassed by him. He did not have to feel the shame for long. His father died of an alcohol-related disease when Michael was young, followed closely by the death of his older brother, apparently for similar reasons. Michael's mother was warm and caring, but she was also the source of feelings of shame, inferiority, and anger. Michael talked once of accompanying his mother to work when he was a small child and watching her go down on her hands and knees to clean the floors in the home of her wealthy white employer. Once again it was too painful for him to verbalize the feelings this provoked.

As with his intelligence, Michael's artistic abilities were recognized early. After high school he received an artistic scholarship. However, despite these opportunities, something always got in the way of his success. As an underpaid, albeit talented artist, he stayed on the periphery of the established art scene, not making the money that symbolized success. As a result, he continued to feel devalued, alone, and outside.

Throughout our work, Michael remained reserved.

He never spoke about the past in any detail or with any emotion. The feelings were probably much too painful. We worked together for only six months and the fact that he told me anything about himself seemed a breakthrough. His negative sense of self and distrust of people made living an emotionally connected life difficult.

Michael did continue to moderate his drinking until the end. I provided a holding environment where he felt heard, understood, and accepted for who he was, and where he could succeed. He came faithfully to his weekly sessions. The support this gave him was probably greater than he could admit or I could realize at the time. Although I do not think he was ever able to trust me completely, there were brief moments of warmth when I could almost measure the growth of our relationship. A high point came after months of working together when Michael told me he wanted to take a trip home, to the South. We planned together how he could save enough money to buy a round-trip bus ticket, which he did. He traveled home and returned with a feeling of happiness and accomplishment. It was the last time he would ever go home.

It was hard for Michael to admit he needed anyone, but in the end he was able to say so in not so many words. We worked a long time toward termination as I knew I would be leaving the agency. Michael was to be transferred to his third and final social worker and I was involved in the choice. I wanted to make sure the selection would be made more carefully this time, that the clinician would continue to support Michael as I had, and that she would be with him until the end, which she was.

For our final session, Michael appeared in a pale yellow polo shirt and conventional slacks. Although I personally preferred his flamboyant, creative look, I understood that his new image was not for me but for him. I think it was important for him to symbolize how much he had changed. To show me that his inner core was still thriving, he brought one last poem that day. As always, he read it to me. It was about a little black boy, his feelings of love and anger. It was the most beautiful and intimate of all the poems he had read.

Together Michael and I had fought a policy that would have put up an impenetrable wall between us, depriving him of the only consistent support he had. Michael succeeded in helping himself and won an important battle, which allowed him a better quality of life for the little time he had left. And I learned an important lesson. If I had yielded to agency pressure, I would not have seen the person Michael was; I would have seen only the *denial* and *manipulation*. But instead of viewing him as a *problem*, I began my work with him anew, treating him the way I did all my clients. I worked in his best interest, I trusted him, I accepted him, I listened to him, and I worked with his resistance around treatment.

I know Michael would not have accepted treatment in a 12-step or any structured rehabilitation program, but even if he had, I believe he would have failed. The failure would not only have harmed him physically but would have added yet another failure to the long list of others in his life. Instead, by working as we did, he succeeded. He set his own rules, carried them out, and was able to take care of himself. He carried this accomplishment with him until he died. This treatment approach would not have worked for everyone, but it did for Michael. And I cannot imagine what the rest of his life would have been like if it had not.

Commentary by Andrew Tatarsky

What stands out at the beginning of the story is Hammer's statement that she was uncomfortable focusing on Michael's drinking before she had a chance to get to know him. Her primary instinct and sense of the proper way to begin her work with Michael were up against an agency policy that initially clouded her better judgment and nearly derailed the work before it began.

Hammer was given an agency mandate or directive in dealing with Michael that was clearly an example of a one-size-fits-all model cure for compulsive substance use. The fact that the client was drinking was enough information to warrant a whole set of generally devaluing assumptions to be made about him which, in turn, were used to justify coercing him into a particular predetermined set of treatment recommendations.

Assumptions dominate the social milieu of social welfare agencies: that the substance user is manipulative and needs to be coerced; that the compulsive substance user needs a more structured rehab program; that the agency knows what the client needs before discussing it with him; that alcohol users cannot benefit from psychotherapy; that substance users cannot be trusted to tell the truth; and that they don't want help.

Hammer describes how the agency mandate prevented her from being able to see Michael clearly in the first meeting and influenced how she moved the session along according to her agenda rather than his. This nearly sabotaged their work because it left him feeling unsafe and angry rather than safe and in the presence of someone who was genuinely interested in getting to know and help him. She says, "I was a beginning social worker at the time and inexperienced in the treatment of substance use." It is not hard to imagine that the only reason Michael came back was because of his need for financial assistance. If this were not the case and he was just coming for counseling, would he have returned? Would anyone have?

Unfortunately, this is an example of something that happens all the time out in the field of substance use treatment. It is easy to see from Hammer's description how many clients may be turned off from seeking treatment, as nearly occurred with Michael, just at the moment they are most open, the first visit. This is likely to explain the motives of the majority of substance-using people who decide not to return for help after a first visit with a professional.

Beyond turning people off to treatment, which is bad enough, there is an arguably more damaging potential consequence of this prejudiced and coercive approach. It mirrors situations in earlier important relationships in which needs and feelings were not recognized and responded to in helpful ways. Because of that, it can trigger reactions similar to those from the earlier situations and seem like a confirmation of what one concluded from the disappointment, frustration, and shame of the earlier experiences. "I was right not to expect help when I am in need." "I am really on my own in this world." "People can't be trusted, they don't really care, they just follow their own agendas." In this case, Michael was lucky. After Hammer examined her first meeting with Michael, she realized that her preoccupation with the agency's policy had prevented her from establishing a safe, trusting collaborative relationship with him. She knew that to insist on her supervisor's stance would lose Michael, and she decided to oppose the recommendations and start over with his interests in mind.

This courageous decision, to buck agency policy and get to know Michael before deciding what course to take with him, enabled her to find the approach that fit his needs. It also contributed to a strong alliance between them because it led to Michael feeling respected and listened to, with offerings of help that suited his deepest needs. Ultimately it led to therapy that supported Michael in achieving his own goal of moderation.

Hammer started from where Michael was, creating a sense of safety in the psychotherapeutic relationship. This led to a strong working alliance between them, resulting in a therapeutic process that helped Michael achieve his goals.

As in prior stories, the themes of courage, creativity, and relationship were important ingredients in the success of this psychotherapy.

Michael drank for comfort and to ease loneliness, but in the course of the therapy, he also drank as a way to test Hammer's sincerity. Would she continue to work with him without trying to control or judge him? In this case the most important thing she needed to do was to be true to her commitment, not controlling or judging, but assessing danger and expressing concern and interest in the meaning of his drinking. Apparently she passed the test and there were no more incidents of heavy drinking.

The first concern of the therapist is pulse-taking, a process of attunement to the subtle emotional needs and vulnerabilities of the client. In this story, we hear how Hammer adjusted her attention in order to respect Michael's need to feel he had authority to make his own decisions. As Michael received the respect of his therapist, which for him was a human experience altogether rare, he began to feel respected in life. This change in self-status with regard to his environment was expressed by his change in appearance, the cessation of his defiant impulse to flamboyant dress even in the midst of danger. The right fit in terms of therapeutic attunement or attention or sensitivity can have profound therapeutic benefits reflected throughout the client's life patterns and habits.

References

Marlatt, G.A. (Ed.). (1998). *Harm Reduction: Pragmatic Strategies for Managing High Risk Behaviors.* New York: Guilford Press.

Miller, W. R. and Rollnick, S. (1991). *Motivational Interviewing: Preparing People to Change Addictive Behavior.* New York: Guilford Press.

Peele, S., Bufe, C. and Brodsky, A. (2000). *Resisting 12-Step Coercion: How to Fight Forced Participation in AA, NA, or 12-Step Treatment.* Tucson, AZ: See Sharp Press.

Prochaska, J. O. and DiClemente, C. C. (1992). Stages of change in the modification of problem behaviors. In L. M. Vernon, R. M. Eisler, and P. M. Miller (Eds.), *Progress in Behavioral Modification* (pp. 184–214). Sycamore, IL: Sycamore Press.

Tatarsky, A. and Washton, A. (1987). Intensive Outpatient Treatment. In B.C. Wallace (Ed.) (1992), *The Chemically Dependent: Phases of Treatment and Recovery.* New York: Brunner/Mazel.

Wallace, B. C. (Ed.). (1992). *The Chemically Dependent: Phases of Treatment and Recovery.* New York: Brunner/Mazel.

5

Complex Problems Require Complex Solutions

Donnie: A Life Apart
—Valerie Frankfeldt

S ubstance use problems in the context of severe emotional, interpersonal, and sociological difficulties generally require treatments that are sophisticated, complex, intensive, and long. This chapter discusses the intensity and complexity of the problems often associated with severe substance use problems.

The complexity of substance use problems and what contributes to them are often grossly underestimated in our society. Substance use is often portrayed as simply a response to peer pressure or bad judgment. It's easier to stigmatize substance users with one-liners than to think deeply about the issues; we imagine that drug use is simply due to media glamorization or due to a personal lack of discipline.

DENIAL OF MEANING AND COMPLEXITY

Prevalent social attitudes of the current paradigm about substance use mirror or recapitulate addictive behavior. Our prevailing drug policy focuses on the substance and not the psychospiritual and sociological roots of the drive to alter consciousness. We have forgotten to examine the total emotional, interpersonal, and socioeconomic matrix of the user. If drug use can be isolated from this matrix, then none of these difficult issues need be addressed. All the focus can stay on the drug use, the question of using or not, and all other factors contributing to a decision to use can be avoided. Similarly, an addictive relationship is one in which the individual's desire is focused on the object of the addiction, whether drugs, food, sex, or money, as an attempt to address feelings and needs that are never fully acknowledged. The addictive object is invested with the symbolic power to cure everything. The focus of the addiction is on getting and having the addictive object rather than on finding real solutions or satisfactions for the needs that are driving the addictive search. In the investment in the addictive object there is a denial of what the actual needs are or that there is somethng very wrong inside that must be discovered and addressed. The denial is a response that protects the individual from some anxiety or threat conjured by the deeper need. The problem is that because the drug, fantasy, or symbolic solution to the denied needs is not a real solution, the needs are never met and the user is never satisfied. The needs get more intense, and frequently, the addictive search intensifies.

UNDERESTIMATING THE COMPLEXITY OF DRUG USE PROBLEMS IS A SETUP FOR FAILURE

Society's denial of the complexity of the issues contributing to drug use seems to serve the same function. Placing all the emphasis on the drug out of its context allows an avoidance of the threatening issues that we don't want to confront. The prevailing social emphasis on the mono-cure of abstinence-only is a similar syndrome. The reductionist "Just Say No" campaign has had repercussions in our social attitudes and treatment of users, in the methods of treatment of available, in the punitive enforcement of abstinence as mass-cure, and in the domains of drug enforcement.

These ineffectual policies and methods have contributed to unfathomable suffering on a mass scale. The underestimation of the problem gives rise to unrealistic expectations held by both users and nonusers about the nature of these problems, the process of change, and what is required to support change. Unrealistic expectations give rise to inadequate measures that set up users to fail and to blame themselves for the failure. Unrealistic expectations set up family and friends to feel unreasonably disappointed, frustrated, scared, and angry at themselves and the user. Unrealistic expectations set governments and policy makers up to support inadequate treatment and blame the "failing" users for not really wanting to change, punishing them with criminal justice interventions rather than providing support for better treatment and other interventions into the social conditions contributing to the suffering that often leads to substance use.

I often see these attitudes in users and friends and families of users who consult me for help. They tend to get easily frustrated that the user isn't quickly able to stop once he has recognized that there is a problem. Just as the user wants a quick fix with the drug, so we all seem to want a quick fix when it comes to changing. When users don't change as easily as they would like to, it often leads them to become angry with themselves, despairing of ever changing. This inevitably intensifies their substance use. Family and friends often become unduly frightened and angry, thinking the user can never change or does not really want to change. Policy makers support inadequate programs that are underfunded, understaffed, too short in duration, and have unreasonable expectations of how quickly or easily patients should be able to make changes. Many programs will terminate patients from their programs if they are unable to stop using almost immediately, as if the threat of this punitive action will enhance motivation to change. Unfortunately, more often than not, this strategy fails and the user is banished from treatment for having the problem he came to remedy.

MULTIPLE PERSONAL MEANINGS OF DRUGS VARY WIDELY

In fact, one of the most important things I have learned in my career is that the nature of substance use problems and the meanings and functions that they can have for people vary so broadly that it is almost impossible to make generalizations about why people use and develop these problems. Generalizations about the specific meanings and functions of substance use run the risk of missing the unique roles that substances play in each person's life. I have come to think of substances as being multipurpose tools that can be used by almost everyone to perform a variety of different functions. Thus, for some the use of substances is a simple straightforward affair easily addressed through education and good judgment. However, for others, substances take on multiple meanings and functions in the context of the most complex and severe emotional, interpersonal, and socioeconomic problems. For these people, the process of changing will be difficult and uncertain, and treatment will generally need to be sophisticated, intensive, and long. This distinction may not be obvious at the outset.

I have chosen a story for this chapter that is an example of how complex and severe the issues contributing to substance use can be and the kind of treatment that is generally required in this situation. "A Life Apart" by Valerie Frankfeldt is the story of her six-year-long psychotherapy work with Donnie, a young man who was severely dependent on a variety of drugs, including alcohol. His substance use was intertwined with severe emotional, communication, and social problems that grew out of a childhood history of terrible sexual and physical abuse and neglect. At the beginning of the story, we hear that the author could not tell if Donnie was schizophrenic, mentally retarded, or severely drug dependent, and she often could barely understand what he was saying.

The story poignantly shows how the right kind of psychotherapy matched to the specific needs of the client can facilitate virtually unimaginable change. This is a message that can be inspiring for anyone. In this case, Frankfeldt was pulled to use a harm reduction approach in spite of her prior training in abstinence-only treatment. She took her cues from the nature of her patient, for if she had insisted on abstinence only, group therapy, or institutionalized care, she would have driven the patient away from their therapeutic course and toward disaster.

Valerie Frankfeldt used a therapy based on an integration of

Modern psychoanalysis and the 12-step philosophy of Alcoholics Anonymous. Modern psychoanalysis is a school of psychoanalytic work that was developed by Hyman Spotnitz (1985).

A Life Apart
by Valerie R. L. Frankfeldt

When I opened the door of my office to greet my new patient, Donnie, I found a small and thin young man, perhaps in his mid-twenties, disheveled like an urchin child, his dirty blonde hair in need of a haircut. He made no eye contact. My immediate sense of him was that he was a disenfranchised person, someone very uncomfortable in his own skin. When I tried to find out what brought him to therapy, I couldn't decipher his speech at all as he mumbled incoherently in deep tones below the audible range. In fact, it seemed he could barely talk. At first I wondered if he might be stoned.

There was an aura of violence beneath the mumbling that made me anxious. I felt immediately curious; I wanted to understand him as I sensed there was a paradox or riddle ready to reveal itself. It was clear this was a person who, although in great need of help, could not or did not want to connect. I felt challenged by the complex task in store for us. As time went on, it became clear what an understatement that was, as I vacillated between diagnosing him as mentally retarded, paranoid schizophrenic, or deeply in the throes of addiction. In view of what was to come during his six-year treatment, my initial anxiety was justified.

Fortunately, Donnie was quite well motivated and he proved himself willing and able to show up more often than not. His verbal production was so muffled and chaotic, I often had to guess at what he might be saying. He indicated that he was using an array of drugs. Which ones, and to what extent, it was impossible for me to tell. Nevertheless, he seemed to be able to manage as an outpatient; his addiction did not require hospitalization at this point in time. Early in the treatment, Donnie alluded to something ominous, something about people being after him. My anxiety rose: It sounded as if his pursuers might be dangerous drug dealers. My concern was twofold: Was he paranoid, or was he in actual physical danger, or both? He did not appear to be a person who could handle himself if attacked, even while sober. To protect himself, he carried a hefty Indian knife in his backpack. Because of his aura of violence, and his unpredictability, I asked him to leave the backpack (with the knife) outside my office door, which he was willing to do.

Over time, I ferreted out the following information:

Donnie was the youngest of four brothers born to an alcoholic single mother in a dilapidated tenement in Queens, New York. He never knew his father nor anything about him. When he was 7 years old, his mother, who evidently could not cope with the pressures of poverty and child rearing, turned one of his brothers over to a relative, put Donnie and his brother into an orphanage, and kept the favorite at home. In the orphanage Donnie was repeatedly attacked, beaten, and sodomized by his brother and the other boys. In the dark of night, the boys would take Donnie by surprise after he had fallen asleep. Donnie had suffered sleep problems ever since. He had no protectors or allies. His mother took him back after a few years only to return him to the orphanage for another year. One winter's day, she picked him up and let him know he would live with her from then on. At that time she had a lover, who also molested him. After the mother and "stepfather" separated, Donnie was sent on visits to the stepfather, and he invariably would be used sexually on these occasions. He tried to run away to avoid the visits, but the stepfather could always find him. Whenever Donnie mentioned the stepfather's abuse to his mother, she accused him of lying. Apparently she needed to get the child out of her hair more than she needed to take him seriously.

Somehow he managed to make it through high school. At the time of treatment he was living with a brother and working a menial night shift job at the post office. Because of his orphanage trauma, Donnie was able to sleep better during the day. Donnie's post office work was simple and structured and he felt relatively safe and comfortable once he was given assignments. He was able to do the jobs competently, and to his credit, periodically received merit raises.

About a year before Donnie commenced his treatment, he was working at the post office and living in a housing project with two brothers. When Donnie went to work each night, the oldest one shot heroin with friends in Donnie's apartment. One day Donnie returned home to find his brother's corpse. Donnie responded to this trauma by making all the funeral arrangements and paying for the funeral with his life savings of $3,000. Donnie's other brothers were substance abusers as well. The oldest one had done better with his life: He held a lucrative job, was married, and had children.

In the beginning of treatment, I worked to get Donnie to show up weekly. Given his erratic substance abuse and his need to fend people off, I knew he could not be relied upon to make a regular appearance. I began to discover patterns in his drug use as I questioned and tracked interferences and resistances to his showing up for appointments. Donnie was more likely to show in the middle of the week than at the beginning. His drugging and drinking occurred most seriously on the weekends. On weekdays, he would drink up to a six-pack of beer. Most of the time the weekday drinking did not impair his functioning. On weekends he couldn't stand to be alone with unstructured time. He couldn't make a plan for himself, and he certainly didn't want to do anything that had to do with people. He avoided people as much as possible. His job was tolerable because he was virtually alone on the night shift.

For a while I couldn't understand what prevented Donnie from showing for appointments. First of all, it took a long time to track and comprehend his speech. His fear of people and his wariness contributed to these verbal obscurations. The psychological and neurological aftereffects of drinking further clouded his thought. Rather than communicate verbally, Donnie used impulsive gestures and actions both within the room and beyond in order to weave his own language. Because I could not rely on his ability to talk or my ability to reach him with mere words, I began to use behavioral techniques to make an impact. If he did not show for a session without giving twenty-four hours' notice, I would not immediately grant a request for a new appointment. I would first ask that he call me at a given time to make the next appointment, and if he was able to comply I would give him a new appointment. If he did not call at the assigned time, but called at another time, I would give him yet another time to call for an appointment.

I have found that in order to be successful with an impulsive patient, one must address the impulsivity. This technique slows down action-oriented impulsivity in clients who demonstrate their negative feelings in actions rather than words. It also opens the opportunity for further cooperation between client and therapist without reinforcing the uncooperative behavior of the past. Last but not least, it clearly saves the therapist the trouble of multiple strings of broken appointments.

I hoped that by responding to Donnie's broken sessions (acts of impulsivity in the context of the therapy) and requests for next appointments in a slow, deliberate, and strategic fashion, that I might "train" him, in tiny increments, to develop more capacity for planning. I stress the importance of this experiential training going on within the treatment. Once a therapeutic relationship is in place, this kind of training helps to mature the client. He can then carry the learning into the outside world. Other examples of the use of treatment to deal directly with impulsivity are the exploration of any actions in the treatment room, such as the patient bringing in coffee, smoking, getting up and walking around, asking to use the therapist's phone, and so on. The point is to get the patient to put into words the feelings that motivated the action. For example, if an alcoholic patient (with whom I have a good working relationship) brings coffee into the room, I may ask, "Am I driving you to drink?"

Donnie often delivered strong nonverbal messages that I should keep a personal distance. For this reason, I remained quiet in sessions, except to interject a question or two. The questions would be informational in nature about people or situations in his life rather than dealing in any way with his internal state. I took this approach to avoid intrusion. Because he did not ask me any questions, I inquired from time to time whether or not I should be doing anything about the problems he raised as a way of bringing myself into his awareness. I wanted, gradually, to establish a sense of partnership in this terribly isolated person, a man who had experienced nothing but trouble and danger at the hands of others. This approach was helpful because it allowed Donnie to control our shared space. He alone determined the pace of the interactions, as much as he could comfortably handle, without any demands from me for a relationship.

About this issue, Unger (1978) has written:

> I know therapists who talk a lot to alcoholic patients, but in a way that is supportive; they answer questions, provide a lot of personal information, and help the patient with problems. This appears to make patients momentarily comfortable, but I think it makes long-range progress impossible and also offers a degree of intimacy that can be anxiety-producing for

the patient. Many alcoholics report a pattern of becoming intensely involved with people, only to break off relationships when things get too close. [p. 165]

I think by keeping such a low profile I enabled Donnie to begin to emerge from his protective isolation, to verbalize more, and to become more understandable as well as more open. He began revealing more information about himself: his reactions to life, his drinking, and his feelings about drinking. In time, the air of danger and paranoia began to evaporate, including his drugging, and his stories of notorious drug dealers ceased to hang over the treatment.

I carefully approached the idea of Donnie's attending Alcoholics Anonymous and was not surprised at his initial response: changing the subject. I brought AA up periodically for a year or two before I got much of a direct response. Eventually, through small revelations, Donnie explained that he was afraid of people; people were dangerous. He lived the life of a mole on purpose. He had never had a friend or a date. He slept by day while his brother worked and slipped out of the house soon after his brother's return. Anything he could do to avoid people was lifesaving for him. Going to AA was tantamount, emotionally, to going back to the nightmare of the orphanage. He was able to come to sessions to meet with me, another human being, because he had been referred to the clinic by a doctor (this seemed to confer some sense of reputability), and I was the person doing the job. It was a formal situation that had structure and purpose. That was acceptable.

Donnie's first clear communications covered his extremely mixed feelings about his drinking. He certainly did not want to consider giving it up, but it was causing him significant problems. He felt out of control; he was dismayed at what he spent on alcohol as well as by the unpredictability of how long he would stay in a bar when he had planned to be home at a given time. He hated the physical discomfort of the aftermath of drinking; he was distressed by the uncertainty of how his Monday would go, whether he could get to work and function if he got there. He could not plan Monday therapy sessions because he might not make it.

I was poignantly struck by the wild tension between his burning desire to grow and the force of his addiction. I felt alternately protective and exasperated. Because the drinking was taking over and starting to contaminate the week as well as the weekends, we did focus more on what incidents seemed to be precipitating drinking. He began to make efforts to curtail his habit. The pattern began to change with his increased interest in the therapeutic relationship, his first relationship. He had become sufficiently involved in the treatment to want to comply with a twenty-four-hour sobriety rule prior to sessions. While I felt I could not insist on his going to AA or to an inpatient rehabilitation facility immediately, I did observe that our work was severely compromised by the drinking. It was evident that when he was hung over or still somewhat under the influence, he could not express himself fully and I could not have much success in reaching him.

I found that it had become virtually useless for me to try to do therapy when Donnie was inebriated because it was so destructive to our communication. Trying to maintain twenty-four hours of abstinence, Donnie used whatever resources he could find to cooperate. He often found that he was incapable of cooperating, even though he consciously wanted to. In the process, we did obtain more grist for the mill with regard to his powerlessness to control his drinking. He was able, most of the time, to manage twenty-four hours without a drink. This led him to feel more hopeful about trying longer periods of abstinence. The reduction of drinking around sessions also had the salutary effect of increasingly his ability to talk, to remember, and to feel.

Life often takes a turn for the worse when people begin to reduce their drinking. Donnie had been previously unaware of his strong death wish. One day he came into our session wounded and badly bandaged. Someone had smashed a bottle over his head at the bar. He didn't remember what had led up to the fight, but he was clear that the drinking played a part in it. I, of course, was alarmed. He could have been blinded, maimed for life, or killed! In any other case, I would have started working to erode the client's resistances to entering a rehab program but with Donnie's history, I knew that direction would be futile. I redoubled my efforts to get him into AA. I persistently explored all the reasons AA was scary and all the things that would keep him from going, in the hope that he could get there before his self-destructive behaviors ended his life.

He was convinced that the people in AA could not help him; he was contemptuous about alcoholics helping alcoholics, and he was sure that they would push him around and tell him what to do. I emphasized the fact that he could control his participation at the meeting. He did not have to sit with anyone, talk to anyone, or give out his telephone number. He did not have to stay the whole time, come on time, or wait until the end to leave. He could arrange his attendance in such a way as to make sure he was comfortable. He did not have to do or say anything. He did not have to like it. He did not have to commit to going. All I was recommending was that he check it out once, if only for five minutes. For him, the most important piece was the reassurance that he did not have to have any personal contact with anyone. He called AA and found out where the meetings were. That was about all he could do for many months. For a while all the meetings near him were somehow inconvenient: wrong time, wrong place, too close to home (someone might see him going in), too far from home, and so on. However, he now had a goal and was oriented to an identifiable location. This made the idea more real as we continued to discuss the possible dangers, discomforts, and bad surprises that lurked behind the four walls of that church.

The discussion of his fantasies of what the people in AA could do to him had a very positive effect on Donnie before he ever set foot in a meeting. It exposed his fears about the destructiveness of people and relationships. These self-revelations coincided with renewed courage, motivation, and curiosity strong enough to apply for a job on the day shift. He was successful. This represented an enormous internal change: It showed that he was ready, albeit marginally, to put himself into the world of people.

At about that time, astonishing to me, he demonstrated a dormant high intelligence and capacity for learning by acquiring a computer, hooking it up, and teaching himself to use it. This was not as easy a task then as it is now. This occurred in the time before computers became user-friendly and before they became a household commonplace. I had previously judged Donnie as brain damaged or retarded, and now he was engaging with the system that would become the Internet. It was not known as the Internet at that time and cruising along the information highway was an activity known only to the most determined hackers. Through this world, Donnie began relating to people. He made acquaintances with people all over the country, and further, began a foray into the world of heterosexuality. In fact, he became one of the unsung pioneers of compusex as he discovered the world of women this way. The computer served as a safe transition from total isolation over to distance connection to the human race. Subsequently, Donnie went to a party held in New York City for members of a special interest group and met some of his female correspondents in person for the first time. Though it

was still early for these connections to have consequence, the fact that he was able to try did provide
plenty of material for therapy and represented tremendous growth.

To my amazement, Donnie revealed to me at this
time that he was carrying on some conversations with
a young woman at work. His description had a dis-
tinctly romantic tinge. For two years, his active social
life via computer had been assisted and informed by
therapy. This combination of distance relating and
therapy provided a bridge to the world of human
relationships. Donnie had learned enough long distance to guide his face-to-face conversations at the
workplace toward getting to know this young woman,
to dating, and to some first sexual activity. He soon
discovered that his new friend was deeply troubled,
living a chaotic and dangerous life herself. Donnie
found himself rapidly taking on a caretaking role. It
seemed he was either doing for her what he wished
someone had done for him or symbolically rescuing his
brothers and mother as he felt he had done earlier in
life. After numerous crises, which he obviously could
not resolve for her, he let go of the relationship.

Donnie's personal crises did not stop. Up until this
time, he rarely talked about his brother at home. Now
he began focusing exclusively on his concerns about
his brother, who was not getting out of bed, was
working only sporadically, and was not bathing or
eating properly. Donnie wanted to help his brother. We
discussed what steps he might take. He was not having
success persuading him to get psychological help. The
man seemed to be drowning in depression and was
unresponsive to Donnie's suggestions. Donnie spent
a number of sessions talking about his desperation
about his brother's deterioration. After Donnie finally
persuaded his brother to get medication and the situation still worsened, Donnie grew frantic. Donnie came
to therapy one day looking ashen with the news that

last week he returned home to find his brother dead, hanging from a rope.

It is indicative of Donnie's isolation that he didn't call me when this happened. He dutifully made funeral arrangements and waited for his regular session time. He was planning to use all of his savings, for the second time, to bury his second brother. I was horrified by the whole turn of events and outraged that he should sacrifice himself for this brother, no matter how guilty he felt. I questioned at length his need to deplete his savings, but to no avail.

The second suicide of a sibling in three years did not help Donnie's control of his alcoholism. Donnie began instigating fights in bars. He was arrested and jailed overnight. On one occasion he was taken to the emergency room by the police. He really needed to be in a rehab program, but I knew that if I gave him an ultimatum that he go into rehab as a condition of continuing our treatment, he would have refused and would have ended the treatment. He was still too people-phobic to put himself in an institutional setting. His earlier life-threatening experiences with institutions were still too overwhelming to his thoughts and feelings. Our work was his only lifeline. Donnie's attendance to our sessions had improved enormously; it had been years since a missed appointment until the day when he called me from the hospital after a drunken car crash. At that time I realized that if Donnie couldn't put into words his desire for death, that I would have to do so myself.

I didn't think giving an interpretation, such as telling him that he was suicidal, would have much effect; he would have denied it. Also, he may not have cared. I tried an approach that I hoped would be more likely to reach him emotionally. I made it a point to say, in every session, something about my certainty that he was now on his last legs. I began questioning him if I would be hearing news of him next from the morgue. My high anxiety earlier in the treatment was nothing compared to what it became now. I did ask myself seriously whether I should impose an ultimatum about rehab; I am not shy of making threats when I think they will be helpful, but each time I felt sure that such a threat would be the death knell to any possibility of his remaining in treatment. Nor was the rehab idea palatable to him when I brought it up for consideration. I had to wonder which would come first, recovery or death. I felt on tenterhooks every time I thought of him, which was frequently. I dreaded opening the door to see him, not knowing what sort of damage would confront me. It was a race against time, against Donnie's now very powerful death force.

This emotionally laden, shocking language about Donnie's rapid spiral toward death helped break through his denial barrier about the severity of his suicidal behavior. In addition to using this form of confrontation, I also resorted to another rather unorthodox technique: I yelled at him! He was going on and on in his usual monotone about the latest drinking binge, saying that he couldn't find the time to go to AA, and I would yell, "You mean you don't have time for Donnie Taylor?!" Or, "You're sitting there telling me it's not that bad and you just called me last week from a hospital bed? What's next?!" I have written elsewhere about the need for the therapist to go to any lengths to change traditional modes of relating to patients when the patient is in this level of denial and aimed toward death (Levinson, 1986).

Working in the addiction field has led me to ponder the nature of what I am calling the "death force," called by Freud the "death wish" or "death instinct." I wonder what compels some people to court death until they are successful, as opposed to those who make it just to death's door only to stumble upon, or consciously decide, to accept help and live. I believe there must be a confluence of circumstances that move one toward a

premature death, which, after all, goes against a natural striving to live. I also believe that anyone who
succeeded at being conceived and who survived gesta-
tion is, in nature, imbued with a striving toward life.
Individuals working their way toward death later in life
are often those who grew up in an emotional atmosphere conducive to death: perceiving self to be un-
wanted by the parents, the recipient of conscious or
unconscious parental death wishes unmitigated by
feelings of love, acceptance, and appreciation. In addition, the stage must be set by the child's not having the
capacity to comment on what he perceives to be true,
either because he has not achieved enough separation
from the parents to be able to be objective and can only
attack himself, or because such expression would be
unacceptable in the family and must be bottled up,
probably also resulting in self-attack.

In the case of some addicts, and probably others
who live out an unconsciously suicidal lifestyle, there
must also be an absence of the ability, which parents
must inculcate, to think, plan, fantasize, imagine, and
talk. Instead, the individual knows only to go into
immediate action to relieve tension. Action not mediated by thought and planning tends to be destructive.
It is much easier and faster to destroy than to create.
Destructive impulsivity tends to result in counterag-
gression from the environment, setting up a vicious
cycle of negativity. This is the central problem in
addiction: Efforts to alleviate tension result in situations that cause even more tension, necessitating wild
activity to escape chaos, confusion, and increasingly
insoluble problems. In the case of addiction to chemicals, there is not only the psychological dependency
as described previously, but also, progressively, the
physical dependency, making it completely impossible
to stop without medical intervention. Then, too, the individual who has grown up isolated from, and right-
fully distrustful of, others' ability to be of help, is most

likely unwilling and unknowledgeable as to how to avail himself of help. These three factors—early destructive relations with murderous caregivers, impulsivity, and, ultimately, physical dependency on drugs—predispose an individual to have no choice but to aim for death.

Donnie was expressing through his actions some powerful wishes to have a premature ending to his life, and he couldn't tap his life force sufficiently to move toward life, other than to come to sessions. Seeing this clearly, I used my own wish for him to live to try to reach him. This did seem to have the effect of mobilizing him, for he now took a look at AA. Literally. He walked himself to the building, looked through the doorway, and left. That was the best he could do. But taking a step in the direction of AA produced a counterforce to the pull the addiction had on him. Very slowly, and in very small steps, his drinking and other self-destructive behaviors began to give way. It took him a whole year to move from outside the AA room to let himself be, solidly, inside the room. He described his first reaction to a stranger's welcoming approach. He said he had glared so ferociously that the welcoming committee and all potential candidates for a welcoming committee left him alone. He wanted and needed not to interact with anyone for the first year.

During this time another helpful event took place. Donnie's remaining brother, the higher functioning one, was jailed for drunken driving, and got the AA message while in jail. The brother then took Donnie to meetings every now and then and, by his own example, helped ease Donnie's navigation into the program. I believe Donnie's brother's active wish for Donnie's continued life was an important contributing factor to Donnie's eventual success.

Over the course of the next year, the fourth year of treatment, Donnie moved from the periphery of the AA room to the front. He gradually became able to exchange telephone numbers with people and to use

them. His drinking continued, but the crises secondary to drinking abated. He requested and got increasingly responsible positions at work, including working
the service window at the post office. Working the
service window requires some degree of diplomacy
because it involves relating to a variety of personalities.
This was an important affirmation of his ability to
function in a world of people.

At this point, late in our work together, an event took
place that was particularly telling about Donnie's ability to care for himself.

Donnie came for a session in the midst of a blinding
snowstorm. He was wearing sneakers that were sop-
ping wet with ice water. I asked him if he had been
caught unprepared for the storm. That was not the
problem. He seemed to think there was nothing
strange about his wearing sneakers in this weather;
besides, he did not have boots. It never occurred to him
to clothe himself properly. Adequate self-care was not
in his repertoire. He was very cold and uncomfortable,
and so he was receptive to the idea that he get himself
protected from bad weather. Left to his own devices, he
treated himself as the virtually motherless orphan he
had been. My educating him about how to be the good
mother to himself was what he needed to begin to
nurture himself, now that he was not hell bent on
self-destruction.

After a year in AA, Donnie found a sponsor, a very
constructive person who helped continue the educational and nurturing process. At the end of that year,
Donnie became disgusted with his drinking and was
fairly successful with periods of abstinence. He heard
about Antabuse in AA and requested a referral from me
to a physician who could prescribe the drug. He found
the Antabuse to be helpful. He remained sober for eight
months, slipping only once, by plan. (He went off the
Antabuse and drank during my vacation in August.)
Exploring his acting out enabled him to "own" his

anger and dependent longings and express them directly to me. He went back on the Antabuse and remained sober. After another six months of sobriety, he went off the Antabuse and remained sober.

Toward the end of a year's sobriety, Donnie deemed himself ready for termination from therapy. Although it was hard for me to say good-bye, I saw nothing wrong with his trying his wings at this time. It had been an uneventful year! He was sober and making good connections in AA. We parted after Donnie's one-year anniversary of sobriety.

This man never ceased to amaze me. Another few years went by. I received an announcement from Donnie of his marriage. After another year I received a notice, and photo, of his new son! I am quite sure that if someone had told us the outcome at the beginning of this treatment, neither of us would have believed it.

Epilogue

This case validated the helpfulness of maintaining the treatment, for a long time, while the patient was still drinking. The concept of harm reduction was not in vogue in the mid-1980s. My training in substance abuse, and the attitudes of alcoholism clinics who employed me, led me to believe that I was enabling the patient's addiction if I continued to work with him, still drinking, beyond a few months, certainly beyond a year (Levinson and Straussner, 1978). However, the intensity of the patient's involvement in treatment, his increasing interest in stopping drinking (which evolved over time), and my having uppermost in mind the goal of training the patient to feel and talk rather than to act, gave me faith that it would be worthwhile to persist in working together.

Commentary by Andrew Tatarsky

This story reveals much about how good psychotherapy facilitates breakthroughs and long-term change. It is another dramatic example of the necessity of using a gradual, harm reduction approach to achieve success. Frankfeldt had to work with Donnie for many years while he continued to use substances in order to build the foundation in their relationship that made it possible for him to stop using. Here the patient was able to engage powerfully with therapy while still drinking, addressing a range of other problems. Once these problems were addressed, measures toward moderation came more naturally. Frankfeldt knew that, despite her concerns, the therapy would have been derailed if she had insisted on abstinence or institutionalized treatment.

THE IMPORTANCE OF THE THERAPEUTIC RELATIONSHIP

The story reveals how Frankfeldt followed Donnie's lead in developing an appropriate relationship. Her sensitivity to the needs and clues of his nature helped to gradually decommission real threats and dangers present in his life and psyche. We learn about some of the elements that she used to facilitate a relationship in which the patient was able to have a new experience of safety and support. She consistently met and matched Donnie where he lives, respecting his needs for personal distance, respecting his intimacy fears by limiting her own self-disclosure, allowing him to set the pace and agenda in their relationship as well as his substance usage. Frankfeldt's growing understanding of the multiple meanings and functions that alcohol had for Donnie helped her to work with him gradually and effectively. Her awareness of his vulnerabilities guided her away from her training in abstinence-only and institutionalized care, guiding her into a new, effective approach.

TAKING AS MUCH TIME AS WAS NEEDED

This story summarizes a six-year treatment, demonstrating that six years was the duration required to help this client meet his goals of stable sobriety as well as unforeseen dramatic improvements in the emotional, vocational, and interpersonal spheres of his life.

THE COURAGE TO BREAK THE RULES AND RESPOND TO THE UNIQUENESS OF THE PATIENT

For Frankfeldt, harm reduction went against her original training and against the voices of authorities from school. However, she knew that if she insisted on abstinence in her patient, he would have left treatment. This level of authenticity is clearly read by the client, who now finds a refuge from social stigmatization as well as a partner in a shared discovery and healing process. This can be a powerful seed for self-esteem and trust in relationships and an antidote to the damage done by early traumatic experiences.

INTEGRATING APPROACHES

Though Frankfeldt calls herself a modern psychoanalyst, she is also freely and creatively integrating cognitive, behavioral, and other more unconventional strategies. She does almost anything she thinks she has to do to encourage positive change in Donnie; she shares her authentic fears and feelings with him, and she takes his pulse and waits for the right time to encourage his participation in AA. Frankfeldt uses eccentric behavior, even yells at Donnie, to break the denial barriers when his life is in danger. This is in keeping with what good therapists always try to do. Jerome Levin and Ronna Weiss (1994) edited a seminal book on the subject of flexibility and variability of technique for substance abuse. *The Dynamics and Treatment of Alcoholism: Essential Papers* includes documents by the leading psychoanalytic addiction theorists throughout the history of psychoanalysis. These papers all suggest flexibility, a variety of active techniques, and the encouragement of a real relationship in which the therapist/analyst shares personal feelings with the patient.

ENCOURAGING INVOLVEMENT IN ALCOHOLICS ANONYMOUS

Frankfeldt clearly thought Alcoholics Anonymous would be a useful support for a number of reasons. However, she accepted that Donnie's problems prevented him from making use of that program. Rather than addressing his resistance as the problem, she explored his reluctance to go to AA as a means to identify and address a full range of themes and memories that conjured obstacles to his forming human relationships.

THE TALKING CURE

Frankfeldt created space in the relationship in which an isolated and disorganized man could feel safe enough to learn how to identify his feelings and put them into words. Their talking eventually dispelled an aura of threat that accompanied his drugging and paranoia in their first phase of treatment. Trying to put one's experience into words can clarify and give form to vague, free-floating feelings, thereby providing the client and therapist an object for focused observation. Donnel Stern (1997) calls this the process of fomulating, or making meaning out of what was previously unformulated experience.

References

Levin, Jerome D. and Weiss, Ronna H. (Eds.). (1994). *The Dynamics and Treatment of Alcoholism: Essential Papers.* Northvale, N.J.: Jason Aronson Inc.

Levinson, V. and Straussner, S. L. A. (1978). Social workers as "enablers" in the treatment of alcoholics. *Social Casework*, 59: 14–20.

Levinson, V. (1996). The alcoholic's self-destructiveness and the therapist's role in mobilizing survival energies. *Alcoholism Treatment Quarterly*, 3(3): 23–35.

Spotnitz, Hyman (1985). *Modern Psychoanalysis of the Schizophrenic Patient.* New York: Human Sciences Press, Inc.

Unger, R. (1978). Sustaining transference in the treatment of alcoholism. *Modern Psychoanalysis*, 3(2): 155–172.

6

Drug Use as an Attempt to Cope

Gary: A Transformation in Self
  —Edward Khantzian

People develop problems with substances for many reasons that are personally meaningful to them. Properly understanding this principle holds one of the most important keys to helping people to correct the problematic aspects of their substance use. Attempts to find the one reason common to all substance use problems are doomed to fail because they don't make room for this diversity. Each user has a unique relationship to the substance that may contain or embody numerous personal meanings and functions. Often, asking people to give up their drug use before these meanings have been clarified is experienced by clients as a negation of the important parts of them expressed through using. By not starting the therapeutic relationship with the requirement that the user give up their use, harm reduction inherently embraces the idea that drug use is tied up with personal meaning to the user. Once the meaning of drug use has become clear, it becomes possible to consider which goals are realistic for the user.

UNWRAPPING THE DESIRE TO USE

Substances can be thought of as multipurpose tools that can be used in several ways to address or express a seemingly infinite variety of meanings.

As the therapist and client hold to this principle, it encourages us to unwrap the desire to use substances. As the wrapper is taken off, it becomes possible to untangle the multiple meanings expressed by this desire. It encourages the user to ask questions such as, "What does my use of substances mean to me?" "What polarities am I seeking to explore through the use of this substance?" "What purpose or function am I using this substance to fulfill?" "Is it working?" "Is it serving the purpose for which I am using it?" "Is there a better tool or strategy I might use for this job?" "What am I trying to say through my use of this substance?"

DEVELOPING THE CAPACITY TO CHANGE

This perspective also encourages the development of a set of qualities that I see as essential prerequisites to changing one's behavior and oneself. These transformative qualities include nonjudgmental curiosity about one's own behaviors; self-reflective awareness; an exploration of one's reasons for using; a concern about whether one is meeting one's needs and desires in the best possible way; and the search for the needs, feelings, wishes, and other aspects of oneself that are being expressed in the desire to use.

We might think of the development, strengthening, or focusing of these qualities or capacities as part of the first step in the process of making personal changes. In fact, there is a relatively new idea evolving in behavioral change and personal growth circles that proposes that before people can make important changes in themselves, a number of different things may have to happen in preparation for these changes. Dr. William Miller at the University of New Mexico in Albuquerque has called this the preparation stage of change (Miller and Rollnick, 1991). A lack of adequate preparation is a major factor contributing to the failure of many well-intentioned people to make the changes they set out to make, whether it is to stop smoking cigarettes, cut down on drinking, kick heroin, or get to the gym more often. Once developed, the transformative qualities described previously become a set of cognitive capacities or skills that can be used in the service of making many personal changes. I would add to Miller's view that the personal development of one's internal witness, watcher, scientist, or self-transformer begins to separate the self from one's behaviors. We begin to see that we are not our behaviors. As one cultivates nonjudgmental compassion for one's behaviors and patterns as a witness, we separate ourselves from these and thereby have more facility in moving and changing them like materials in our hands.

PERSONAL MEANING AND THE DIVERSITY OF USERS

This view also allows us to understand the fact that many different kinds of people with diverse personal strengths and vulnerabilities use substances for multiple reasons and in different ways. In my experience, the substance users that I have known intimately as clients, colleagues, and friends have been as diverse a group as any other group of people. This awareness can be a kind of corrective to the tendency in our society to lump all substance users in one category and then to argue about which category is the right one. This tendency is reflected in the professional, academic world in the failed but persisting search for "the addictive personality" and the ongoing debate about which psychological or sociological theory is right. These efforts assume that there is one factor predisposing to addiction. It is also reflected in popular generalizations, most rather degrading, that are made about substance users. Substance users are described as weak, sociopathic, selfish, untrustworthy, infantile, rebels, and artists. The fact is, as I have observed, some people who use and misuse substances have each of these qualities. But, as a group, substance users are as diverse as any other group.

Does this mean there are no generalizations to be made about substance abuse? I would posit that substances are often used to connect to the matrix of life more effectively. The causes of our alienation from this matrix are varied and manifold, as well as the complexes, behaviors, and compensations that arise in the face of this alienation. The alienation leading to excessive or compulsive drug use is certainly worsened by societal stigmatization, by generalizations about addicts, and by aversions to certain states of being and states of consciousness. Generalizations, stereotyping, and mass-cure methods exacerbate the alienation that addicted humans are seeking to relieve.

VULNERABILITY TO PROBLEMATIC DRUG USE

A more effective question than the generalized one about what is the cause of addiction may be what are the factors that constitute vulnerabilities to developing drug problems.

Whether these vulnerabilities will actually lead to problematic use hinges on many other factors that may support or work against using or abusing substances. There are a variety of factors—psychological, social, cultural, economic, and biological—that make people more vulnerable to excessive use. A particular combination of and interaction among factors that is unique for each person gives rise to that person finding substances compelling or not and then problematic or not. We are learning more and more about these vulnerability factors generally. However, a way out of the bind of problem use for each individual will be found through a personal exploration that leads to an identification of the factors for that particular individual. This can then lead to a personal plan for change that addresses each of these vulnerability factors as it arises.

PERSONAL MEANING AND THE PSYCHOANALYTIC TRADITION

The psychoanalytic tradition, beginning with the founder of psychoanalysis, Sigmund Freud, has been most interested in exploring the role of meaning in substance use and abuse. There are many psychoanalytic ideas about substance use; some I have found to be more useful than others. To me, what is most interesting about the psychoanalytic endeavor is the process of inquiry as opposed to the particular theoretical results of this inquiry. The theories that make up the body of psychoanalytic literature were derived from collaborative psychoanalytic explorations between individual practitioners and individual patients in analysis. The ideas of psychoanalysis reflect a deep inquiry into the inner lives of the many people who have engaged in the process for more than a century. The ideas derived from this endeavor are likely to have had some truth for some people. I likewise consider that they may or may not be useful to those who are trying to understand themselves and others. The very process of personal discovery between client and clinician is a healing factor that can be undermined by referencing generalizations in the body of the literature.

THE ADAPTIVE VALUE OF DRUGS: ATTEMPTS TO COPE

In this chapter, I will explore the use of drugs as an attempt to cope with a variety of personal and social difficulties. This has been called the "adaptive value" of drug use. In later chapters I will discuss other possible meanings that substance use may carry.

Many of the ideas I will discuss here were first put forward by one of the most important contributors to this area, Dr. Edward Khantzian of Harvard University. He is also the writer whose story I have selected to illustrate this chapter, because many of the themes I will discuss here are illustrated in his story. He along with two others whose work reflects this tradition, Leon Wurmser (1978) and Henry Krystal (1999), had formative influences on my own thinking twenty years ago. Their ideas helped me to develop a perspective that has enabled me to feel very hopeful about the possibilities that people have for making dramatic, positive changes in their drug use and the personal issues connected to it. My view is that when these personal meanings can be discovered or recognized, it becomes possible to consider whether there are other better ways to address the needs, feelings, desires, wishes, or fantasies their use is expressing.

Dr. Khantzian's work very much reflects the general perspective that has informed much of psychoanalytic thinking about substance use problems, particularly in the last forty years. This tendency is to consider that, at least initially if not throughout, people use substances for *adaptive* reasons, that is, as a way of coping with external challenges and stresses or with internal difficulties.

Self-selection Hypothesis

In the 1970s, Khantzian (1975) observed that substance users generally sample many different drugs and discover the effects of one most appealing. He further saw that people generally seem to use particular drugs to address, manage, or soothe specific feeling states. He observed that people tend to find stimulants like cocaine and amphetamine useful to deal with depression; heroin is particularly effective in quelling anger; marijuana and psychedelics are useful for managing boredom; and alcohol and other relaxing drugs like Valium are good for dealing with anxiety, fear, and stress. He called this idea the self-selection hypothesis.

Self-medication Hypothesis

Ten years later, Khantzian (1985) offered a more general model, the self-medication hypothesis. This has become one of the most widely accepted basic principles for understanding substance use that is also consistent with cognitive-behavioral, sociocultural, and biological perspectives. Essentially, this idea states that people use substances as an attempt to address inner difficulties that they are unable to resolve in other ways. In contrast to the earlier view that substance users are simply bad, morally deficient, or just thrill seeking, all of which may be true for some users, this idea emphasizes that people for whom substance use has become problematic, compulsive, and severe are trying to deal with some inner suffering that they are unable to heal in other ways.

The beauty of this idea is that it replaces earlier devaluing ideas about substance users as not caring about themselves or others with the view that these folks are actually trying to take care of themselves, though in a way that may not ultimately work for many. It leads to the compassionate question of what is wrong and how might these people best take care of what hurts. It also answers the often asked question, "Why do people often continue to use drugs when they begin to experience negative consequences from their use?" The answer is that the drug did or still does provide relief from some difficulty despite the pain it may now be causing.

Sectors of Vulnerability

One of the most recent developments in Khantzian's work is a refinement of the self-medication hypothesis. Through his work with large numbers of people struggling with drug problems, he has identified a set of general aspects of psychological functioning that seem to make people particularly vulnerable to self-medicating with drugs. Here the link is made between the personal meaning that drug use has for people and personality factors. Instead of the earlier idea of an addictive personality, this theory suggests that there are several general aspects of personality that make one more vulnerable to finding drugs compelling. The four "sectors of vulnerability" that he identifies are problems with self-esteem, problems in relating to other people, problems dealing with emotions, and difficulties that people have in how they take care of themselves (Khantzian, 1990).

I have found this useful as a guide in thinking about what might be the areas of greatest vulnerability for a given person. While these areas tend to overlap and interact with one another, people may find they resonate more with some than with others.

As you read through the stories in this book you might try to read them with an eye to seeing which of these sectors seem most present for the client in the story and how an awareness of the sectors was useful to the client in making positive changes.

The story I have chosen for this chapter, the case of Gary, was adapted from a longer article published by Khantzian called "Alcoholics Anonymous—Cult or Corrective: A Case Study" (1995). In the article, he uses Gary's story to illustrate both how many of the psychological sectors of vulnerability contributed to Gary's problematic use of drugs and alcohol and how a combination of 12-step program participation and psychotherapy with Khantzian contributed not only to his stopping all drug use, but also to significant change in the personal vulnerabilities related to it. While I believe that people may achieve profound changes in substance use by a variety of paths, as is evident in the collection of stories in this book, I do not think these changes will be stable and long-lasting unless the personal meanings of the drug use and the personal issues connected to them are also addressed, as they were in Gary's story. While Gary's treatment was a traditional abstinence-oriented treatment, I see it as falling within the harm reduction umbrella. From a harm reduction perspective, when the user's drug use is so significantly out of control as to be life-threatening or impairing of the user's capacity to function, the recommendation of an abstinence treatment can be good harm reduction, particularly if the user is motivated and able to make use of it as the client in this story was.

Gary: A Transformation in Self
by Edward J. Khantzian

Gary is a handsome, intense, and determined 30-year-old married anesthesiologist in training, whose decision to pursue medicine initially was postponed, probably because of certain personality traits, an unrecognized drug dependency, and financial considerations. Although he finally got on track with his medical training, he was crushed when his long-planned-for dream to become a medical practitioner was abruptly interrupted in the middle of his residency training with the discovery of an addiction to Fentanyl®, a short-acting, rapid-onset synthetic opiate used in anesthesia. At first Gary reacted by vehemently denying wrongdoing or addiction and resisted the intervention that was imposed on him. However, once in treatment, his qualities of determination resurfaced and began to allow him to pursue recovery as earnestly as he had pursued his career.

Gary's boyish, attractive, and casual manner made him appear youthful, in stunning contrast to a commanding presence and articulate and precise speech, which made him seem old and wise. Although Gary was average in height, his compact and rugged physique and imposing style made him an even more formidable character. All in all, he was an attractive and admirable man, notwithstanding that his personal and professional identity and future were in doubt because the discovery of his addiction had left him personally shaken, unemployed, and without a license to practice.

I heard his voice on his answering machine before seeing him in person. He had reached my answering service when he called to arrange aftercare treatment. He had been released from an eleven-week inpatient rehabilitation program about one month before. When I returned his call, I was greeted by an upbeat, outspoken voice with the Southern swagger of a gunslinging cowboy; his greeting ended with the exhortation "you-all leave a message—you heah." I was put off by the swagger in the recording and anticipated meeting some kind of difficult rogue as I set up an appointment for his evaluation. As soon as we met face-to-face I no longer felt this aversion; my impression was and continued to be as positive and admiring as I have already described.

From the onset it seemed to me his recovery program was working, in the sense that it had already initiated a healthy process of self-examination and self-reflection. He began the interview by indicating that his admission to problems with drugs and alcohol allowed him to realize that he had always been a "stimulus-seeking risk taker." He realized that he was "an addict" before he ever touched a drink. Gary then abruptly shifted to describing other aspects of himself, saying he was "blessed" with a good mind and athletic ability, which allowed him to excel as a student and athlete. He was first in his high school class of 400 and a four-sport athlete. His rapid-fire characterization of himself was as revealing in a series of side notes, as was his impressive roster of accomplishments and activities. In describing his gift to read people and relate socially, he casually inserted that he "had a body and mind built for excess." He joined a fraternity in college where drinking and drugging were heavy and pervasive, and he said that he fit right in, yet stayed at the top of his class. When asked, he speculated that the alcohol and marijuana, which he preferred, enhanced his "outgoing" style. When I asked him if it was easy to be outgoing, he immediately offered that he was a "serious child." He then emphasized that he found thrill in reaching his achievements, he liked the attention he derived, especially the "rush" of winning. Yet it was never enough and he was always anticipating his next conquest.

After heavy experimentation with drug and alcohol use through college and graduate school, and various behavioral excesses that earned him the labels of "maverick" and "diamond in the rough," Gary began to curtail his drug use as he commenced medical school. Looking back, he now realized that his offbeat style and excess offended people and had delayed his acceptance to medical school. Heavy drinking continued but was limited to social functions where it was considered acceptable.

This relative pattern of moderation, especially his curtailment of drugs, continued upon the commencement of his residency training, but became even more limited with a change in residence; he was too busy to pursue friends and contacts and these changes interrupted his previous pattern. As Gary neared the final phase of his training program, his workload increased, and he was in demand or on-call because the clinic was short of staff. At a time when he was totally inactive physically and suffering many colds and flu-like symptoms, he said he reached for Fentanyl. The drug primarily provided a numbing antidote to the progressive sense of feeling tired, sick, and lonely.

In retrospect, Gary realized that his resorting to drugs at that time had occurred in a context of feeling that he was "never happy and had no skills in reaching out or asking for help." He felt his wife was doing the best she could, and he felt he could not reach out to her or anybody else about his anxiety concerning his upcoming boards, his sense of lagging behind in his workload, and his mental and emotional exhaustion.

So much for my initial encounter with Gary as my patient—his strengths, his vulnerabilities, his personality, which served him and defined him—qualities that were ultimately subsumed by the discovery of his Fentanyl dependence. This initial introduction to Gary's strengths in no way prepared me for the unique ways in which he would apply those strengths toward deep changes that began to make themselves known two months later.

It was clear that the 12-step program was serving him well to counter his denial and sense of invincibility and catalyzing an extraordinary process of self-examination, admission of vulnerability, and emotional awakening. He learned how to reach out and ask for help. The session followed a five-day reunion with his wife. The discovery of his Fentanyl dependence had coincided with her being offered a position back home in the Midwest, which, with his encouragement, she had accepted. They had not been with each other for several months at the time of their reunion. He had anticipated this reunion with considerable apprehension, knowing that one source of his "never being happy" was a sense that he had long felt that his marriage was a mistake. They had been living together when he was accepted for medical school. It was she who suggested marriage at that time, and he had just "gone along" with her desires. In a session before his visit with her, he had opened a discussion about pursuing a divorce.

In the next session, five days following the dreaded reunion with his wife, Gary chose to begin with another issue entirely. After some preliminary social amenities, he began by telling me that he was physically sore, explaining that he and a friend had recently climbed one of the highest mountains in our region. He commented that "it's near winter up there," and we both spontaneously acknowledged that he was characteristically and once again "near the edge." As we went on, however, he seemed as if he was near something else as well, and that his ascent to the top of the mountain was also a metaphor for other transformations that were taking place. After clarifying that he and his friend had been painstaking in planning, timing, and safely tooling themselves for this climb, I realized he was describing his growth in caution and self-care. He described the beauty and "near spiritual quality" of the climb. It was then that he went on to review the tense, painful, but emotionally satisfying visit with his wife. Gary said, "We talked and talked, including my intention to seek a divorce. I shared my darkest and worst fear: that our marriage was a mistake." His wife was not surprised, admitting that she had given thought to divorce, and she shared her own apprehensions about his addictive illness, recovery, and their future prospects. Although he felt relieved and "off the hook" by her reactions, he went on, nevertheless, to reveal how they openly wept together and continued to open up to secrets they had not previously shared. "By way of making amends," he confessed to old secrets about money he had used for drugs and two affairs.

As he continued, I was impressed by his self-reflection, his openness, and his vulnerability, thinking he was changing as fast as anyone does, in or out of psychotherapy. I remembered that on a recent attempt to call him, I noticed that the message on his answering machine had changed. It was an ordinary message asking for the name, telephone number, and best time for a return call. I chose to comment on the changes, including the one on his answering machine. I observed that there was no trace of bravado—that he seemed less shielded and more open. Gary said that he had given a lot of thought to and worry about shame, regret, and what could have happened. He emphasized his realization that he needed to know and speak his own feelings. As he did so, he filled up, openly wept, even sobbed.

When I asked where his feelings were coming from, he expressed regret that he had never been able to experience and express his own feelings. This inability had kept him from speaking his heart and making authentic decisions. In part, he was referring to the deceit in his marriage, but he meant more. He said, "It all has to do with regret about not being open, not being a feeling, human being." He made reference to dodging problems rather than going through them. As he faced his problems and allowed feelings, he felt better. He had seen clearly how secrecy and not feeling held him back. On the mountaintop he felt as free spiritually and mentally as he ever had. He had no fears of looking back, no fears of facing clearly his old manipulations and conniving. He had opened to his family and felt they were there for him; he expressed the conviction that people thought more of him than ever before, and this made him feel "joyful." He under-scored the benefit of "dumping" his problems with his family, friends, and me, and thus no longer being burdened by guilt.

I have presented Gary's case because he provides illuminating insight into the strengths, vulnerabilities, and pitfalls of compulsive substance use. Even more importantly, in what follows, he also reveals the strengths and benefits of 12-step programs. With very little prompting, he provided a point-by-point description of how his recovery program appropriately addresses his emotional and relational handicaps, including related self-esteem and self-care deficiencies. The program effectively responds to and serves as correctives to the defensive personality style that shielded him from being and becoming a more comfortable, satisfied, and satisfying person.

After reviewing the remainder of this session, in which he gives his own account of this transformation, I will review and elaborate on what it is that is disordered in the person (or personality) of substance-dependent patients, and what I believe are some of the crucial elements of effective recovery programs that provide corrective experience for the disordered person or self that suffers these illnesses.

I said, "It seems your program has had a transforming effect on you." He said that when he first entered Alcoholics Anonymous, he had told his counselor that he felt he could go no further downward in his personal and professional descent. The prompt retort of the counselor implied, "not quite, you had six more feet to go." The counselor had commented on his bravado, how he had not felt anything in a long time. Gary contrasted that exchange early in his recovery with the present: he said, "I cry on a dime now, and it feels natural." He reflected that the program was his last chance, alluding to one of the guidelines of the program: "Try it for 60 days, and if you don't like it we'll hand back your misery in full." Gary observed that the program had provided some "spark for a sense of self." He elaborated that rehab helped to put things in an "I/we, first person" form, helping him to ask what he needed and express what he felt. He said, "I found out I wasn't such a bad guy down in there with all my dire consequences—no job or license, and a likely divorce. Since beginning AA I have more meaningful care and relationships than I have ever had." I asked him to elaborate a bit more. He explained that he now had the ability to get his secrets out and to find, "I am better than I thought." He continued in his description; he said his family, his friends, and his wife embrace him. He said he now felt he could call people whom he feared—his chief of service, the director of the Physician's Health Program, and colleagues. Once face-to-face with the authorities, he realized they wanted his company, for example for the upcoming holiday dinner.

As the end of the hour approached, I reflected out loud more about his transformations and requested that I might use his experience to help others to appreciate how AA helps people to change and correct their vulnerabilities. He simply and generously agreed. We talked about the distinctions between abstinence and sobriety. The program works beyond the establishment of abstinence; it works because it firmly establishes sobriety by assessing and modifying vulnerabilities involving emotions, relationships, self-esteem, and self-care. I added that his efforts and work during these past weeks and months had gotten him to the top of the mountain, literally and figuratively, in a different way. He described the exquisite timing of his suspension from work, and how things work out; in this case, how free time away from work coincided with his wife's visit and gave them the space together to address their relationship, one of his most daunting problems. He concluded the hour with the thought, "coincidences are God's way of maintaining his anonymity."

Commentary by Andrew Tatarsky

In this story, we can see how Gary used drugs and alcohol to correct problems in the four sectors of vulnerability about which Khantzian has written. Gary is a man who suffered serious self-esteem problems. He masked and tried to compensate for them by developing a social front of "bravado, swagger, and counterdependency," suggesting that he felt great about himself and didn't need anything from anyone. He also tried to prop up his deficient sense of self by proving to himself and others that he was better than he felt he was by taking tremendous personal risks and making achievement and conquest more important than anything else. That this confident exterior was only a front was proven by the fact that the "rush" he got from winning was short-lived and never enough. His insatiable need for attention and reassurance was never satisfied.

Early on, he used alcohol and marijuana to "enhance" this social facade. These substances supported him in self-presentation to the world. This worked for him through college and graduate school. When he entered medical school he became relatively moderate in his drug and alcohol use, Khantzian says, "because he had changed locations, was too busy, and had few friends or contacts to persist in his previous pattern." This is a good example of how the personal vulnerabilities I have been talking about don't in and of themselves explain drug use. When Gary's social and professional life no longer supported excessive drug use and actually conflicted with it, his use became more moderate. However, his self-esteem and other personal vulnerabilities set him up to return to using during a crisis while completing his residency in anesthesiology.

Toward the end of his training he had an extra case load, was more on-call at the hospital, was physically inactive, and was feeling increasingly tired, sick, lonely, and unhappy. He was also feeling anxious about his upcoming exams and felt that he was not keeping up. He said that he "had no skills for reaching out or asking for help" and began using Fentanyl, a powerful painkiller like heroin, to numb the pain. Here we see all four of Khantzian's sectors of vulnerability conspiring to set him up to return to drug use in an effort to cope with intense suffering. The demanding circumstances facing Gary created a set of painful feelings with which he was not equipped to deal. His problems caring for himself no doubt contributed to Gary getting himself in this situation to begin with; for example, agreeing to take on more work than he could handle and being physically inactive. He also had no resources for effectively dealing with how badly he was feeling and, looking back after some time in treatment, he was able to recognize that he "had never been able to experience and express his own feelings." This captures some of the complexity of what many people with problems effectively managing feelings experience. For many people, they are related to having trouble both identifying feelings and knowing what to do with them once they have been identified. Gary's self-esteem problems contributed to his feeling anxious, ashamed, and overwhelmed by his workload. His problems relating to other people were expressed in his inability to reach out to others for help. This combination of personality traits interacting with his extreme circumstance made him vulnerable to seeing the drug as the most desirable way to try to take care of himself. The drug enabled him to feel somewhat better without having to ask for help. As he had done in college, he used the drug in an effort to maintain the facade of being able to handle things, thereby continuing to look good to others when in fact he was feeling terrible inside. As is often the case when people turn to drugs for this kind of help, while the drug did help in some way, it also further isolated him from the help he really needed and contributed to his feeling worse. This is part of the vicious cycle inherent to drug use problems.

Gary's story also shows that his ability to stay away from drugs was related to how well he was able to identify and address the personal issues related to his drug use in treatment. In this case, treatment was the combination of an initial 12-step–based inpatient rehabilitation program followed by individual psychotherapy with Khantzian and ongoing attendance at 12-step meetings.

In his story, Khantzian emphasizes the power of the community and group in the rehab and 12-step meetings in helping Gary address the personal issues related to his addiction. Like many people with drug problems, Gary's shame and fear of how others might react to him if his drug use and personal problems were discovered led him to hide what was going on. Paradoxically, this left him alone with his frightening fantasies and sealed him off from getting real feedback from others about himself. Once in treatment, exposed and without reason to hide, he could be open with others and discover that he was not the terrible person he thought he was in other people's eyes. In fact, people had a lot of compassion for him and could see the good qualities in him that he could not see. These experiences with peers, only available in group treatment or self-help situations, can begin to counter long-standing self-esteem problems and the additional bad feelings about oneself often accompanying excessive drug use. They can be the kernel of a new, more positive sense of self that can counter shame and hopelessness and inspire a commitment to change in all areas of one's life.

Gary also had his sessions with Khantzian to process and make sense of the experiences that he was having in his self-help meetings. In the process of telling the story of important discoveries he was making about himself to Khantzian, Gary got to formulate them in words that he could then further integrate. He did this in the presence of a well-known and well-respected substance abuse specialist who clearly cared about, liked, respected, and supported Gary in making the changes he was making in himself. While Khantzian doesn't give himself the credit in his story, I think these are some of the intangible ways in which the therapist helps the client make the changes he is working toward. The therapist is also a person, and generally one invested by the client with a lot of symbolic power, who sees all the qualities in the client about which he is most ashamed. If, in spite of this, Khantzian could still respect and care for Gary, this can also help correct the negative feelings Gary had about himself. Here again we see the importance of the therapist's personal feelings toward the client in supporting the client's growth and change.

For Gary, this combination of treatment elements was the right fit and created the necessary conditions of safety for him to begin a process that led to profound change in himself in a relatively short time. Most of the changes we read about seem to have occurred by Gary's sixth month into his treatment. While I have had many clients like Gary, this is not always the case. Gary had a particular combination of personal and external factors that supported this rapid progress. Firstly, he is a man with many personal strengths that enabled him to function at a very high level for many years despite his personal difficulties. His accomplishments were also at stake: a marriage, a career, and a public image that was very important to him. These risks no doubt helped to motivate him to mobilize many of these strengths in his work on his drug problem and other issues. His personal vulnerabilities may also have supported his efforts in an interesting way. Once his addiction was exposed, his intense need for approval from others and his intense desire to be successful became additional spurs for his efforts in treatment. Finally, his substance use had not been intense continuously over a long period of time. Thus he had shown before a capacity to get himself on track when necessary. One thing we do not know is how these changes lasted over time for him.

THE IMPORTANCE OF ALCOHOLICS ANONYMOUS

Khantzian gives a lot of credit to Gary's 12-step program involvement. I have my own perspective on that. I have known clients, colleagues, family members, and friends who, like Gary, have found Alcoholics Anonymous and other 12-step programs to be lifesaving support systems for dealing with drug and alcohol problems and related personal issues. AA came into being in the 1930s at a time when people with drug problems were severely stigmatized by professionals and nonprofessionals and there were few if any good treatments available. Over the course of this history, a large international network community has grown that people can join when they start attending meetings. In most communities, there are free meetings around the clock that people may attend for support, structure, and concrete help in staying away from drugs and alcohol, if that is what one is pursuing. There is also a structured program of specific recommendations, the Twelve Steps, for how people can achieve and maintain abstinence. Also, there is a large body of unofficial knowledge about "staying clean and sober" that people can tap into. For these reasons, AA has a unique set of powerful qualities to offer to drug or alcohol users with "a desire to stop using."

So much has been written about the effectiveness of AA from many different theoretical points of view that it seems like AA can be almost all things to all people. People develop their difficulties in living in groups, families, peer groups, and larger communities, and for some people, these human problems are best solved in groups that can heal. Khantzian says that AA has particular effectiveness in helping people attend and persist because it is able to create "conditions of interdependence, safety, and comfort." I think this is so for many of the qualities I discussed previously.

THE NEED FOR AN ALTERNATIVE TO ALCOHOLICS ANONYMOUS

However, there are many people who do not find Alcoholics Anonymous appealing; some studies claim this is the majority of people with drug and alcohol problems. This may be for many reasons. Two prominent reasons frequently cited by people who reject AA are its emphasis on the acceptance of a higher power and the need to admit powerlessness over alcohol as prerequisites for getting sober. These are ideas that I think people can interpret and find useful in many different ways. Alcoholics Anonymous supports this personal interpretation in statements like "take what you need and leave the rest" and "you can make your higher power anything you like." People who feel that they are no longer in control of their drug using and don't know how to make changes may find it very reassuring to know that they don't have to figure it out on their own and that there is a higher power in the community of people in 12-step recovery that they can turn to for guidance.

Nonetheless, many people simply do not find AA appealing and need something else. Without criticizing AA, we can simply acknowledge that humans with substance problems are a tremendously diverse group who differ widely in many ways: goals, philosophy, readiness to change, and preferences. Like my good friend Dr. Michler Bishop said at a conference once, "Some of us prefer Chinese food, some prefer Mexican, and some Italian. Why should we assume that everyone will prefer the same self-help program?" Luckily, in recent years there has been a proliferation of self-help programs for people with different interests, goals, and preferences. Smart Recovery is an alternative self-help program for people working toward abstaining from drugs and alcohol. This program sees drug and alcohol problems in more explicit cognitive-behavioral terms as bad or maladaptive habits that people can actively change by learning a set of skills for actively changing these behaviors. It may be particularly appealing to people who have trouble with Alcoholics Anonymous's idea of powerlessness, because it asserts that people do have the power to make changes in themselves and it tries to support this power in people. An alternative self-help program for people who are considering whether moderate use is a realistic option for themselves is Moderation Management (MM) (Kishline, 1994). MM is generally targeting those drinkers whose drinking has become problematic but not seriously debilitating, the so-called "problem drinker." Although this is often a gray area, all are welcome who are considering moderation. The program aims to support people in discovering whether this is a realistic goal and supports stable moderation and abstinence as outcomes for people who attend the meetings. This encouragement and support for a serious exploration of this question is what really distinguishes MM from the other self-help programs. It relies on many of the same behavioral ideas that Smart Recovery does and also encourages an exploration of the personal meanings and functions that drugs have had for people. Both of these programs offer many of the nonspecific benefits that AA does: community, structure, peer support, and advice, though on a much smaller scale. They are programs still in the process of coming into being to a great extent, with the shortcomings and benefits that that may have for different people.

References

Khantzian, E. J., Halliday, K. S., and McAuliffe, W. E. (1990). *Addiction and the Vulnerable Self: Modified Dynamic Group Therapy for Substance Abusers.* New York: Guilford Press.
Khantzian, E. J., and Mack, J. E. (1989). Alcoholics Anonymous and contemporary psychodynamic theory. In M. Galanter

(Ed.). *Recent Developments in Alcoholism.* Vol. 7 (pp. 67–89). New York: Plenum.

Krystal, Henry (1977). *Self and Object Representations in Alcoholism and other Drug Dependence: Implications for Therapy in Psychodynamics of Drug Dependence.* Research Monograph 12, pp. 88–100. National Institute of Drug Abuse.

Miller, W. R. and Rollnick, S. (1991). *Motivational Interviewing: Preparing People to Change Addictive Behavior.* New York: Guilford Press.

Wurmser, L. (1978). *The Hidden Dimension: Psychodynamics in Compulsive Drug Use.* Northvale, NJ: Jason Aronson Inc.

The Impact of Trauma

Sally: A Dynamic Cure
—Jerome David Levin

As we have seen, the multiple meanings that drug use can have for people reflect personal issues that we have called personality vulnerabilities. For some people, like Gary in Chapter 6, recognizing the role that drugs play in addressing these vulnerabilities is the key to exploring other drug-free ways of addressing these issues more effectively. An important part of this work hinges on interrupting the connection between these vulnerabilities and the desire to use a drug, in order to find other solutions to these issues. Concerning self-esteem, for example, one might look at how we talk to ourselves, and what is the system of judgment that we use that inevitably leads us to feel that we don't measure up. Rather than using a drug to support trying to live up to these unrealistic standards or to deal with the pain of living up to them, an individual might modify these standards to reflect a more realistic, compassionate set of expectations. In the domain of feelings, interpersonal relationships, and self-care, one can take inventory of the skills that one lacks and work on developing these. Learning to relax when tense, to be more assertive at work and not agree to take on more work than you can handle, or to know your limits and when to take breaks so you don't burn yourself out are all examples of good self-management skills that can reduce the desire to use drugs because they offer better ways of addressing these needs.

ROLE OF CHILDHOOD RELATIONSHIPS

However, all of these vulnerabilities were, to some extent, learned or shaped in childhood relationships with parents and significant others: siblings, teachers, clergy, and peers. For some people, these vulnerabilities are the scars of serious, traumatic neglect or abuse, whether verbal, physical, or sexual. I have found in my work that, in general, the more difficult the childhood history, the more likely it is that this history will have to be examined in the course of working on a client's drug use and associated vulnerability issues.

As we work on personality vulnerabilities, we often discover that it is necessary to re-work beliefs about and internalized relationships to the significant others in our formative years. For example, claiming the right and the power to care for oneself can be like taking that power away from a parent who was possesive of that power, one who said, in effect, "You need me to care for you because you are not able to do so for yourself." The process of change can unearth overt or covert negative and often crippling suggestions such as this made by one's parents. In this process, we begin to understand that they were wrong, and that we psychically dread the dire consequences of making them wrong. This recognition is followed by the more manageable but still difficult subsequent feelings of disappointment, guilt, and grief.

A good example of this is the experience of a 28-year-old man that I have been seeing in psychotherapy for about a year. He was brought up by parents who always seemed to him to be away working or traveling. They knew little of his inner life and provided little structure for guidance to him. He grew up feeling alone, adrift in the world without a compass and with a profound sense that he didn't matter to them or to anyone else. He concluded at a very early age that he must have been at fault, that is, not worth their time and attention. This neglect instilled rage, which was "naturally" directed at himself because he had concluded that his parents' neglect was due to his worthlessness. These feelings frequently took the form of active wishes to kill himself. This combination of feelings of worthlessness and self-hate pervaded his life until he discovered marijuana and other drugs that gave him some relief by helping him to feel hopeful for the first time.

He came for help with his drug use when he began to see that while it lessened the pain of his self-hate and despair, it didn't resolve these feelings. In working on getting past his tendency to direct hatred toward himself, it became clear that his self-hate had been his way of identifying with or agreeing with his parents because of his childhood need to see them as people upon whom he could rely. Without this sense of security, his early life would have been too frightening. Challenging his self-hate entailed really seeing their neglect as wrong. This put him in touch with a deep, powerful grief that he had never allowed himself to feel before. On the other hand, it also allowed him to begin to have greater compassion and acceptance for himself, locating the kernel of a strong, healthy self-esteem.

WHEN EXPERIENCES BECOME TRAUMATIC

Everyone has experienced some level of suffering in the normal course of events, and many of these events are a necessary part of growth and development. However, events are traumatic when they are so painful, threatening, or intense that they are more than the individual is psychologically equipped to handle. Physical or sexual abuse are common traumatic experiences in the histories of individuals with substance use problems. Trauma can also result from less obvious relational binds such as a relationship with a significant other who demands that the child conform to his wishes and suppress vital aspects of her uniqueness while punishing violations by shaming the child or withdrawing love. More problematic than the physical acts themselves, the trauma is related to the intense irreconcilable conflict the child experiences between feeling unsafe, hurt, violated, and ignored by a person upon whom the child is emotionally and physically dependent. The intensity of associated feelings creates intense anxiety that overwhelms one's capacity to process, or handle the event. This can lead the victim to resort to extreme self-protective measures to handle the conflict and anxiety such as dissociation, or actively keeping apart conflictual or contradictory aspects of oneself or significant others in consciousness (Kernberg, 1984). These defensive measures generate a wide range of different feelings, psychological states, behaviors, and attitudes that contribute to the vulnerability factors that can lead to a desire to use drugs.

In terms of difficulties managing feelings, trauma can leave people frequently filled with grief, rage, anxiety, loneliness, despair, tension, self-hate, unhappiness, depression, fear, and mistrust, often with little sense of why. The feelings generally have a global, vague, disorganizing, physical quality that makes it hard to know what to do to help oneself to feel better. This is, in part, because the memories of the traumatic events are often not available, either because they were never recorded or they were forgotten as a way of trying to deal with the pain. So the feelings live on without being connected to the events that caused them. These feelings can also be provoked by events in the present that have some relation to the earlier trauma. Because this level of feeling clearly is not warranted, it can leave the individual confused and ashamed.

Drugs are often used in an effort to feel better when there is nothing else that seems to work. They are a way of coping with what is otherwise unmanageable, a way to feel differently, to not feel, or to get one's mind off the feeling.

Feelings about oneself and other people may reflect direct and indirect messages received in the context of these early experiences, or the way the child's mind attempted to make sense of them. For example, an abused child may think, "If my father is beating me it must mean that I deserve to be beaten." A neglected child might believe, "Because I never knew when I would be attended to or ignored by my parents who were off working, drinking, or fighting, I can never count on others to be there consistently for me and need not to depend on anyone for anything."

Self-esteem problems often result from trauma for several reasons. Victims of trauma feel somehow responsible. They think they must have done something to deserve this or they are at fault because they didn't do something to prevent it. People can also feel badly about themselves because they have these bad feelings that they can't understand and can't seem to do anything to fix, except by using drugs, which are not really solutions.

Relationship problems can result from trauma in many ways. People can fear or expect that the traumatic event that occurred in the past will happen again: "Because the people most important to me let me down, why should I ever trust anyone?" Trauma victims also can feel afraid to let others get close to them because of shame about their histories and fear of how others will regard them if they were to find out. Because current relationships can provoke those intense feelings from the past trauma, the past can make the present stormy and very difficult for the victim and the other. People may use drugs to quiet these stormy feelings in order to try to protect the relationship.

Self-care problems can reflect a general disregard for oneself because of these other issues. They may also reflect, paradoxically, other ways in which trauma victims attempt to take care of themselves. The overwhelming feeling states resulting from trauma can be handled by resorting to extreme modes of self-protection such as freezing or dulling one's capacity to feel, by thinking rather than feeling, or by acting rather than feeling. All of these responses cut one off from the natural feeling responses to life such as fear in dangerous situations. Without natural feeling responses to life, people don't have them as guides to rely on for exercising proper care in those situations. This can result in an individual finding himself in terrible situations with no sense of how he got there, or taking inordinate risks without really being aware of the risk. These ways of coping can also leave people feeling dead, lifeless, confused about who they are, impulsive, compulsive and obsessive, all with little sense of why.

THE TENDENCY TO REPEAT EARLY TRAUMA IN THE PRESENT

Another process that can impact on all the vulnerabilities as a result of conflictual or traumatic early experiences is the tendency to repeat old patterns by moving toward negative situations that in some way are reminiscent of earlier situations. This is what Freud first called the repetition compulsion (Freud, 1919). A common example is one in which people find themselves getting into relationships with different partners who have the same disturbing characteristics, such as the woman who keeps dating men who don't care what she thinks or the man who keeps dating women who turn out to be very critical and controlling. The strangest thing to these folks is that these people share this disturbing trait with the opposite gender parent. Unusual sexual interests can also reflect this process. The frightening or shameful abuse experienced as a child may create in later years a sexual charge. This pattern can result in the person repeatedly feeling the same set of intensely upsetting feelings that were experienced as a child in relation to a parent. This leaves the person vulnerable to using drugs as a way to manage repetitive trauma. Drugs can be used to set up significant others in one's current life to act in ways that are uncannily similar to how earlier figures in one's life acted. For example, repeated alcohol binges may provoke a loving partner to become enraged and physically abusive. This scene recapitulates an earlier experience of having been beaten and humiliated by an out-of-control parent.

How might we understand this tendency to repeat? It seems to reflect a common human trait to return to difficult situations in an effort to master them. This is no doubt involved in the more everyday interest in frightening things like roller coasters and horror films. If we can set up a situation that is like an earlier one in which we were the victim but, this time, go back by choice and survive it, we can have some sense of undoing the damage done originally.

Dangerous drug use itself can also serve this purpose.

HISTORIES OF TRAUMA AND THE CHALLENGES OF CHANGING

For people who have experienced difficult childhood histories, the nature of the personal issues connected to drug use and the meanings that drugs have for them are typically more complex than for people whose early lives were not as painful. The road to successful change is typically longer and more challenging for these folks.

One of the biggest setups for failure can be for an individual to underestimate the difficulty, complexity, and time it may take to achieve his goals. This can lead to the unwarranted conclusion that change is not possible and raise questions about intentions or seriousness. It's like setting out to climb a tall mountain expecting to get to the peak by afternoon without maps, adequate equipment, or proper planning. This often leads people to lose hope and abandon the project that they've barely begun. The problem may be compounded by caring and well-intentioned family, friends, and professionals, who share many of the same misconceptions about how challenging and time-consuming the process can be.

Often the beliefs and feelings are as tenacious and well-hidden as the early experiences were strong and well-buried. This creates the illusion of resistance. For some, discovering the roots of current feelings and beliefs in the early experiences of one's past can help loosen their grip in the present. The work may entail seeing the connection between the meaning that drug use has and one's personal vulnerabilities, and then making the connections between these vulnerabilities and their early roots. Sometimes these connections are easily and quickly made. For many people, however, the process of discovering these connections is more gradual.

I am frequently asked by clients, "Do I need to go back and explore my childhood in order to make these changes I wish to make in my life today?" My answer is, "We'll see." Because each of us is unique, the needs and directions of change work can only be discovered in time.

I suggest what I call a two-pronged approach to making change. The first prong is an active, direct focus on the behavior that you want to change. The second, to the extent that it seems necessary, is a focus on the feelings and experiences related to the past that seem to be driving, expressed through, or locking in these beliefs, feelings, and behaviors.

Therefore, individuals may go into their past if they believe it is useful. Not only can it assist the change process, but there are other benefits to be reaped.

THE VALUE OF DISCOVERING THE PAST IN THE PRESENT

Discovering the past in the present is a way of finding the sense in what may appear to be senseless. Making sense of one's experience may change it, and it will give it context, making it more coherent and therefore more acceptable and manageable. If individuals know that their feelings and actions may not make complete sense in terms of the present but do in terms of the past, it can help lessen the sense of confusion and shame frequently associated with these feelings. It can also help one to have greater compassion and acceptance for oneself and one's "difficulties."

Seeing that one's feelings make sense in the context of past relationships can also lead to a reevaluation of the past in terms of what one now knows. This can lead to new conclusions about the past that have relevance for the present. Let's consider, for example, George's discovery that his inability to take pleasure in any of his achievements was a reflection of his parents' hyper-critical, perfectionistic expectations of him. As he considered this in therapy, he was able to see that their inability to feel satisfied with his achievements was not a reflection of his shortcomings but rather a reflection of their own perfectionism. This perfectionism made it impossible for them to ever feel satisfied with themselves, so they looked to his achievements in an effort to make up for their own sense of failure. This series of connections helped George to begin to feel better about being less than perfect, to have greater understanding and compassion for his parents, and to relax more in the face of other people's criticisms of him, particularly all of those who had different criteria for perfection than what was reflected in his true will.

The story I have chosen to illustrate this topic is "Sally: A Dynamic Cure," by Jerome David Levin. Sally came for therapy to address a wide range of problems that were the consequence of severe childhood trauma related to parental alcoholism. Her own substance abuse problem and its relationship to childhood trauma was not revealed until some time into the psychotherapy. The story gives a good illustration of how early trauma can affect one's emotional life and increase one's vulnerability to compulsive drug use. It shows how complex and challenging psychotherapy can be for client and therapist, and presents some of the ingredients necessary for success.

Sally: A Dynamic Cure
by Jerome David Levin

Sally was the most terrified patient I have ever treated. Looking cadaverous, she cringed in the waiting room, flattening herself against a wall as if she wished to be absorbed by it. Hands turned, palms against the wall, this nearly anorexic-appearing woman radiated sheer terror. My office is a flight above the waiting room. When I would call her in, she would go up the stairs half-twisted to keep her back against the wall, not relaxing (if moving from terror to tension and anxiety can be called relaxing) until she entered the office and I closed the door. In her mid-thirties, she was potentially attractive, given a dramatic reduction in her tension level and a twenty-pound gain in weight, but her distress made her no more appealing than a frightened animal. Not only her movements and her body language, but also her eyes radiated fear. Although I wouldn't have described her as fragile, her tension was so great that I feared she might break, even shatter. I mean this not metaphorically, but concretely—bodily. It took some time before the basis of her fear—guilty secrets and terror of her alcoholic and abusive father— became apparent. As she sat rigidly on the couch, the tension in the room was palpable. It made me anxious. I figured that I wasn't going to be able to be very helpful to her unless I could reduce my anxiety level, but this proved elusive; I couldn't do it. It was as if the terror were contagious. Perhaps I too believed that her father would kill me. I think I also sensed the infinite rage behind her fear, and it frightened me as well.

Sally's anxiety level was so high that it was almost impossible for her to speak. She sat rigidly, not quite trembling although threatening to, and said little. Her initial communications made little sense. She told me a garbled account of triangles, squares, and circles, which evidently had special, perhaps magical meaning for her. Try as I did to understand their significance, I could not. Did they have some sort of sexual symbolism? Triangles could represent both the male (penis plus two testicles) and the female (pattern of pubic hair, two breasts and vagina) genitals. The circle—the breast? And the square? This sort of analysis was a dead end. It went nowhere. Eventually it became clear that the geometric shapes represented modes of confinement, of being imprisoned within them, but for the moment, they seemed to be representative of the magic world of the schizophrenic. Was my patient schizophrenic? I began to think so. She was unemployed, terribly worried about finances, and struggling to find work. She was able to talk about this with difficulty. I also learned that she was married, but not much else.

We did manage to reach a contract, in which time and fee were set. She agreed to twice-weekly sessions; she agreed to say what came to mind. The fee would be paid by her husband's insurance; her circumstances made treatment impossible without that third-party payment.

Terror and hesitant speech were our mode of being together for some time, until Sally asked, "May I sit on the floor?" adding, "I'll feel more comfortable there." Without really thinking, I nodded, and she did so. In retrospect, I wonder where I was coming from. With almost any other patient, I would have "analyzed" her request. "Tell me more about wanting to sit on the floor." "What does sitting on the floor bring to mind?" "I wonder why you are asking me that now?" I think I nodded unreflectively because I wanted a tension reduction at almost any cost. I wanted the impasse broken. Sally needed to control something, and where she sat was one thing she could control. Though I was proceeding on unconscious intuition, it is true that to have analyzed her request would have increased the distance between us, further reducing her self-esteem and increasing her fear. The longer I practice, the less I say. If I don't get in the way, most patients cure themselves. Sally immediately moved to the floor. Once there, she looked up at me imploringly, yet with the first manifestation of warmth I had seen in her, and asked, "Will you join me here?" Sensing nothing seductive in her request, I did. We sat silently for a long time; she was no longer terrified. Then she said, "I used to sit like this with my mother, eating the cookies we baked together or just playing." After that, the therapy, hitherto frozen, exploded.

A TRAUMATIC DE-REPRESSION

What followed was the most rapid recovery of repressed images, feelings, and thoughts that I have ever witnessed. A series of hitherto inaccessible memories flooded the patient. The earliest concerned the physical abuse by her mother—throwing her against a wall. This abuse was apparently episodic and rare. The way it came to consciousness was interesting. Sally had been to a chiropractor who had discovered that she had a cracked coccyx. He had treated her kindly, and she had had a strong attachment to him. His kindness had reminded her of the warm side of her mother, and when I sat on the floor with her, the relationship with her chiropractor, which had echoes of the good aspects of her relationship with her mother, transferred to me.

Feeling safely and firmly held by the "good mother," she was able to tolerate memories of the "bad mother." The recovered memories of being between her parents, her father throwing her aside and her mother throwing her against the wall disorganized her. (Did he throw her aside when she got in the way of his sexual advances toward the mother, or in the midst of a physical assault on the mother?) In frozen terror, she became hysterical. Her father's hostility was not news, but her mother's was. Devastating news. A child needs a parent with whom he or she can feel safe, and lacking one, the child uses the best material available to create one.

It was as if an unconscious reenactment of her relationship with her "good mother," brought about by our "making cookies on the floor," provided the security and safety needed to experience the bad aspects of her relationship with her mother. This safety with me and the de-repression it enabled were facilitated by Sally's positive experiences with her chiropractor; her rapport with him accrued to me before she even walked in my door. Without it she would have been too afraid to enter psychological treatment.

The chiropractor had another impact on Sally's recovery of the repressed trauma. He told her that her X-rays showed an old fracture of the coccyx. Had she been injured? This information—the existence of a fracture—became operative within the safety of her relationship to me. We were sitting quietly on the floor when Sally's face turned wooden; contact seemed broken as she retreated inward. Then she started screaming; the screaming was brief, followed by prolonged, broken, haunting sobbing. I said nothing. Her convulsive sobbing continued. Gradually quieting, she cried herself to exhaustion. Tears became whimpering, and then ceased. After an interlude, Sally said, "She broke my back." Over the next week, Sally recalled how her mother, in an uncontrolled fury, had picked her up and smashed her against a wall. She was about 5 years old when that occurred. The rememberance was devastating. Mother had been the stable, caring parent, while Father, nightly drunk, had been cold, uncaring, hostile, withdrawn, and sometimes violent. The threatened loss of Mother as a stable, loving parent was almost unbearable. Was the broken coccyx a screen memory for many such happenings? A screen memory is a memory that conceals as much as it reveals. Freud suggested that they be analyzed much in the same way as a dream, with the patient free-associating to each element of the screen memory. Sally's memory didn't appear to be a screen for multiple abuses. The mother of Sally's infancy, toddlerhood, and latency had been remarkably caring in a home of persistent hostility and violent arguments. That love had been interrupted by a small number of brutalities. (An array of similar episodes, widely separated in time, were uncovered.)

Having little history, I knew nothing at that time of her parents' drinking. After about three weeks of alternating disbelief and all-too-convincing belief that her beloved mother had so mistreated her, Sally stopped talking about her mother's abuse and began talking about her parents' drinking. She had perfect recall of most of this, and she proceeded to relate how her father, who always worked and who used his status as a "good provider" to justify doing anything he damn well pleased, drank every single night. He "held it well," meaning that he rarely slurred or staggered. What he did do was scream and argue, virtually continuously. Utterly self-centered, Father could not tolerate not having his way. When he could not dominate, he ranted. Sally's memory of the "baseline" status of her childhood home was of parental fighting: loud, vulgar, occasionally physical, and always terrifying.

The terror she had exhibited in the waiting room trying to disappear into the wall was the terror she had lived with night after night as a small child. The attempt to disappear was a re-creation of her earlier attempts to disappear, which was her way of coping.

She literally hid in the closet or under the bed; when older, she hid in the woods in back of the house. Constant fighting meant constant terror. Sometimes Sally's mother interposed her, "literally frequently, and metaphorically constantly" between herself (the mother) and the father. Sally was monkey-in-the-middle with a vengeance. Her mother's use of her as a shield was totally repressed until these episodes flooded back during the period of traumatic de-repression in therapy. They, too, were traumatically disillusioning. Sally was tossed around—pushed aside by her father and sometimes flung across the room. Although not quite explicit, it was clear that what the mother was using Sally to protect herself from was sex. Sally was almost literally penetrated by her father as he thrust toward her mother. "How could she? I thought she adored me," sobbed Sally in a thousand variations. Children need to idealize their parents; clearly her father was not idealizable, so she turned the upward gaze to Mother. Disillusionment is inevitable and normal—nontraumatic, gradual disillusionment. This was not possible for Sally. Being thrown against a wall so hard that her coccyx was broken and being put between Mother and her enraged father could not be integrated with Mother, the loving baker.

When Sally was thrust in front of Mother, Father was not physically violent toward her. Rather, his attitude was one of scorn, rejection, hostility, and barely repressed rage. He had contempt for "girls." Her older brother, although hardly well-treated, was more accepted and later sent to college. Sally, in what was one of the most damaging of the many injuries inflicted on her, was not sent to school. Father didn't believe in education for girls; he thought it a waste because they married anyway. Needless to say, the fact that this highly intelligent woman was aggressively deprived of education had survival consequences in terms of her earning power and the skill to navigate her true will toward meaningful and satisfying work. This went far beyond the already indelible psychological damage that her father's dismissal of her as insignificant had inflicted.

Besides the sexualized fighting between the parents, there were other instances of physical brutality. When Sally was trying to disappear, she sometimes had temper tantrums. Her rage had to have some outlet. When she was 4, she had a particularly intense prolonged one. Her father came, pulled down her pants, put her across his knee, and spanked her with a strap. Her conscious memory was of the experience being humiliating and enraging. Yet, as an adult, she sometimes found being spanked highly sexually exciting. This was one of her most guilty secrets. In addition to that which was a secret to herself (the repressed), Sally had a number of guilty secrets that she had confided to no one. Her pleasure in erotic spankings was one of them; she blushed scarlet when she finally told me about this. Sally was ashamed of the pleasure she gleaned from being spanked. That shame was threefold: it seemed perverse; it had first occurred within what she considered a shameful affair; and most saliently, the idea that the original spanking by her hated father had been sexually stimulating was repugnant and violently unacceptable.

Sally tried to detach her pleasure in erotic spanking from her father, saying that a reddening of the skin of her buttocks was physically stimulating and had no psychological meaning. I pointed out that her temper tantrums were states of high arousal from which the spanking, which had not been so painful for the pain to override the pleasurable cutaneous stimulation of the spanks, had brought a resolution, a sort of climax. The pulling down of her pants, the father's attention, the father's sexual excitement, her own state of arousal, all fixated this experience in her mind so it was one she returned to in adulthood with intense, highly guilty pleasure. Sally then said, "My father got an erection when he spanked me. I think I can remember feeling it.

That's why he stopped." I said, "He stopped because he came." I went on to suggest that it was no accident that she first experienced this form of eroticism in a relationship with a man who was in many ways like her father.

I return to Sally's parents' drinking. As the years went on, the parents' fighting intensified. The father's alcoholism was stable in the sense that he continued to drink in the same way, with the same effects of sullenness, barely contained rage, and contempt. He often repeated that he had never wanted children and that they were a burden he couldn't wait to shake off. When Sally was in her early teens, her mother started to drink heavily. She did not drink well. Unlike the father, she staggered, vomited, slurred, and was a public humiliation. Her drinking hastened her premature death from a series of strokes. Sally's parents finally separated and divorced when she was in her late teens. At the time Sally came to treatment, her father was dying of cirrhosis of the liver.

Sally's account of her mother's alcoholism gave me an opportunity to offer her a possible explanation for her mother's unusual, cruel behavior, a reconstruction that allowed her to regain some self-esteem and proved vital in her rehabilitation. I told her, "Your mother must have been drinking, even drunk, when she threw you against a wall, and when she interposed you between her and your furious father. You remember her alcoholism as developing in your teens, but it is highly unlikely that she started drinking then. She went downhill too fast. It is far more likely that she had drunk episodically for years and was ashamed of it because she could hardly drink and object to your father's drinking in the way she did. She must have drunk secretly, and it was when she was drunk that she involved you in their fighting and broke your coccyx."

"Do you really think that is so?" she asked pathetically, pleadingly, so strong was her need to make sense of her mother's behavior and to feel loved by her. "Yes," I said. "I can't be sure, but it fits, makes sense. Why else would your loving mother, who usually protected you from your father, act in that way?" Sally's relief was enormous. It was her mother's alcoholism, not her hatred, that injured.

During this period of de-repression, Sally's behavior and demeanor would alter abruptly and totally. One minute she would be engaged, in the room on the floor with me, the next minute she would "leave," either freezing in terror, or going into a cold, withdrawn, immobile rage (not experienced as rage) reminiscent of the catatonic patients I encountered in my psychiatric hospital days. Her utterly frigid rages were unnerving. I tensed when she went into them, sometimes for reasons that I could not discern, and sometimes in response to some slight disturbance in our relationship—the phone ringing, or my being two minutes late, or a perceived failure of empathy on my part. These withdrawals, with their psychotic quality, were frightening. I worried that she might not come out of them; they were too close to psychosis, and regression is sometimes irreversible. They also angered me; I don't like to be cut off. When she did speak, it was of suicide.

I didn't want Sally to suicide. Neither did I want her to limp through life terrified and half-alive. Therapy is a serious and sometimes dangerous business. All therapists take risks and expose themselves to emotional injury. If they are never on the edge, they aren't doing their job. On the other hand, failure to protect patients as fully as we can is inexcusable. What should I do with Sally? Hospitalize her? Not if I could help it. The injury to one's self-esteem caused by hospitalization is profound, and it would have been experienced as a violation of the tenuous trust we had established. Naturally, I would rather lose the case than lose the patient, but damn it, I didn't want to lose the case. Things were happening and Sally just might go far if she could live through the violence of traumatic de-repression. So I decided not to press for hospitalization at that time. It was a decision that cost me no little sleep.

The question of the diagnosis that I preferred not to make reoccurred. Was Sally psychotic? Were her catatonic-like states more than repeats, in relation to me, of her rage at and flight from the traumatic occurrences of her childhood? I decided she was probably not psychotic, and that the intensity of her reactions to "minor" disturbances in our relationships were reflections of her intense need for all of me and all of my attention and understanding for her to feel safe enough to do the work that she was doing. As it turned out, she reacted as she did largely because any lapse on my part meant that I could no longer protect her from her father's vengeance, which would be to murder her. If not psychotic, what then? For quite a while, I thought that I was working with a multiple-personality disorder. So rapid and so total were the shifts in her state of being that I considered consultation with a multiple-personality specialist. Her third-party payment diagnosis was dysthymic disorder, which was true enough.

Just as things seemed to settle down, Sally was hit by—and that was what it seemed—another wave of de-repression, this time of sexual abuse by her father. This was possible only after my interpretation of her mother's violent behavior toward her as being an early manifestation of her mother's chronic alcoholism, which helped Sally feel loved and protected by her mother once again. After that interpretation, an interlude of relative serenity was certainly welcomed by me and must have been by her. However, that interlude was brief, and Sally's extreme terror returned. She spent several sessions rigid and far away. There was little communication, and I could not seem to make contact with her. In the fourth such session, I was worried that she might be slipping into psychosis, when Sally erupted in convulsive, prolonged sobs.

When Sally sobbed in that way, which I had seen before, her face reflected all the pain of a heartbroken child. As her tears poured forth, the triangle formed by her eyes and nose seemed to regress inward, so that her face split into two planes, much like a crushed cardboard box. At first I though my visual impression was hallucinatory, and to some extent it was, but I now believe that her musculature actually changed her physiognomy. After about 15 minutes, Sally started speaking through her sobs, and her face regained its normal contours.

"He tore me; he's going to kill me for telling you. When I was 3 and 4 and 5, Mother worked nights as a waitress, and he would baby-sit me. He hated it; taking care of kids was woman's work. When he put me to bed, he would lie beside me and hold me very tight. At first I liked being held; it made me feel secure, but then he would hold me too tight, very tight. It hurt, and I was scared. He would rub up against me and I would feel something hard. I guess he would come; maybe I partly liked it. I don't know." (More convulsive sobbing, during which Sally again retreated far inside herself.) "One time—one time—one time." (Silence.) "One time," I prompted her. "Oh, it hurt, it hurt. He tore me. There was blood. Then he took my panties and threw them out, telling my mother I had wet them. I think that happened. I know the rubbing did; I'm not sure about the rest—oh, it hurt."

During the ensuing month, Sally's terror reached an apogee. Her petrification against—into—the walls of my waiting room became continuous unless she was sitting on my floor. She moved her head rapidly, searching for danger.

I told her I thought that the events she remembered were real, that they had actually occurred. Could I be sure? No. But here is a problem that has vexed psychoanalysis from the beginning. Were the confessions of Freud's hysterics about childhood seduction true? (Seduction is an odd word for what is sometimes rape and always involves an extreme power differential, which says something about the need of the old-time adult theorists [of childhood sexuality] to exculpate adults.) Or were they fantasies? Historical truth or narrative truth? Although Freud himself abandoned his seduction theory, he never denied that adults sexually abused children and that such abuse is traumatic and etiologically powerful in the formation of neurosis.

On the other hand, there is currently an atmosphere of near hysteria in which any physical affection expressed by an adult toward a little girl is suspect. I do not wish to contribute to that hysteria and make no general statement judging the veracity of accusations by children, or by adults remembering childhood, of sexual abuse. However, I am inclined to believe my patients, at least without evidence to the contrary. In Sally's case, her father drank heavily every night and was certainly near drunk when he "baby-sat" her, and we know that sexual abuse is highly correlated with alcoholism. Sally's father was in a constant rage because his wife was "cold," and Sally was involved in their violent quarrels over his sexual demands. Further, the way Sally "remembered" this "seduction," and the emotionality accompanying that remembering, only made sense if her memory was a memory of a real event. The only possible alternate explanation was that she was crazy, and/or that her remembered father was a projection of her own pathological rage. Did I believe that? No way. I was there, Sally's struggle to *not* remember was at least as powerful as the affects that accompanied that remembering.

I concluded that Sally wasn't crazy, but I was concerned that she was becoming so. Maybe she just couldn't handle knowing that both parents had so little loved her that they had each violently attacked her. Even more ominous, she remained convinced that her father, now old, seriously ill, and 2,000 miles away, was going to kill her in my waiting room. That did seem near psychotic. I asked her if he had threatened to kill her if she "told." I was convinced that he had, but Sally couldn't remember such a threat, only that she had always been terrified of him. I tried reassurance to no avail. I wondered if a need for punishment was fueling her delusional fear, if it was delusional. Was he capable of coming north and killing her, if he knew of her "betrayal" of him? Did she need to be killed because she had experienced some pleasure in her father's rubbing against her genitals? Did she have other (conscious or unconscious) guilty secrets? I was soon to find out. Sally was poorly differentiated. During the first years of treatment, she would relate incidents that I interpreted as incidents in which she lost her identity in merger with casual acquaintances, in which she would be overwhelmed by their misfortunes. It was as if she became them, especially when they shared great pain with her. Was her lack of firm boundaries between herself and others contributing to her terror? I asked her if she thought her father could read her thoughts. She replied, "I don't know." My telling her that he couldn't did not help. Confessing her "guilty secret" did.

Like so many adult children of alcoholics (ACOAs), Sally had married an alcoholic. In the early years of their marriage, he was daily drunk, frequently unemployed, and totally irresponsible. In a sense, she had traded down; at least her father had consistently worked. She had also traded up, as we shall see. Freud described "object finding being a refinding," meaning that humans tend to want to marry a gal (or guy) "just like" the girl (boy) who married good old Mom (Dad). When the relationship with the parents was problematic and painful, the unconscious wish to repeat is strong. Hank wasn't only an alcoholic, and Sally's "object finding being a refinding" was complex, being simultaneously a refinding of her father and refinding of her "good" mother. Sally and Hank recapitulated her parents' arguments. Finally, she emotionally detached, threatening divorce if he didn't stop drinking.

At that time, Sally was working for a physician as a sort of all-around assistant and untrained nurse. Outwardly, he looked as different from her father as possible, a nondrinking educated professional. Needless to say, she became his mistress. He too was unhappily married. (As someone once said, clichés are clichés because they are true.) Sally became friendly with the wife, and was quickly monkey-in-the-middle, just as she had been as a child. Further, Steven turned out to be a dominating tyrant who used the power differential (employer-employee, upper middle class-working class) between them to exploit her sexually and otherwise; he demanded long working hours and total devotion. Steven did give her something in return: He taught her a great deal about medicine. For Sally, grievously hurt by her lack of education, this affiliation was, among other things, an attempt at remediation. It raised her self-esteem and gave her vicarious if not real status.

Steven, whatever his character defects, was masterly at his profession, and Sally adored that. At first their sex had been mutual and highly gratifying. Then Hank stopped drinking to save his marriage, and Sally grew close to him. The sober Hank was remarkably different from drinking Hank: loving, considerate, responsible. Sally no longer wanted sex with her employer. He pressed her relentlessly, demeaning her and belittling her—"Who else would employ you?"—and she usually gave in. When she didn't, he would grab her in an empty examining room and push her head down on his penis; when she swallowed his ejaculate, which she enjoyed doing and then was sexually aroused in spite of herself, he ranted, "That was disgusting. Only whores swallow cum." She came to hate him, yet couldn't break with him. Now that she was in love with her husband, Sally's guilt knew no bounds. Finally, she quit her job, but her guilt never left her.

Her guilt was exacerbated by her naïveté and lack of caution in agreeing to go for a ride with her podiatrist, who raped her. He threatened to kill her if she told, and fear of him added to her already great fear of her father. Sally continued to have lunch with her physician ex-employer, hating it but not knowing why she did so.

Confessing to her affair and discussing the rape somewhat lessened her terror, one source of which was her fear that she would confess to her husband; telling me obviated that need and removed that component of her terror. Sally didn't connect Steven with her father. I made the connection for her, saying: "When your father forced himself on you and tore your vulva, you had no choice. You were powerless. When you found Steven, who as employer was a father of sorts and shared your father's domination, self-centeredness, and ruthlessness, you unconsciously repeated your relationship with your father, but you were now choosing it instead of having it inflicted upon you. In choosing it, you were active—doing it rather than having it done to you so that you didn't feel so powerless. Your relationship with Steven was an attempt to master a trauma by repetition." That was the most I had said for months. My interpretation was instantly understood, and the response to it was profoundly emotional. Neither Sally's terror nor her guilt left her, but the intensity of both abated.

In the next session, Sally arrived with a large paper bag, blushing beet red. "Can I show you something?" I nodded. Whether or not she was a multiple personality or psychotic, I had by now come to trust Sally's drive for health and let it direct the treatment. After all, she had opened things up with her move to the floor, had bonded with me to enable her to experience and integrate her childhood traumas, and had told me a destructive secret that she feared she would tell her husband. Out of the paper bag came Charlie—a large and obviously well-loved teddy bear. Sally, looking about 2 years old, cuddled Charlie. At last she felt safe.

Charlie, and Sally's relationship to him, was a creative act, an illusion if you prefer, but an illusion that
worked for her. Sally had provided herself with a
reliable object, one who cared and loved, and could be
cared for and loved. She was doing as an adult in
treatment what she hadn't been able to do for herself in
childhood. Few of my patients have had Sally's gift for
creative, restitutional healing by allowing herself to be
a child again. We spent many sessions talking about
Sally's relationship with Charlie. I offered no interpre-
tations. It was during this relatively serene period of
our work together that Sally revealed other sources of
her strength—her love for nature and her reading of
Norman Vincent Peale.

We stopped "doing therapy" and talked about hiking,
woods trails, and mountains, and how the power of
positive thinking had prevented her from suiciding
during the episodes of submission to Steven's sexual
demands. Should I have analyzed instead of shared?
No way. You don't take away before replacing. Trian-
gular relationships in psychoanalysis don't usually
refer to patient, therapist, and teddy bear, but this
particular triangle bore fruit. Did I enjoy regressing
with Sally? You're damn right I did. Is such regression
on the therapist's part dangerous? Sure, but therapy is
a dangerous business. The trick is to have binocular
vision; to regress and not regress simultaneously. I
decided to risk being too tolerant of my patient's
therapeutic regression, rather than to risk distancing
myself and inflicting a wound to her self-esteem by
making her feel foolish.

Charlie enabled Sally's next, and vital, "confession."
Out of the blue, Sally said, "I don't know how to tell you
this, but I'm addicted to amphetamines. I get them
from Dr. X., my diet doctor. If I get fat, I'll kill myself. I
can't stand being fat. I went off them once, but I got so
depressed I nearly suicided. I've never wanted to live,
and I'm afraid if I go off, I'll kill myself."

Sally's fears of suicide were all too real. I was taken

aback. I shouldn't have been. So many adult children of alcoholics themselves become addicted to alcohol or marry alcoholics that such behavior is predictable. Addiction to other drugs or to compulsive activities is also extremely common among ACOAs, yet I had totally missed Sally's addiction. Looking back, I could see that her extreme tension, body rigidity, fear, anorexia, runaway anxiety, and near psychotic ideation, whatever their psychodynamic determinants, were pathognomic of amphetamine addiction. I'm an addiction specialist, and I should have spotted this. Sally's diagnosis was becoming clearer. She was an ACOA and amphetamine-dependent.

Sally once told me that she had smoked pot a lot in the past, and sometimes drank too much, but had minimized this, putting it all well back in time. She felt ashamed not only of her addiction, but of having "lied" to me through minimization and omission.

Amphetamine, a "good mother" psychodynamically and an antidepressant pharmacologically, seemed to be something that she couldn't live without. She also couldn't live with it, not anymore: the guilt and shame and self-hatred were too great. That is why she "confessed" her addiction.

Here was the missing piece of Sally's terror. Her need to be punished because of the guilt she felt for her addiction was handily projected onto her all-too-terrifying father. Of course, he would kill her; she deserved to be killed. Her use of pills and, as it turned out, more than a little pot, also contributed to her poor ability to distinguish fantasy from objective reality and her tendency to lose her identity by over-identifying with others. "Can't live with and can't live without it," is the terminal point of all addictions. It is a dangerous point always. Suicide is an ideal way out for any addict at this point, and Sally had long been suicidal. I again considered hospitalization, deciding against it. Instead, I kept her talking about her shame, her need to lie and evade, her constant fear that her husband would find out, her need to play money games for her supplies, her fear that Dr. Feelgood might cut her off. She repeatedly tried to cut back, always failing. The more we talked about drugs, the more she wanted to be off them, but she could not do it; her fear was too great. Now I discussed a rehab program, but she would have none of it. Hank would find out she had been deceiving him about her drug use if she went into rehab. Unlike an alcoholic at a parallel stage of the "disease," her physical health was not immediately threatened, nor was she pharmacologically deteriorating under the impact of her drug consumption in such a way that therapeutic gains were swept away and meaningful relationship was impossible. Her consumption was stable. For several months, we were at an (apparent) impasse.

A CREATIVELY CURATIVE REQUEST

Then Sally made another one of her creatively curative moves. She came to session more frightened than I had seen her for a long time. With trembling lips and shaking voice, she asked, "May I pray?" I was taken aback, although I don't think I showed it. I nodded. Speaking now in a low but increasingly firm voice, she prayed, starting: "When two are gathered together in My Name," (which made me, being neither a Christian nor a believer, vaguely uncomfortable), and went on to ask God "to help Dr. Levin help me get off of amphet-amines." At her final "Amen," I almost cried. That prayer was what has been called a "performative ut-terance," a use of language not to denote, connote, or emote, but rather to act. Such speech is an action. Sally's petition was clearly self-fulfilling. The act of asking God to help me help her, released her, even if not entirely, from her paralyzing fear. It was also a commitment at a deep emotional and psychic level to getting off drugs. I knew at that moment that Sally would soon be drug-free. It was her "surrender," her admission that the two of us were powerless over her addiction. For her performative utterance to be efficacious, I too had to surrender—admit my powerlessness, thereby becoming a participant in her sanctifying and enabling ritual. It was humbling, and that was good. If, in her surrender, she relinquished a grandiose illusion of control in order to transfer that control to an idealized object (that is, something or somebody we experience as all good and all powerful)—God—then I, too, relinquished a part of my grandiosity and transferred my illusion of control to an idealized object—the anabolic forces of the universe manifest in the therapeutic process. It was a healing moment for both of us.

We were not yet home free. I tried to send her to a psychiatric consultant to determine how much amphetamine she was on and to propose a safe withdrawal schedule. Sally resisted this referral, not wanting to tell anyone else of her addiction. Finally, I sent her pills to the consultant, who identified them and worked out a detoxification schedule without actually seeing her. I was angry about this, but she was adamant.

Fortunately, we got by that and Sally started cutting down. All went well until we approached ground zero. At that point, Sally panicked and upped her dosage. We went around that merry-go-round several times. I was then doing a lot of analyzing and interpreting. I pointed out as many meanings of her addiction as I was aware of starting with the unconscious identification with her mother's and father's addictions, of which she had been unaware, and ending with amphetamine's role as an idealized, magical object that would soothe, satisfy, thin, and mood-elevate. I told her that contrary to her expectations, she would feel better "off" the drugs, her self-esteem would get a huge boost, and her self-hatred diminish. I was very active, very didactic, and very firm in my assertion that things could only get better for her if she were drug-free. It finally worked, and there she was feeling bereft, naked, more vulnerable than ever, after I reassured her that she would feel better without the drugs. She was angry as she dared to be with me. I repeatedly urged her to go to Narcotics Anonymous (NA) meetings. She resisted but finally went. Sally never became a deeply committed member of the 12-step movement (so-called for AA's Twelve Steps of Recovery), but her intermittent, rather tepid involvement significantly helped. It reduced her shame and lessened her social isolation.

Sally dealt with her fear of people by superciliousness and contempt, which kept her socially isolated. Of course, her fear that people would "know" that she was an addict and adulteress made matters worse. Fortunately, neither was now nearly as salient, and NA provided her with a first socialization experience in an alcohol- and drug-free environment. She was still too troubled and struggling too hard to ward off depression to become socially involved outside of NA, but a seed had been planted, and she became less defensively contemptuous of others. A year later, she would start to have lunch with fellow workers and develop some friendships with women, but that was yet to come. For the present, she had only Hank and me.

Psychotherapeutically, "curing" an addiction always involves a transfer from dependence on a substance (seemingly much safer) to dependence on people. Relationship cures. Therein lies both the opportunity and the problem. Sally's dependence on me was so overwhelming (for both of us) that the slightest deviance on my part (e.g., being a few minutes late) threw her into a panic, and she responded to a perceived injury to her core self with intense rage, punishing me with catatonic-like withdrawals (which were also self-protections), suicidal threats (not experienced as threats), and frantic calls at all hours of the day and night. I understood her desperation, yet I felt enraged and controlled. I did not for a long time point out the aggression behind much of this behavior. She would not have understood such an interpretation. Instead, I set such limits as I needed to function and otherwise remained tolerant of and empathic toward her need to cling, control, and position. That behavior diminished only slowly. Even more troublesome, Sally lived in dread of my going away, which inevitably would occur.

At this point, her fear of her father returned. Now I pressed for and encouraged her to express her rage toward him. Fearing fatal retaliation, this was very difficult for her. However, our bond was now so strong (confining and infuriating as I sometimes experienced it to be) that she was able to do this work.

Her most characteristic way of reducing the anxiety generated by the anger she had for her father was turning the anger against herself. I actively intervened when she would tear into herself. During a particularly virulent orgy of self-deprecation in which she insisted on her "worthlessness," I said, "It isn't you but your father who is worthless." That opened things up. Once begun, her rage at him was poured out volcanically, yet her fear didn't abate. She oscillated wildly between wanting to kill him and wanting to kill herself. I pointed out this confusion. She asked me if she should call him and express her feelings. Technical neutrality would have been disastrous. Sally needed to actively experience and express anger to her father and not be killed. I actively and strongly encouraged her. Technical neutrality refers not only to the analyst's noninvolvement in the patient's life but also to the analyst's neutrality toward conflicting aspects of the mind, equidistancing him or herself between needs and wishes, reality considerations, and conscience. It is a technique of extraordinary power and efficacy when used appropriately. This simply was not such a situation.

After several weeks of "I will" and "I can't" (confront Father), Sally came in and said, "I called him and told him I hoped that his prick would fall off, and hung up." I shook her hand. Sally fully expected to be murdered, but the longer nothing happened, the less fearful she became. Several months later, her father died. His death was liberation for her. Probably for the first time in her life, Sally wasn't terrified. What she feared may have been a memory, but the death of the objective correlative of that memory dislodged it and, so to speak, it was expelled. Sally felt no guilt, or at least none I could detect—and I probed for it. Her only regret was not seeing him buried, so that she would be absolutely sure he was gone. I wondered if she would have driven a stake through his heart if she had been at the funeral.

The momentous events following Sally's ceasing to take amphetamines were largely adaptive. However, she certainly experienced a "postwithdrawal crash depression." Amphetamine withdrawal is dangerous because of the rebound depression. Such depressions can and often do lead to suicide, hence my making myself available as much as possible during that period. Whatever nonpharmacological psychological and emotional determinants her behavior had at that time, it was powerfully psychopharmacologically driven, and her "clinging behavior" was the clinging of a drowning person to a life raft. In other words, it was necessary and restitutional.

THE LIBERATING POWER OF HATRED

If love and forgiveness can liberate and cure, so can hate. We don't give hate its proper place in the restoration of the self. Sally's hatred of her father, a well-earned hatred, remembered, experienced, and expressed, was the singly most potent force driving and enabling her recovery. I deliberately say "hate" and not "rage," for it was truly hatred. Therapists, generally identifying themselves with the angels, are usually uncomfortable with hatred, especially hatred of parents. It goes against the grain of our professional self-images as healers and restorers of harmony. Some things can't and shouldn't be fixed, and some families and some parents are toxic. We need to help our patients hate them, and use that hatred in the service of establishing a separate identity. Sally's boundaries firmed up once her internalized father ceased tormenting her. Of course, being off of amphetamines also helped her differentiate. The pills, which she literally internalized and ingested, symbolized an all-powerful, loving mother as well as her hateful and hating father—safer within her than without her, yet, like him, tormenting and persecuting her. Part of her fear of giving up the pills was a fear that he, no longer symbolically within, would be even more dangerous without. I told her all of this while she was still struggling for abstinence and warned her that she would suffer a rebound depression—a rebound crash—that would be neurochemical, intensely painful, but self-limiting and without emotional or symbolic meaning.

After prolonged work on these issues, all went well until my vacation grew closer. Sally regressed to near psychosis. Her phone calls became more frequent and increasingly unmanageable. I now found them invasive and intolerable. Sally's voice assumed the same remoteness that her face expressed during her quasi-catatonic withdrawals. Glacial, dead, and astral were some of the adjectives that came to mind listening to her calls. She seemed to be a different person. Was she indeed a multiple-personality disorder who split into multiple selves, perhaps to prevent complete and total fragmentation when her anxiety reached panic proportions? Sally constantly threatened, although she didn't experience it as a threat, to return to her old friend amphetamine.

My impending abandonment (i.e., vacation) threatened the ultimate blow to her self-esteem, destruction of the self. She protected herself against that threat by going away, by not being there, and by cold, murderous fury. Her rage could easily prove fatal. I was fully convinced that Sally was capable of killing herself as the ultimate way of not being there, of avoiding annihilation, and of punishing me for my abandonment. An eye for an eye, a tooth for a tooth. I was abandoning her; she would abandon me. This time I decided to make hospitalization a condition of treatment if things didn't change before I left. Now I suggested that aggression and rage were behind her frantic calls and suicidal ideation. She couldn't hear it, although much later she did and was able to use it. I went back to empathizing with her terror. I emphasized that it *felt as if* she would shatter, but that it wouldn't happen. It worked. Sally now asked, in a less enraged, albeit still desperate way, "How can I survive your vacation?" She then had another one of her creatively curative breakthroughs. She asked, "Can I come and sit in your waiting room (which was shared and accessible) during the times we would be having our appointments?" I was relieved that the hospital, which would have been shattering for her, wouldn't be needed. I spontaneously went her one better and said, "I'll give you the key to my office, and you can go in and sit in the usual place, at our regularly scheduled times." She now had her safe place, and panicked terror of annihilation turned into more ordinary forms of separation anxiety.

The security of knowing that she would be able to stay in my office stabilized Sally. And she had a dream, the associations to which led her to one of the most traumatic events of her life. This wasn't really, strictly speaking, repressed, but it had never come up, and Sally didn't connect it to her present panic. When she was 12, her mother, by then far advanced in her alcoholism, stated, screaming, "I can't stand you fucking kids anymore. I'm leaving." And she did. She got in her wreck of a car and drove away, not returning for weeks, and only then because she couldn't make it on her own. Sally was devastated. She was abandoned, on the verge of adolescence, to the mercies of her drunken, sexually obsessed father. The weeks her mother was gone were sheer hell for her. All security and safety, however meager, vanished. Nothing dramatic happened during her mother's absence, and the incident was never discussed. Life, such as it was, slowly returned to the status quo, but things were never the same for Sally again. It was Mother's second traumatic failure: a broken coccyx and a broken heart—strange legacies from a good mother. The primary meaning of my leaving was now apparent. I, like Mother, was abandoning her to Father, who would kill her horribly, sexually mutilating her, if she didn't kill herself first.

A wall had been breached. Sally's frozen, furious withdrawal was no more. Now sorrow and fear, rage and fury poured forth. I pounded away at the transferential link between these feelings and her relationships with her parents. Time and time again, I took her back to Mother, also pointing out that I wasn't Mother (which in her near psychotic transference, that is, experiencing me as her mother not only in fantasy, but in reality, was not always clear to her), and that Father was dead. Much was accomplished before I left. As the date of my departure neared, Sally's fear, as was to be expected, escalated again. I insisted that she see a covering therapist, as well as sit in my office. With surprisingly little resistance, she agreed. Ensuing vacations were almost equally traumatic for her, but each was a little less traumatic than the last, and as the years went on, Sally steadily improved. It took her several years to be completely comfortable without amphetamines or pot. She knew few people who weren't into drinking or drugs, but as her defensive devaluation of people subsided, her social anxiety abated, and she made new connections. (Her defensive devaluation of people was really a fear of rejection and fear of a consuming and losing her identity by emotionally melting into others. Her self-esteem rose, and her anxiety level fell, as she progressively became her own person.)

An enduring current injury was lack of meaningful or fulfilling work, a constant source of pain that I could do little, beyond empathizing, to alleviate. She came to terms with her father: "I don't forgive him, yet I understand him more now. He never wanted children and resented us. If there is an afterlife, perhaps his punishment could be helping me now. He owes it to me, and I deserve it." She also experienced more active and overt rage toward her mother. She did a lot of grief work, and it paid off. Sally's rage seemed to separate her from her mother, her bond to me giving her the security to do so. She was becoming more and more her own person.

My next vacation approached. Sally, as usual, was upset, but this time she was more nervous than terrified. Just before I left she said, "I'll miss you." That wasn't transference. That was here and now "real" relationship stuff. I said, "You are going to miss me because you are you, and I am I, and you like being with me, but I will be away. You used to think that you would cease to exist if I went away because you could not be, except as a part of me. Now you are secure in your own identity, as evidenced by your growing interest in intellectual activities, hiking, and bicycle riding. And you don't need me in the same way. Your missing me isn't about your mother, it's about us.

"You used to get confused with your mother. You weren't sure what was you and what was her, but the more we talked about her dying and your feelings about her dying, and of her earlier leaving, the less confused you became about who you are and who she was. You knew perfectly well that Mother wasn't you in the sense that you had separate bodies and were separate people, but in your mind, you had images of you and your mother that were blurred, confused, and merged. Now those images in your mind are clearly demarcated. When you get very upset, they may temporarily blur again, and when that happens, I will point it out to you; however, you have moved on to a different space, a different way of being, and that achievement is indelibly yours. It was only after you separated, in your mind and heart, from your mother, finally felt her loss, experienced her as a whole person, good and bad, loving and hating, there for you and not there for you, that you yourself could become a full person, loving and hating, joining and separating, joyful and sorrowful, fearful and secure, and it was only after your mourning allowed you to experience your mother as separate and whole, forever gone and forever a part of you, but not be confused with you, that you could experience yourself as separate and whole with all the feelings you have about that separation and wholeness; that you became able to experience me as separate and whole, as there and not there, as focused on you and as having my own needs, as magnificently capable of helping you and as frequently flawed and sometimes inadequate. It is you, the separate, individuated, and whole Sally who will miss me as a separate, individuated, and tired therapist. I will miss you too, but not so much that I won't have a hell of a good time."

Sally wept a little, but she was not fearful. "I hate your going away, but I hope you have a good time, if you know what I mean." I did, and said so.

Commentary by Andrew Tatarsky

Sally's story begins with a chilling description of the crippling impact that physical and sexual abuse in early childhood still had on her thirty years later. When Sally came for help, initially she was barely able to enter Levin's office because she was so "terrified," and her words were so confused that Levin could not understand her. Levin gives us a daring, honest account of the terror and confusion that he felt in himself, and how he worked to contain and understand these feelings and his own uncertainty in the service of trying to be helpful to Sally. Thus Levin gives us a window into how ultimately successful psychotherapies with people who have suffered severe difficulties in childhood often begin and why the work can be so challenging for client and therapist.

Then Sally makes a most unusual request: "May I sit on the floor?" Then she asked him to join her on the floor and he did. This moment enabled the therapy to take off: "She was no longer terrified . . . the therapy exploded."

This is one of those magical moments that happens in good therapy. Client and therapist, interacting spontaneously, two people working together to create the conditions of trust and collaboration necessary to move on to address the tough issues ahead. The client's traumatic history left her unable to put into words what she was afraid of and what she needed to go forward; she could barely communicate. Yet she was able to find a way to put Levin to the test. Would he be able respond to what she needed even if she couldn't tell him why? Would he have enough respect for her? Would he be sensitive and caring enough not to shame her by refusing or analyzing her motives?

Levin gives us a wonderful demonstration of the art of good psychotherapy. As much as there is a body of thought about how to understand people's suffering and how to support their change and growth, there is much uncertainty along the way that requires the therapist to act spontaneously, on intuition, and to respond to the client as a person rather than by the book. It is these moments that, more than anything else, can communicate that the therapist is willing and able to respect and sensitively respond to the client's needs in a way that creates the sense that it is safe enough to go forward.

All of us, and more so where there is trauma in one's past, need to know and feel that we are in a safe place before we will reveal to another what we are most afraid or ashamed of. This theme is repeated in many of the stories in this book: finding the right fit that creates a sense of safety. Clients have specific things that they need from a therapist that help them know that they are safe enough to move forward.

This relates to another important issue highlighted by Sally's story. The client is ultimately in charge of the direction and flow of the therapy. Levin took his lead from Sally. She decided what she needed from him, namely, for him to join her on the floor. She decided when she felt ready to talk about certain issues: her affair, her history of abuse, her drug use. Levin respected her need to determine when she was ready to talk about these issues. He believed in her "ability to self-cure." Good therapists know that the client will tell them what they need. If a client doesn't get what she needs from one therapist, ultimately the client will, and should, fire that therapist and find another that will be able to do what is needed.

Sally's therapy seemed to me to move in phases that revealed more to both Sally and her therapist. This is how therapy is really a process of discovery for both client and therapist. Neither can know the ultimate outcome, because there is much that is not known at the beginning of the road. The issues Sally initially brought into therapy led to an exploration of her history of abuse. This led to an exploration of her drug use. The sequence in which the issues were addressed had an inner logic that could not have been otherwise.

Sally's drug use is particularly noteworthy in several ways. Firstly, it should be noted that much of value occurred in the therapy before Sally ever mentioned her drug use while she was actively using on a daily basis. There is, I believe, a misguided and dangerous truism out there that people cannot benefit from therapy while they are actively using drugs. Further, it is said, people cannot process the information revealed in therapy while using and must first work on stopping, getting "clean" before entering into therapy. As we can see in Sally's case, there was much work that she needed to do and was well able to do in her therapy before she felt ready to bring her drug use up with Levin. It is arguable that her drug use may have made it possible to do the work she needed to do. Sally needed a harm reduction approach that accepted her active drug use as one of her conditions of the therapy. Had the therapist drug tested her, discovered her active drug use and required her to stop, it is hard to imagine Sally would have been able to remain in therapy.

This relates to another noteworthy aspect of her drug use. For several reasons, Sally believed that she needed her drugs to stay alive. It took care of her like a "good mother"; it countered her dangerous suicidal depression, and it helped her stay thin when she felt that she couldn't live with herself if she gained weight. This is a reflection of her intense self-hate. Sally needed to have enough faith in her therapy with Levin ("Relationship cures" as Levin says) and see the possibility of being able to survive without drugs before she could reveal her drug use in therapy. As Levin says, you don't take something of value away from the client until there is something better and available to replace the long-useful compensation. If Levin had tried to force her to talk about her drug use before she was ready, would it not have been experienced by her as another form of abuse? She felt she needed amphetamines to stay alive. If Levin had insisted on taking them away, she very well might have perceived him as an enemy to her survival. This would have slowed down the therapeutic process considerably. She may have seen in Levin a lack of awareness, sensitivity, understanding, and compassion for her needs and boundaries, reminiscent of her parents' abuses and neglect. Did Sally's relationship with Levin give her an experience of safety and satisfaction that she had never had before and thereby a real reason to feel hopeful about relationships in her life outside the therapy room? This is one of the most powerful ways in which the therapeutic relationship heals.

The therapeutic relationship also helped Sally feel safe enough to finally confront the intense hatred that she felt toward her father, hatred she had been too terrified and guilty to fully acknowledge and had turned toward herself. Feeling and expressing these feelings toward her father, and having the direct experience that her father didn't kill her, left her free to a great extent from the fear and guilt that had plagued her since childhood. Here we see the liberating power of hatred. This act helped her feel better about herself (self-esteem), feel safer in relationships, feel clearer about and more comfortable with her feelings, and become better able to care for herself.

References

Freud, S. (1919). The Uncanny. *The Standard Edition of the Complete Psychological Works of Sigmund Freud.* Vol. 17 (pp. 219–252). London: The Hogarth Press.

Khantzian, E. J., and Mack, J. E. (1989). Alcoholics Anonymous and contemporary psychodynamic theory. In M. Galanter (Ed.), *Recent Developments in Alcoholism.* Vol. 7 (pp. 67–89). New York: Plenum.

8

Drug Use as Rebellion against the Inner Critical Voice

Diana: The Fear of Feelings and the Love of Wine
—Patt Denning

THE CRITICAL VOICE AND THE FALSE SELF

Substance use may express a revolt against a critical inner voice, known by some as the "inner critic." This voice says, "You are no good as you are, and you aren't allowed to express your true feelings or be yourself in the world if you want to be loved or safe." This voice exists in all of us to some extent, whether we rebel against it with drugs or not.

This voice may be recognized as the early childhood imprint of mother or father, or our own voice that accepted parental authority, rules, and power. The voice demands compliance or submission. For the voice also makes threats: "If you do not hide yourself, lie to the world, show them what they want to see, or be 'good,' you will be unloved, rejected, despised, abandoned, or killed."

The universality of this voice is rooted in the power and authority of parents over us as children. We accept their authority because of our need for their love and caretaking, and our need to believe in some blueprint for how to live safely in the world. Without parents or adults to structure our lives, we would have found ourselves in a chaotic and terrifying world. So out of deference to our survival instinct, we learned to suppress, hide, and deny true feelings, wishes, and needs that were deemed unacceptable. We created a "false" self for public consumption. British psychoanalyst Winnicott (1965) said that this is an inevitable development in human socialization.

The false personality can get along very well, achieving great safety and success in life. However, we pay a price in the maintenance of this persona. In complying with this voice, we believe its claims that we are no good and will be unloved if we express ourselves honestly in the world. The potential for direct experience, authentic feeling, and new possibilities is obscured and confounded. Our compensations, compliance, and the manufacture and artifice of outward success hides a stirring sense of worthlessness, shame, and fear of being discovered. The voice punishes transgressions by shaming and guilt-tripping. This punishment takes the form of self-hate and self-criticism that create shame, guilt, anxiety, and depression: "Why did you say that, stupid jerk? Now you've really blown it! You will never learn, and you deserve whatever rejection or punishment follows your thoughtless expression of feeling!"

DISCONNECTION FROM INNER NEEDS

Many people discover that it is easier to play the game successfully if they stop those true feelings from creeping into awareness. Successful compliance in the service of survival is traded for a connection at the deepest levels to our authentic wants and needs.

Some people accomplish survival by freezing their capacity to feel, numbing through tension and constriction in the body. Others do it by creating a kind of separation or split between their conscious, mental experience of themselves, the false personality, and the feeling-full body that is experienced as "not me" or "bad me" as Harry Stack Sullivan put it (1953). The first approach leaves people feeling mechanical, numb, dead, disconnected, and unreal, while the second one leaves people experiencing their feelings as confusing, scary, vague, threatening, and other. The feeling self becomes a threat rather than what it is, a source of essential important information about who we are and what we need to live a healthy, satisfying life.

Some individuals continue to feel and understand their feelings, but to the extent that they have bought into the critical inner voice, they tend to mistrust or criticize their feelings and assume that there is something wrong with them: "I am too sensitive." "I am nuts." "I am evil."

Our lives inevitably reflect this blunting of life force, as we eventually realize the life we are leading has been constructed by the wishes of others rather than our own. In our relationships, we become increasingly aware that we are not getting something that we need, even though we try hard to please others. Finally, though we may not even know why, some of us become increasingly unable to stand it. We feel tense, angry, but unable to express it; we want to get away.

As we identify with this critical voice and submit to its demands or threats, where is the rebellion? Here is where it gets interesting.

THE SPLIT WITHIN

While the dominant, public, conscious part of us may be buying into the critical voice, another part of us, the feeling, needing, wishing part, feels increasingly frustrated, unhappy, unloved, and furious; it longs to be free of the tyranny of this voice. Many people know this "split" inner experience very well as a struggle between "the good me" and "the bad me," the angel and the devil. They know this longing to be free in phrases like "I want to be bad" or "I gotta break out." Because these hidden needs and longings have been put in the bad, unlovable category, by definition they cannot be comfortably expressed in the open but can be expressed in bad, that is, socially unacceptable, ways.

THE REBELLION

For many people, drugs can set the hidden, feeling, needful, bad part free, or create an experience of setting it free in fantasy. Otto

Fenichel (1945) said, "The superego (his term for the inner critic) is that part of the personality that is dissolved in alcohol." Drug use can be a revolt against the critical voice and an experience of mutiny and self-liberation, the temporary experience of being true to those parts of the self that have been driven underground.

Sometimes the revolt is symbolic and sometimes it is all too real.

Because drug use is forbidden, as is overdoing it with alcohol, the act of using a drug or taking that extra drink is a symbolic way of bucking authority, the authority of that voice that says you must follow others' rules to be safe and loved. It is an act of symbolic rebellion that expresses the fact that this voice does not control me completely. This rebellion is often done in private, so deep is the belief that release of hidden aspects will cost one everything: "While I will play at being what you say I should be in public, in private I am free and powerful enough to do whatever I want." The forbidden nature of drug use is what makes it available for this purpose.

This process can also be expressed in relation to others in the following way. If I can "put" the critical voice in you by imagining and assuming that you believe what the critical voice believes, I can then experience you as one who does not accept me as I am. You are the one trying to control me, and I can "defy" you as the projection of my critical voice by using drugs as an expression of my freedom from your control.

In these strategies, drug use becomes the symbol of rebellion.

A real revolt is possible in the following way. If the voice tells me that my feelings are wrong and should be shut away and ignored, taking a drug, like alcohol, that quiets this voice and helps me to reconnect with and express my true feelings and needs is a revolutionary, self-affirming act. If a drug can help me ease the fear that I feel about expressing myself freely with others, using a drug is a means to challenge the authority of this voice and to affirm those parts of myself that I have kept hidden. It may help to free me in the world to be myself. This explains the "nice" person who becomes an "angry drunk," or the shy person who becomes assertive under alcohol. It explains the creativity liberated by marijuana and other similar transformations brought about by the use of drugs.

So is there a problem with using drugs to quiet the inner critic?

Not necessarily, but often there are.

LIBERATION THROUGH DRUG USE

The impulse to alter one's consciousness is as old as human culture, and it is found in countless human pastimes. For many people, drugs are so desirable and compelling because they lead to the rarely felt experience of being able to connect more fully with split-off feelings and needs (Krystal, 1977). Drugs are used to explore the domain between the polarities of total self-constraint and self-expression, self-love and self-hate, chaos and order, selfishness and selflessness, and emotionality and stoicism. Drugs have served as the keys to or initiators of first experiences of authentic, hidden aspects of self. People fall in love with drugs because under their influence they are temporarily opened to the possibility of being more free to feel more fully, to feel more accepting of parts of themselves that they had despised. This experience of open freedom with others temporarily disarms and decommissions the inner critic's dire warnings. People often enter into this using behavior driven by a need to learn and explore, to come closer to who they are. They are generally propelled by a deep urge to heal. They embark on this exploration seeking potential therapeutic value, to embolden themselves to make lasting changes, to encounter unchartered frontier. However, these positive experiences can also lead to serious problems.

THE INNER CRITIC'S REVENGE

The problem with these acts of rebellion is that they often don't lead to real liberation. The critical voice may be put to sleep, but eventually it wakes up. The temporary liberation doesn't educate the critic that the newfound behavior is acceptable. Often the

newfound behavior is still raw, infantile, untrained, uninte-
grated, and dangerous; it isn't acceptable by society's standards. We don't live in a society that gives safe structure to this
kind of exploration; we find no safe reentry into the sober world.
After waking up, the critic reasserts its power and domination
with a vengeance leading to intense feelings of remorse, self-
hatred, shame, and guilt, sometimes of suicidal proportions and
fervent recommitments to be good; that is, to once again re-
nounce and devalue those aspects of the self forbidden by the
critical voice.

LIBERATION AND LOSS OF CONTROL

There is another common, potentially dangerous side effect of
using drugs to rebel in this way. Once the denied aspects of self
get out of their prison, they may not willingly return. Because
drugs have been the key to freedom, the way to stay free is to
continue to use. This can lead to the binge or the bender, the
so-called loss of control. The longer the binge goes on, the
greater the potential threat to other aspects of life that need
attention. Health, money, work, and relationships, become secondary to the exploration of this new state. This dynamic
explains the endlessly repeating cycle of binging and quitting
that is so familiar to many excessive drug users. Rebellion
follows submission, followed by rebellion, followed by submission, ad nauseam.

REINFORCING THE CRITIC'S CLAIMS

These acts of rebellion can actually lead to a reinforcement of the
inner critic's claims. After all, the critic might argue: "Look what
happens when you let those needs out, they just run amok!"
"You see, you really are an irresponsible, no good, worthless,
disgusting baby who can't take care of yourself! You only think of
yourself!" We might even consider that the choice of drugging or
drinking in a self-defeating way is both a means to express the
wish for freedom and self-expression while, at the same time,

buying into the inner critic's claims that our deeper feelings are unacceptable and should be hidden. This is an example of a classic psychoanalytic idea: a good way to resolve a conflict between two contradictory ideas or feelings is to create a solution (what can be called a symptom) that embodies both sides of the conflict at the same time (Freud, 1896). It resolves the conflict in a way that keeps it alive and leads to no real change. Users who are familiar with this cycle ask themselves why they keep finding themselves in the same spot while they are simultaneously driven to change.

The user in this relationship to using is in a serious bind. Rebellion that leads to loss of control followed by self-hatred, abstinence, and buying into the judgments, demands, and threats of a devaluing inner critic are two unstable, undesirable options. What is the way out of this bind?

HARM REDUCTION PSYCHOTHERAPY AND THE WAY OUT OF THE BIND

The way out of this bind is to stop playing the submit/rebel game. To disengage from it, one must be able to become aware of how it plays out and watch it compassionately with some distance. In the psychotherapeutic space, client and psychotherapist can join together in making the connections between the impulse to use drugs and these various factors. As stated previously, often before it is possible to work on making changes in oneself, it is necessary to first develop the capacity to observe oneself more fully.

Harm reduction accepts that there may be much work on this phase to be done before there can be a consideration of what to do about one's drug use. Harm reduction also accepts that many active drug users can and must enter into therapy while continuing to use drugs during this phase of developing the capacities necessary to make changes. The therapist supports the development or strengthening of the part of the client that can observe and reflect on her experience. As the client develops this capacity, it becomes possible to witness dispassionately the critical voice and the rebellious impulse with curiosity and compassion. When the client can recognize the voice of the inner critic and see the adaptations he has made to its claims, the submission through the false public self that pleases others, and the rebellion against the critic and false self through excessive drug use, it becomes possible to rework his relationship to the critic. As the client becomes aware of these meaningful elements—the feelings, needs, desires, and wishes that compose the desire to use a drug—this opens up the possibility of making different decisions in relationship to those desires and feelings.

The harm reduction stance of not coming with presumptions about drug use, and of not taking sides in the client's inner battle to use or not to use, particularly lends itself to forging an alliance with the observing part of the client. The therapist stands outside of the conflict between the critic and rebellious aspect, inviting the client to also stand outside of it and observe it, understanding more fully what the conflict is about.

This also makes it more difficult for the client to imagine that the critic aspect is in the therapist, which would leave the client with his desire to use/rebel and feel in conflict with the therapist. Because the harm reduction psychotherapist does not take an a priori stance about the client's drug use, the fantasy that the therapist is in alignment with the critic can more easily be challenged.

Therapist and client can then consider together the value of the claims of the inner critic, considering how realistic and practical these claims have been for survival purposes. They can explore the origins of these voices. They can review them as meaningful in the context of early childhood but not necessarily in the present context.

It can be useful to encourage the client to have an inner dialogue with the critic and express what she really believes about the critic's claims. In this way, an alternative or revised point of view begins to form in the client's inner experience. This can be followed by experimentation. New ways of being in relationship to others can be tried out that challenge the critic's claims. If the client want to be very cautious, start small, in situations where the risk is not as great. For example, if the client's critic has been telling him that he can not safely disagree with his friend because the friend will find it unacceptable (as his parents did), he can look for an area of low-risk disagreement, such as when choosing a movie or a restaurant, and make a contrary stand and see how the friend reacts. The awareness and conviction that the critic is wrong may not yet be enough to change the critic's mind. It may take several experiences of trying something new that softens or eliminates the critic's claims about these matters. Small successes and self-affirming voices based on empirical evidence lead to greater confidence and safety.

The therapeutic relationship is also an arena in which this work can go on directly as well. To some extent, clients inevitably bring the interpersonal expectations and adaptations based on the inner critic's claims into their relationship to the therapist. These can be identified in the fantasies and expectations that the client has of the therapist. As these are identified and linked to the critic and early messages in childhood, it becomes possible to consider and try out new ways of being with the therapist.

There are other ways to disengage the self-punish and rebel reflex. The therapist might observe how the impulse to rebel with drug use first makes itself known. What precedes it in time? What thoughts, events, or body sensations are present at the first moment of awareness of the impulse? Unwrap this impulse to rebel through drug use. Tease out what feelings, desires, and needs are being expressed in that impulse. What is that impulse saying? What words or feelings does it carry? A self-affirming way to rebel against the inner critic is to find ways to express these parts of oneself directly in one's life rather than through drug use. Experiences that lead to success can be used to modify the critic's beliefs.

To unwrap these impulses, one must also develop the skill or capacity to stop the action, sit with the impulse, take it apart, or get inside of it. Some people are able to identify their forbidden feelings and desires, while others have lost contact with feelings. Practice in sitting with the impulse rather than acting on the impulse opens the capacity to do this work and the possibility for radical behavioral change. These capacities and skills can be learned. Various people refer to them as "self-management skills," "ego skills," "emotional intelligence," "awareness," and being aware without getting swept up by the moment-to-moment onslaught of one's sensual, emotional, and mental experiences. Being able to sit with or tolerate one's experience allows one to consider alternative ways to relate to them.

In the following story, "Diana: The Fear of Feelings and the Love of Wine," Patt Denning describes Diana's struggle with a harsh inner critic mediated by a 20-year course of alcohol abuse. Patt Denning compares Diana's previous psychotherapy, which lasted for ten years with less visible results, with Patt and Diana's subsequent harm reduction approach, which addressed the deeper, pivotal issues before significant change took place. The story shows how abstinence was not a realistic goal for Diana, because she experienced it as a submission to the critic that triggered her rebellion through excessive drinking. Pursuing moderation enabled Diana to feel freed from this bind, put her in charge of her life, and helped her achieve a successful outcome.

Diana: The Fear of Feelings
and the Love of Wine
by Pat Denning

The story of Diana and her treatment outlines both the principles and the process of conducting psychotherapy with clients with drug or alcohol problems. Diana began treatment in 1992, at a time when I was still formulating my ideas regarding alternative approaches and attempting to use both cognitive/behavioral and psychodynamic perspectives as a guide. The sudden shifts in emphasis, style, and process that are apparent in this story reflect the changes that I went through in order to better match Diana's needs. I have since been able to articulate my views and synthesize a new model for treatment. This narrative of her therapy is punctuated by Diana's own comments and perspectives, which enhance the reader's understanding of how an alternative approach to addictions can be successful.

ENTRY INTO TREATMENT

Diana had just passed her 45th birthday and was increasingly worried about aging. Successful in her career, but "unlucky at love," she had been in psychotherapy on and off for ten years. More ominous, she had been drinking heavily for more than twenty years. Her therapist had seen my advertisement in a national addiction treatment magazine offering alternatives to traditional 12-step–based work. A growing sense of hopelessness must have permeated the therapeutic relationship, because Diana willingly accepted her therapist's referral to me.

Diana: Everyone who ends up looking for a way out of addictive behaviors has reached a point where it is obvious that things can't go on this way anymore. Mine came at the end of three months of drinking more than usual; alarm bells were getting too loud to ignore any longer. Three months previously my cat had been run over and killed, which set off a depression that I couldn't seem to shake. I began to question why I couldn't get over her death, and it seemed apparent to me that it had to do with living alone and being alone much of the time. My cat had been my only intimate friend. Why was I always alone?

Diana arrived well-dressed and carrying herself like the high-powered, competent businesswoman that she is. With few social formalities, she announced that she was an alcoholic and stated firmly, "and I hate AA." She vehemently listed a host of reasons to emphasize her view that Alcoholics Anonymous was useless to her. I told her that she had come to the right place for treatment, because I didn't require the use of AA and I actually agreed with many of her criticisms. With a satisfied "good," she began to tell her story.

Diana: I came to Dr. Patt Denning after twenty years of abusing alcohol in the hope that there was another way outside of AA to finally grapple with my problem. Several years before I had tried AA for about six months, and it never "took." Sometimes the alienation I felt at those meetings—the slogans, the maudlin confessions, and the endless talk about the 12 Steps— drove me to drink as soon as I could get out of there! I was not surprised to read, shortly before coming to Dr. Denning, that AA was successful in the long term for only five percent of all the alcoholics in this country. I kept looking for another way out. More than once the idea of traditional psychotherapy seemed promising, and when I heard that Dr. Denning specialized in, among other things, alcohol treatment alternatives, I made the call.

Diana's pattern of drinking had been stable for most of the past twenty years. Socially she drank in moderation, no more than two glasses of wine, stating that she "hated seeing women drunk." When alone, however, her pattern was different. She would stop after a long day at work at a local specialty wine store and buy an expensive bottle of Cabernet. At home she would begin drinking while still in her work clothes, turn on the TV, and drink until she passed out on the couch. She woke the next morning feeling humiliated and somewhat scared, but quickly exercised, showered, and began the long day again, putting away any feelings or thoughts about her drinking. Diana didn't always intend to drink the entire bottle, but she did drink with a purpose: often to reward herself for a hard day at work, sometimes to soothe hurt feelings from a relationship, always for the pleasure of the taste of a good wine. No one knew she had a drinking problem.

Diana: All of my problem drinking has taken place when I'm alone. A strong concern for what people think has kept me to having only two drinks in social situations. When in the company of interesting people there are far more interesting things to do than to get drunk; it is when I've been home alone that I've gotten into trouble.

Diana described herself as "genetically predisposed" to alcoholism because of her Scandinavian heritage, despite the fact that no one in her family was alcoholic. Her mother went through a brief period of drinking after divorcing Diana's father, but quit because she realized that she couldn't control the amount that she drank. Diana recalls her first taste of alcohol, a fine French cognac, when she was on an ocean-going cruise at age 15. She was amazed at the warmth of cognac and felt soothed, comforted, and loved. This initial positive reaction to one's first drink is often predictive of people who will develop alcohol problems. Diana did not begin drinking until the age of 22, but she quickly developed a pattern of out-of-control drinking.

Diana: Almost immediately I began drinking excessively, mostly alone, always unable to stop once I'd had my first sip. Those were the days of exploration; I tried liqueurs, fortified wines, gin, and other hard liquor. I loved it. But it was not long before I began to wake up in the morning with hangovers, thinking NO MORE BOOZE. My morning resolve not to drink always vanished the same day, after work. It has been said that many people who abuse alcohol are in denial about their addiction throughout much if not all of their lives. This was not the case with me. I knew from almost the beginning that I loved this stuff, way too much. I could not stop, but knew that someday I probably would have to. I kept putting off the someday.

Many people enter treatment for alcohol and drug problems with obvious reluctance. Diana showed very little, easily declaring that she had to "stop drinking." When I suggested that it might entail some difficulty for her, she responded with a businesslike attitude of

"well, let's get down to it." I asked her exactly why she
wanted to quit, and she corrected me by saying that
she didn't want to, she had to. She had recently been
arrested for driving while intoxicated and was very
worried by the danger and her lack of judgment. She
was also aware of feeling slowed down in the mornings,
less able to focus clearly at meetings or when planning
projects that required exacting detail. She was also
frightened by the change in her looks after drinking too
much. She claimed that her eyes got puffy and stated
that she was aging too quickly. Diana firmly believed
that she would not find a man for a committed relationship if she was not young, thin, and feminine in
both looks and demeanor. I silently assumed that she
had to hide her obvious intelligence and competence in
order to achieve this femininity and concluded that she
must trade in her public persona for a much different
one after-hours with a man.

THE DEVELOPMENT OF A NEW MODEL OF
TREATMENT FOR ADDICTIONS

Before beginning to see Diana, I had spent twenty
years working in the public sector as a psychotherapist
and administrator for community mental health programs. I maintained a small private psychotherapy
practice at that time as well, specializing in mood
disorders and borderline personality disorder. When I
began seeing Diana in my private practice, I had just
made the decision to quit my job as the director of a
psychiatric outpatient clinic, partly out of frustration
with diminishing funding and partly out of a wish
to pursue more creative enterprises. I had worked
directly with many seriously disturbed adults and
supervised hundreds of other cases. Many of these
patients' treatments were complicated by their use of
drugs or alcohol. After years of referring these patients

to 12-step meetings or drug treatment programs, I was dissatisfied with the outcome: very few quit drinking or using. Many of those who stayed with Alcoholics Anonymous or Narcotics Anonymous quit taking their psychiatric medications in a misguided attempt to remain "clean and sober." Others wandered in and out of treatment, gaining a reputation for being difficult patients. Dual diagnosis was considered to be "double trouble."

When I tried to work with counselors at drug treatment centers, I experienced little cooperation and much hostility. I was unwilling to see my clients' problems as primarily drug related, and the counselors were not trained in mental health principles. Noting that we belonged to different worlds with different perceptions, styles, and rules for treatment, I began developing the idea of "provider cultures" to account for this phenomena. Mental health clinicians and chemical dependency specialists were, and still are, trained to see the patient in very different ways. Much as the blind people in the proverbial examination of the elephant, we could only describe what we had learned from a partial and fragmented experience. Each one's training and supervised experience molded us to belong to a specific provider culture that guarded its own professional turf. There are many examples of these differences: One is our differing assessments of a client who is unsure about whether to quit all use of drugs. While I might see such considerations as an indication of normal ambivalence, chemical dependency staff would routinely denounce the client's hesitation as denial.

Aware of this dilemma, and aware of my own provider culture, I decided to train myself to think in a more holistic way about people with alcohol and drug problems. The research I found and increasing clinical experience expanded my sphere of competence but, has not, up to this point, changed my basic psychological stance towards these problems. I still believe

that all serious drug problems are embedded in significant emotional difficulties and operate within a social
climate of stigmatization. The prevailing notion that
addiction is a disease still appears to me to be a case of
a good metaphor gone bad—a concretization of what
might have once been a useful analogy to explain the
mysteries of addiction to a client or a clinician or a
public frightened by the harm caused by out of control
use. Neither empirical studies nor treatment outcomes
support such a simplistic theory, but the disease
model has become the primary theory for alcohol and
drug treatment in this country (Alexander, 1987).

One of my specialties is in the area of psychopharmacology, the types of drugs used to treat certain
psychiatric conditions. I expanded this knowledge
base to include the so-called drugs of abuse and was
able over the years to blend physiology with psychology
to form the beginning of a holistic treatment approach
that I call Addiction Treatment Alternatives.

Diana was one of the first patients in my private
practice who presented with significant alcohol abuse
but who also maintained a high level of functioning. I
was more used to seeing patients whose abilities to
function were clearly compromised by their alcohol use
and who had already suffered significant losses associated with it. I was aware that the world was full of
"Dianas" and that she would teach me a great deal
about the more secret, less obviously destructive patterns of alcohol addiction.

Speaking with her previous therapist left me with
the impression that he had primarily attempted to
actively support her shaky self-esteem, especially in
her dealings with men. He seemed confused and frustrated by the lack of progress on that issue, as well as
worried about her continued drinking. He saw her as
desperately fighting off a deep loneliness by overwork-
ing, becoming obsessively involved with a man, and
during alone times, drinking. Diana would not allow

herself to feel any of these needs, he said, pushing herself along at a feverish pace to outrun feelings.

It was difficult for me to evaluate his treatment because we, although both trained psychotherapists, also belonged to different provider cultures. My orientation is psychodynamic and, more recently, cognitive, while he seemed to be trained in a more humanistic style. He used words like "self-esteem," "shame," and "self-actualizing," while I was more apt to use words like "core issues," "deficits," and "ego strengths." Once again I was surprised by the differences among mental health providers and by our inability to translate the particular methodology of our provider culture. Stumbling blocks such as these make it difficult to plan effective treatment for a client. With no real evidence to the contrary, I had to assume that the previous therapy had indeed uncovered important issues that Diana was now aware of and that we could draw on that experience in the present work.

Diana: My relationships with men through the past ten years were intermittent, serially monogamous. Each ended because I had lost interest in the guy. Then I went to the most inappropriate place of all. I met and fell deeply in love with a married man who was charismatic, successful, and quite ineligible. I was to spend ten years waiting for him to leave his wife. He never did. Early on in this relationship I began seeing a new-age psychotherapist, and I continued to see him during the course of this affair. His main aim was to help me see that there was no hope for me ending up with Matt; he would never divorce his wife. I never could bear to see it that way, and continued to wait, suffer, and drink— and see my therapist once a week. We never really talked about my childhood.

THE THERAPEUTIC "FIT"

First impressions influence me in significant ways. I find that my initial reaction to a potential client not only colors the treatment, but often predicts the outcome. I also have to be careful when I meet someone who, despite being the same gender, class background, and race, seems somehow "other" to me. I tend to feel a bit lost and unable to count on my intuition to guide the early stages of treatment, relying instead on standard practices and techniques until I sort out this odd sense of alienation.

My initial reaction to Diana was one of feeling that we were extremely different people despite both being professional women of similar ages. Diana's style and businesslike attitude seemed to allow for little personal interaction between us. I felt very much like the doctor who was being consulted for a specific problem. There was no sense of the two of us as a team getting to know her and together finding solutions to her problems. This impression was so strong that it overpowered my usual interest in the interactional process of psychotherapy and propelled me into a complementary businesslike approach to her presenting problem, alcohol abuse. In this way I artificially created a "good fit" when I didn't actually feel one.

EARLY STAGES OF TREATMENT: ASSESSMENT

Diana was eager to focus on specific ways to quit drinking. She expressed frustration with herself but she also expressed determination. She had some awareness that she drank when she was feeling bad, but was confused by her pattern of drinking when nothing was apparently wrong. I asked her to take a formal assessment test, the Alcohol Use Inventory (Horn, Wanberg, Foster, 1986), to better understand her drinking. This test is unique among alcohol and drug screening devices in that it offers scaled scores that reflect several dimensions of a person's drinking.

The AUI tests for styles of drinking (gregarious, solitary, binge), perceived benefits (improved mood, sociability, focus), and negative consequences (hangover, disruption of important life activities). The resulting profile allows the therapist to develop a more sophisticated view of the client's drinking than can be gleaned from interview data alone.

This test would prove useful for Diana to see how alcohol impacts her life. Her scores were mostly what I had expected. Diana is not a gregarious drinker. She drinks more or less daily and feels that it improves her mood and allows her to forget problems, especially with her boyfriends. She is showing signs of moderate dependence on alcohol and some distressing hangover symptoms. Consistent with her self-report, she shows no decline in professional functioning as a result of her drinking, but she does put off household chores and personal bill paying. She is very worried about her drinking, seeing it as a problem that she needs to grapple with. Surprisingly, however, the AUI also showed that she was extremely resistant to accepting help despite her awareness of the problem. This contradiction became a central theme in the therapy. When I asked Diana (during the third or fourth session) about this part of the test, she replied quite honestly by saying, "I don't let anyone tell me what to do." This statement opened up the topic of her childhood and the source of her fierce independence.

FAMILY HISTORY

Diana was a very precocious and independent child. She had little patience for other children and their toys and games. She was not a "cuddly" child, preferring little contact from others. She was quite assertive and controlling by temperament. Her mother was very disturbed by Diana's personality and saw these characteristics as both unfeminine and too much like her father. She would criticize and control Diana's actions, speech, and activities by predicting that no man would ever marry her because she was too much like her father. Both Diana and her mother were extremely critical of Diana's father, whom Diana describes as eccentric and aloof, saying, "there's something missing in him; he's got some human parts missing." Much to Diana's relief, her mother divorced him when Diana was 17, remarried several years later, and is still with this husband. Diana describes her mother as controlling and demanding, but sweet, and says that her current husband "dotes on her."

Twin brothers were born when Diana was 3 years old, and she remembers this as a traumatic time for her. She was aware that her mother shifted her loving attention from her to the "little princes," as Diana's mother referred to the boys. Despite this loss, Diana continued to idolize her mother and strove to behave like "a little lady." No matter how good she was, though, Diana always felt like a bad girl, aware of her angry feelings and her unsociable nature.

Diana: Early in my life I learned that I was selfish, ill-tempered, and far too smart to be considered feminine enough to attract a husband. My mother passed this information on to me as I was growing up. She was determined that I not take after my selfish, ill-tempered father, and she probably overdid the training. She clearly loved my younger brothers more, for taking after her. Believing that I was inherently unlovable I turned to achievement instead, excelling at school, art, and music. At the same time I learned to control my temper, selfishness, and intelligence. I became cheerful, generous, polite, and enthusiastic to the outside world. I never lost my temper after I was about 10 years old. I did not rebel or act up as a teenager because that sort of thing was simply not tolerated. In short, I learned to deny and fear all negative feelings. I also became a compulsive overeater, swallowing all those negative feelings and washing them down with alcohol.

Diana's description of her childhood indicates that the fit with her mother was less than optimal (paralleling the initial fit with me?). Diana was a strong-willed child who required loving direction with a lot of independence. Her mother saw Diana's personality as a crucial defect and was relentless in her attempts to modify it. Currently, her mother seems to be quite selfish, narcissistic, and increasingly histrionic as she attempts to control the adult Diana as she did the child.

Diana did well in school, showing a distinct intelligence for both sciences and the arts. She sees herself as a passionate person who soaks up everything in the world, having intensely positive or negative, rather than neutral, feelings about things. She studied music and art, but ended up with a degree in architecture, which she sees as part engineering and part art. She has had her own design business for the past ten years and is quite successful.

Diana had a brief, tumultuous marriage when she was a junior at college. After growing up in the confines of a small town in Minnesota, she chose an Ivy League college to expose her to a more exciting world of ideas and people. She met her husband at school and they married after only knowing each other for a few months. He was physically abusive and she stayed with him for two terrifying years before finally leaving him. She has not had a stable relationship since that time.

Diana: I married my college sweetheart, who was as ill tempered and selfish as my father, and ultimately abusive as well. Brilliance can sometimes hide mental illness, and my husband probably fit into that category. My upbringing, however, had put me into a state of unawareness about my true feelings about him. I married a man whom I didn't really love, convincing myself that I did. Inevitably, two-and-a-half years later our

*marriage abruptly ended in divorce. By that time I had
acquired a taste for gin and sherry (not together!) but
still hadn't begun to abuse alcohol. Then came the
divorce. It was traumatic. But even as I was struggling
with suicidal feelings and extremely low self-esteem, I
clearly recall thinking, "Now I can drink!"*

COGNITIVE/BEHAVIORAL INTERVENTIONS

As our treatment progressed, Diana expressed excitement about the prospect of a clear focus and specific
guidelines for her drinking. She had decided that she
wanted to quit, but admitted that she would really
prefer to be able to drink socially. She was not ready to
explore that ambivalence, however, so I began helping
her achieve and maintain abstinence. I opted for a
cognitive/behavioral approach for two reasons: Diana
had already had ten years of insight-oriented psychotherapy, and I assumed at the time that many of her
psychological issues had been uncovered and explored. The fact that this psychotherapy did not help
her quit drinking was not unusual. It is nearly impossible to effect a change in an addictive pattern without
specific attention being paid to that pattern in the
therapy. Secondly, Diana's businesslike presentation
indicated that she would respond to concrete interventions that would enable her to see results, positive or
negative, quickly. Her resistance to being told what to
do stayed in the back of my mind as I formulated
specific tasks for her to do. She would have to understand my rationale and agree with my suggestions;
there would be no following my lead with blind faith for
Diana!

The first step in arriving at strategies is to make sure
that the client is fully conscious of both the wish to quit
drinking and the wish to drink. Too often people
catalogue the list of reasons to quit when they are

suffering the negative consequences of a recent drinking episode, only to repress those reasons as the episode fades over time and the positive associations return to consciousness. Developing a Decisional Balance, or a Motivational Balance (Miller and Rollnick, 1991, Prochaska and DiClemente, 1992), allows the client to list both the positive and negative consequences of a decision to quit drinking (or using any substance). Diana was easily persuaded that this was a worthwhile exercise and produced an interesting profile that I asked her to keep with her at all times:

QUIT DRINKING

Pro	Con
My eyes won't be puffy.	I'll be lonely.
I won't age as quickly and men will find me attractive.	I'll be irritable and bitchy and no man will want me.
I'll think more clearly at work.	
I'll be able to do my bills on time.	
I'll spend more time marketing my work.	
I'll have time for my music.	

Diana was encouraged by her realization that she did indeed have reasons to quit drinking that belonged to *her*, that is, not derived from some external critical, punitive person or organization, which was how she viewed Alcoholics Anonymous. I was concerned that her looks and the issue of aging seemed a primary motivating force, but this was not the time to remind her that she, like all of us, will get old and wrinkly if lucky enough to live that long! There would be time for that issue to surface over and over again and for me to choose a time for confrontation and exploration of her fears and prejudices. In the short run, this Decisional Balance would provide a critical tool for helping Diana deal with her urges to drink.

Most drinkers who are highly functional at work have critical times during the day, or certain days of the week, when drinking is most likely to begin. These times constitute psychophysiological triggers for alcohol cravings that result in a failure to assess the danger objectively. The person is unable to search for coping mechanisms to resist the urges. Critical time periods were easy to establish for Diana because she rarely thought about drinking during the day at work. As she described it, she would find herself driving home and would automatically go to her favorite wine store. Sometimes she was aware as she left work that she felt like she deserved a reward for a hard day's work. Never did she argue with herself about whether she should drink or not. Her resolve of the morning not to drink again had disappeared.

I asked Diana to walk me through the steps from leaving her office to arriving home with a bottle. As she described each segment of the trip, I offered a rule that she could impose on herself. The primary rule was: *Stop what you are doing and read your decisional balance sheet.*

This alternative behavior pattern was meant to stop the automatic processes that ended in Diana being at home drinking wine. We broke down her usual pattern into many steps, each of which could be interrupted by employing the basic rule to stop and read her balance sheet; leaving the office, taking the preferred travel route, pulling into the parking lot of wine shop, picking up a bottle, paying for it, driving home, opening the bottle, drinking the first sip, continued drinking. Diana felt quite confident that she could stop herself up to the point of paying for the bottle. She believed that once she got that far into the process, she was doomed to go home and drink uncontrollably. We began to focus on the earlier stages, counting on her motivation and confidence to increase her chances of success.

INITIAL SUCCESSES

Diana quickly used this strategy to stop herself from drinking. Almost from the first day, she was successful in keeping herself out of the wine store even though at times she actually drove into the parking lot. However, she followed her rule to stop while in the car and read over her decisional balance sheet. This helped her in two ways: She was reminded that she really did have reasons why she didn't want to drink, and it placed a time delay that enabled her to marshal other coping mechanisms. These, in turn, offered clues about her internal dynamics. In order to stop her behavior she would sometimes chastise herself for being immature. Other times she would remind herself that she really wanted to go to the gym or go home and play the piano. Still other times she told herself that she could drink any time she chose; today just wasn't the day. Diana alternated between self-criticism, scaring herself about the ravages of alcohol-related aging, and firm confidence that she could handle this problem. She saw all of these strategies as worthwhile. I was impressed with the amount of self-loathing that Diana could turn to her advantage. I was also, however, nervously waiting for her to turn those feelings against herself, derailing her attempts to take better care of herself.

Over the next few months Diana continued to improve. She rarely drank after work or on weekends. When she did, she was able to see clearly how she let herself violate her decision. She told me that she could hear this voice inside her head saying "Who do you think you are? You can't tell me what to do!" Diana looked at me with a sheepish expression when relating these incidents. She would apologize for her "bad behavior" and berate herself for being so immature. She seemed concerned that she might be rebelling against me and was surprised when I asked her, "Who are you talking to right now?" She blinked a few times and said "Well, my mother."

Diana: Early on in therapy I became aware of a particularly pervasive pattern in my drinking behavior. I would go through several days of not drinking at all and would then report this achievement to Patt in my next therapy session. Almost as soon as the words were out of my mouth, I would begin to smell and taste a glass of wine. Then I would stop at a liquor store on the way home from therapy, buy a bottle, and go off the wagon. It was much like a tiny cloud that appears on the horizon of a clear sky, and an hour later has evolved into yet another day of rain.

This pattern did not occur just sometimes, but always. It was as if as soon as the words of my progress were out of my mouth, another voice inside me was saying, "Oh, you think you're so smart? Well, I know just what you really are, and you're not going to get away with this. We're going to drink tonight, so get used to it."

Whose voice was this? It always had its way with me, and I continued to be bewildered by its power over my choices. I had no freedom of choice in this situation, and always surrendered to its demand to drink until I passed out. Countless times I would wake up at 2:00 A.M. to the test pattern on TV, turn it off, and then crawl into bed and another sleepless night.

In therapy it became apparent that this voice was almost certainly my mother's. She had spoken to me in the same tones many times throughout my early childhood, always in an attempt to control my behavior and shape me into what she thought I should be. The

*message was "You're just like your father when you (do
that) (say that) (make that face)." By all objective standards my father really was a jerk, and early on he
became a symbol to me of all that was bad and
unworthy of love. To be told continuously that I was just
like him taught me to control the expression of any and
all negative feelings. They were simply buried, but of
course could not be eliminated.*

Diana had never seen herself as rebellious as an
adult, although she often longed to rebel when she was
quite young. Her anger at being controlled was buried
at a very young age and did not even surface during
adolescence. Only now, when desperate to control her
own destructive behavior, did this conflict emerge and
threaten to derail her treatment. By restricting my
focus, I almost missed the opportunity to help her deal
with it.

INTERVENING LIFE EVENTS

Throughout the first few months of treatment, I attempted to focus the sessions on Diana's drinking
behavior and her efforts to remain abstinent. I was
tempted to see any other topic as a distraction from the
work at hand. She would often introduce topics about
work or her previous relationship with Matt, who still
called occasionally. It wasn't until Diana met a new
man, Mark, that I realized that she had *not* uncovered
significant psychological dynamics in her previous
therapy. She was displaying behaviors and feelings
that would derail this new relationship as surely as her
treatment was threatened by the narrow focus that I
had defined.

*Diana: Six months into therapy a gift came into my
life. His name was Mark. I had met him the previous fall
when I was still involved with Matt. I found him physically attractive, but far too stiff and arrogant to be of*

*any interest. In any case, a friend of mine, Mary, was
seeing him and I gave him no more thought.*

It was not entirely true that Diana gave Mark no
more thought. In fact, she was a frequent guest at
parties given by her friend Mary. When she told me
that she had started a relationship with him that
would have to remain secret, I decided that the therapy
needed to shift to help Diana see how her underlying
feelings and conflicts were impacting her relationships. It would be difficult to shift the focus of the
treatment from alcohol to relationships and even more
difficult, I thought, to begin confronting Diana on
acting out feelings that she had only a dim awareness
of.

*Diana: There were a couple of tough revelations that
Patt insisted upon. My "meeting" Mark that first night
was no accident, but planned. I had decided to get even
with the not-so-good friend who had been interested in
him by seducing him away from her. I had no intentions
of ever telling Mary about this, but the desire for revenge
made me decide to do it as a lark. That I ended up
falling in love with him came as a complete surprise.*

After hearing Diana tell me about her planned revenge, I realized that she was not, at least in this
instance, unaware of her angry feelings toward her
girlfriend. She revealed, in fact, a long pattern of feeling
put down by Mary but offering no protest. It was
difficult for her to admit that she had wanted to hurt
Mary by her actions. Diana experienced a kind of guilt
that was more self-loathing than feeling empathy for
the other person. With much discussion in therapy,
Diana came to see her behavior as motivated by angry
feelings that she had a responsibility to communicate
but hadn't. Her extreme difficulty acknowledging her
negative feelings without self-hatred and expressing
them assertively became a central theme in her
therapy from this point on.

CHANGING THE FOCUS FROM ALCOHOL TO RELATIONSHIPS

Less than six months into the therapy, I realized that my attempt to separate alcohol from the rest of Diana's life had resulted in a brief period of success for her, followed by relapses that were confusing for both of us. Her initial ability to use the behavioral strategies to control her automatic drinking behavior deteriorated to the point that she was drinking almost as often as before therapy. Her relationship with Mark was going very well and she was preoccupied with issues that arose during their times together. She held a rigid belief that any display of negative emotion was unladylike and would drive him away. She also remembered her mother's teachings about relating to men: Never tell them the truth about yourself. It was clear to me that the pressures of hiding her true feelings and becoming intimate with a man for the first time in her life while trying to manage her drinking were overwhelming to her. Despite her relapses, I chose to shift the therapeutic emphasis to the importance of dealing directly with her feelings with Mark.

Diana: Luckily for us I was also seeing Patt. Many times I would tell her something about myself that was less than appealing, that I felt I had to hide from Mark. Her response was always to get me to do the hard thing, to tell him about whatever it was that I was trying to hide. Another of the imperfections I finally admitted to him was that I drank too much. This did not seem to be a problem for him. It continued to plague me, however. I spent four nights a week with him, drinking two or three glasses of wine at dinner. The other three nights I would spend alone, drinking a bottle a night as I had for many years. Overall, however, I was drinking a lot less than I had in most of my adult years.

Diana had indeed returned to a previous style of drinking. She also became ambivalent about her desire to be abstinent and talked more about wanting to be a social drinker. She saw the two glasses of wine when she was with Mark as an indication that she could be "normal." The fact that Mark was a regular, if moder- ate, drinker and didn't really understand that alcohol was a serious problem for her made it hard for her to settle on a decision. Rather than engage in a struggle with Diana about moderate drinking versus absti- nence, I decided to help her do whatever she thought was best for her. This stance has since become the cornerstone of my work with people who suffer with addictions. At the time, however, it felt like leaping from a cliff, abandoning standard treatment protocol for an experiment with self-control and individual liberties.

The first step in this phase of treatment was to get Diana to articulate a clear goal regarding her drinking. These discussions invariably led to her fears of prema- ture aging and losing sexual attractiveness to Mark if she continued drinking. She worried about gaining weight and losing his interest. The internal battle that had been set up by her mother was now taking place on the center stage of her life. Her question was whether or not she could just be herself (whoever that was!) or whether she had to continue to hide and lie in order to be loved.

Diana: After going through therapy with Dr. Denning, I can look back and know that my ten-year affair with Matt was as intimate a relationship as I could handle at the time. I was always at my best for Matt, never showing anger or asking for anything significant. How hard is it to be charming for two hours a week? I tried to be the best Diana I could be. We never fought. I would capitulate in an instant. I thought this was the way it was supposed to be. Fighting was unfeminine, and no man would want to marry a woman who fought (Moth- er's teaching persisted).

Despite her real-time relationship with Mark, Matt continued to try to persuade her to start up their affair again. Whenever Diana was frustrated with Mark, the temptation was almost irresistible. Matt was every-thing that Mark was not; he was instantly charming, witty, and totally unavailable. While discussing her father one session, Diana told me that she always fantasized as a child that her real father was Clark Gable or Cary Grant, a man with a normal personality, unlike her eccentric father. I asked if Matt was like that for her. Diana realized that her attachment to Matt was primarily motivated by her wish to have a wonderful father who would sweep into town after a business trip and treat her like a queen. This realization had an effect like a thunderbolt. Diana lost her compulsion toward Matt and has never since been tempted by his flirting. From then on, Diana characteristically reacted the same way throughout the treatment. Once she uncovered feelings or motivations that helped her make sense of herself, she was liberated to act in ways that she had been too fearful of in the past.

Diana: Through the following months of therapy, we revisited my childhood, youth, marriage, and ensuing years. I became aware of why I feared and avoided real intimacy. My deepest conviction was that I did, after all, take after my father—that Mother was right. I feared most falling in love with someone who would then discover that, like my father, I was ill-tempered, mean, selfish, humorless, and no fun to be with. As I saw it there would be no room for his acceptance of me, warts and all. He would instead reject me and send me into an even darker place. Repeatedly I was pleasantly surprised to find out that Mark still loved me even after he heard about the real me and had to deal with my moods. It should not have been such a surprise. After all, I was aware of his imperfections and still loved him, so why shouldn't it be the other way? Intimacy was now possible for me.

Diana continued to gain insight into her fears of intimacy and to practice many "confessions" to Mark. She began to see clear links between her anger and her drinking. She continued to drink, however. She would go through periods of drinking a couple of glasses of wine only with Mark and abstaining the rest of the time. This was how she wanted to be. Her occasional solitary binges were always precipitated by some event that angered and/or humiliated her. She easily identified the source of her feelings the next day in the midst of a terrible hangover and marveled that she could remain hidden to herself. Her ability to reflect during the emotional crises did not improve quickly and her drinking bouts, though not as frequent, were still problematic.

THE FINAL LINK: THE EXPERIENCE OF AFFECT

Diana: I became aware that acknowledging success in controlling my drinking was not the only thing that could trigger a binge. A more common one was that something bad would happen during the day, eliciting in me a negative feeling that had to be controlled before it got out. Work stress, anger at Mark for something he had done, anger at just about anything, grief at hearing about something that broke my heart. All of them were there from time to time, but I hadn't a clue as to their existence at the time they were happening. I simply drank them down and then pondered the next day (now with a hangover) what had triggered the binge. There always was a reason, and I learned to identify whatever it was, albeit a day too late. Through therapy I learned to identify these triggers, finally reaching a point where I could recognize them and let them come out, before I could get to a bottle. I learned that they were just feelings, bad but bearable, each of them normal in certain circumstances.

Diana's difficulty recognizing her feelings is typical of people with drug or alcohol problems. In fact, problems with affective experience are often the most obvious therapeutic issue once the behaviors of drug or alcohol use are set aside (Morgenstern and Leeds, 1993). There are four typical problems associated with affective experience: recognizing, modulating, expressing, and accepting (tolerating) various feeling states. In the most serious cases, the person has a kind of alexithymic condition, unable to put words to affective states that are experienced more as bodily sensations than as true emotions. This was not, however, Diana's difficulty. Once aroused, sometimes in the throes of a hangover, her feelings came alive for her. She was able to articulate her feelings with an intensity that was astonishing for someone who appeared so unaware of her internal life.

Neither was modulation of affect a problem for Diana, although she was deeply worried that her feelings were "too much." In fact, she displayed clear, intensely experienced feelings, always appropriate to the situation. She was, however, seriously hampered in her ability to express and accept her feelings, most notably feelings of anger, disappointment, and hate. She was uncomfortable also with the more tender feelings of love and concern. Diana's behavior reflected these deficits. In professional situations she often avoided assertive confrontation with clients and attempted to win points by flattery and a show of acquiescence. Sometimes she was unable to win her point in such an indirect way and the project suffered as a result. More often, however, her business dealings were marked by a cooperative attitude and modulated competitiveness.

It was primarily in one-to-one intimate relationships that Diana's problem with affect caused problems. In such interpersonal relationships, particularly with men, Diana consistently hid her true feelings, obeying her mother's warnings not to be too honest with any man. She rarely asserted her own wishes, praised the other person for being smart, sensitive, and so forth, while plotting indirect ways to get what she wanted.

This passivity invariably led to feelings of anger, disappointment, and disgust with the relationship. Diana would then long to flee from the man rather than talk directly. She would often run to wine to comfort herself or to dilute her angry feelings.

Diana's ongoing relationship with Mark provided her with an excellent practice field for new behaviors. Mark provided a stability, tolerance, and emotional equanimity that would prove essential for Diana to feel secure enough to express scary needs and feelings. Often I suggested that Diana share with Mark a particular need and helped her formulate the words to ask for what she wanted. Other times I would push her to own up to her anger over something he had done. She often looked at me with fear and said, "I can *say* that?" Diana had no idea, no model for how two people could communicate and negotiate a life together. She had spent her life hiding her feelings, denying any needs for dependency and nurturing. The cost for her was enormous in emotional isolation and alcohol dependence. With Mark, she has learned to speak up for herself, and allow herself the freedom to feel and express a wide range of needs and feelings. She is an intense person, a polar opposite of Mark who, while accepting of her, shows little of himself.

Diana came to accept that a kind of dualism had ruled her life. Her real self was a composite of the child who was both needy and independent. She suppressed her needs in relationships and ended up feeling alone. She tried to couch her independent spirit in a softer veil of passivity and built up a storehouse of anger and resentment. She could not be herself for fear of being like her father, and she could not be her mother's daughter because she possessed a drive and independence that her mother lacks. Diana continued to work on these issues and continued to struggle with her use of alcohol as a defense against expressing feelings.

Diana: Throughout much of the therapy I felt a continual ambivalence about whether or not to quit alto-

gether. Patt had me make a pro–con list of the positive and negative sides to continuing to drink, and another list of benefits/losses of not drinking at all. I went on and off the wagon many times, and (to continue the metaphor) most of the time ran alongside it. I was always about ready to almost be about ready to quit but couldn't seem to make the permanent leap. I hoped to quit for a year and then resume drinking in a controlled, moderated way. Patt really pushed for me to quit for a year. Three months into abstinence I fell into a deep depression. I had expected to feel better off the booze, but I actually felt worse. I remember thinking at the time that if I was going to feel this way for the rest of my life, I wasn't sure I wanted to be around for it. Patt had little trouble convincing me that it was time for some meds.

The occurrence of a major depressive episode is not uncommon in women who have spent a lifetime drinking. Despite alcohol being a central nervous system depressant, it often has significant antidepressant effects in women. Alcohol interacts with both the estrogen system and the dopamine system in ways that are just now being studied. In clinical practice, it is not unusual to find women who develop depressive symptoms after periods of abstinence. Whether they were medicating a preexisting depression or if the alcohol had created changes in these systems over time is not known. Once a full depressive syndrome emerges, however, quick relief must be sought in order to avoid a relapse. I referred Diana to my psychiatric consultant for a medication evaluation with a recommendation that she try Wellbutrin, an antidepressant that has dopaminergic effects. I have noticed that this medication often offers significant relief to women with alcohol problems.

Diana: Both Patt and Dr. P. warned me that the meds might have no effect at all. For me the results were quite dramatic, coming on much more quickly than I had expected. Within a few days I was feeling better than I ever had in my life, leading me to wonder if I hadn't been a little depressed since childhood. I was becoming more of my true self. It was as if a part of me had been buried all these years, just out of reach. It sometimes seemed that I had gotten as far as I had with one hand tied behind my back. Now both were free!

The medications allowed Diana to address her problems more directly and with a determined swiftness. Her drinking decreased dramatically, and she began talking about the place of alcohol in her life. She was able to accept that she enjoyed drinking and was resistant to giving it up. Before, whenever she acknowledged her fondness for wine, this acknowledgment contained the self-hatred that she reserved for her most hidden self.

Diana: I think the reason I failed to make the permanent leap was that it involved engaging in a battle; implicit within this was the idea of a dualistic self in which consciousness triumphed over unconsciousness, will power over anarchy, good over evil. I realized that this battle, in fact, was a continuation of what I had learned in early childhood about denying all negative feelings. Only after becoming fully conscious of all that I am, owning it and finally becoming whole, could I change my drinking permanently.

Diana explored the meaning of alcohol in her life, growing more comfortable with the idea that she did not have to quit entirely in order to be a good girl, and that moderate drinking did not make her a bad girl. She continues to fight the urge to react passively to situations and is rewarded with increased closeness in her relationship to Mark and increased success in her business. She does not always have an easy time drinking only one or two glasses of wine (her new rule for herself). The combination of emotional and physiological reactions that make her vulnerable to alcohol's effects will probably always be with her. Diana and I had one final intense interaction that seemed to solidify her resolve to control her drinking because she wanted to take care of the good life she had finally created.

Diana: The final change occurred when I told Patt that I would quit drinking for a while to "save my looks." She immediately confronted me, saying that this was not a good enough reason and that it was bound to fail as surely as I was bound to grow old someday. This upset and angered me greatly. I went home and got royally drunk that night. Because I hadn't been drinking much, the hangover was excruciating. I thought about what had triggered this binge and why I should quit. I stepped back, back as far as I could and took a look at my life and drinking. The rest of my life is as good as it gets. Career, love, music are all in place. Getting drunk alone because I have bad feelings has no place in this life. I don't want to be so alone anymore.

Diana showed great strength and honesty in her struggle with alcohol. Like many people with drug or alcohol problems, she was able to engage in treatment and make significant changes even in the midst of an active addictive process. My acceptance of her ambivalence and the range of her feelings and needs provided the counter to a childhood of restraint and criticism. She was allowed to define her own success. We became a therapeutic team, always standing up for her right to be whoever she discovers herself to be.

Diana: When I first came to Patt my goal was to become a moderate, social drinker. Many, many sessions later I have become all the things that it took to become that, and have gained a whole self in the process. Solo drinking was a symptom, a way of coping with adversity because it was the only way I knew how—a half self can't do much better than that.

Commentary by Andrew Tatarsky

Diana came for help for a twenty-year-long drinking problem that she had been unable to successfully address in a prior ten-year-long psychotherapy. When she initially consulted Patt, she "announced that she was an alcoholic" and said that she didn't want to stop drinking although she knew she "had to quit."

As the story unfolds we learn how her drinking was related to problems with a harsh inner critic in several ways.

She had grown up with a highly critical, controlling mother and a selfish, aloof, ill-tempered father. Idealizing her mother, she tried to gain her attention and love by "acting like a little lady." This meant controlling and suppressing those needs, attributes, and feelings that were unacceptable to her mother. She buried her intelligence, rebelliousness, needs, and anger, eventually losing touch with these feelings, all the while secretly believing herself to be the "bad angry girl" she had internalized from her mother's voices. Here we see how the true self comes to be denied by voices of the parent and remains buried beneath a false persona, continually misperceived as secret badness by the inner critic.

As Diana grew older she "swallowed her feelings (with food) and washed them down with alcohol." Here, excessive eating and drinking were done in the service of submission to her mother's demands, and the inner critical voice acted as mother's representative in her inner life. She suppressed her feelings and controlled herself by drinking to symbolically please mother.

Diana's excessive drinking also expressed her wish to rebel against her mother and inner critic because she drank for pleasure and in order to forget about being a good overly conscientious girl; she simultaneously expressed her anger at being controlled as a child. Drinking enabled her to stop being the good little lady, always trying to please mother/critic. It allowed her to think about her own forbidden needs and feelings, which were selfish in the eyes of the mother/critic. She could temporarily be free of the tyranny of the inner voice by quieting it with alcohol. Her over-drinking was simultaneously and paradoxically a rebellion against the critic's control and a form of self-punishment that reflected the critic's revenge.

This drive to be free of the controlling inner critic coexists with the drive to buy into the critic's self-punishment. This is the self-defeating bind or solution negotiated by compulsive substance use.

THE THERAPY

The first phase of therapy with Patt focused on supporting Diana's initial abstinence goal by suggesting several cognitive-behavioral techniques, including the "decisional balance sheet" and a strategy for applying it to interrupt Diana's typical nightly binge pattern.

These techniques help to clarify conflicting feelings on both sides of the impulse to use a drug; they support the development of skills to observe thoughts, feelings, behaviors, and external circumstances surrounding the impulse. One learns to "sit with" the impulse and interrupt the "automatic" nature of the habit and to consider other options. These are the basic elements that go into conscious behavior changing.

Patt based her initial strategies on fitting them to Diana's "no nonsense" personality style and to Diana's rebellion against authority. We later hear how Diana's initial desire to stop was a form of submission to the critic's demands. Patt's willingness to tailor her approach to Diana's needs enabled them to form an alliance together in the therapy, the essential ingredient. It enabled them to discover together that Diana's difficulty stopping drinking was complex, necessitating a more thorough exploration about the personal meaning of her drinking, which is a prerequisite for change.

This shift in therapy focus came about because Diana's initial six-month success in abstinence was followed by a return to her original drinking pattern. Rather than seeing this as a failure, Patt and Diana were able to see it as suggesting the need to rethink Diana's goal concerning her drinking and to shift and deepen the focus of the therapy.

Here again, as in the other stories, we see the therapist attempting to meet the client where she is in order to establish the alliance.

I've found that many clients like Diana realized that the cognitive, behavioral, self-management, skill-building approach is not enough. It is necessary to delve into the meaning of the substance use. An integrative approach brings together skill development, a cognitive-behavioral approach, with a search for the psychospiritual roots of the problem, the psychodynamic approach to substance use. For many people, the cognitive-behavioral focus can set the stage for the search for meaning. As we set goals and learn the skills for reaching them, we more readily see that there may be forces (dynamics) that prevent us from achieving the goals.

Diana's primary goal was abstinence, which evolved to her ultimate goal of stable, moderate drinking. It was the voice of Diana's inner critic that initially demanded total abstinence from wine, and not the voice of her authentic and true will. Diana's difficulty in achieving abstinence was that this demand could not be enforced by her inner critic, from whom she was continuously rebelling. She could not ultimately submit to the will of her inner critic, but would have to locate her true will and alignment with that true will to create conditions for wholeness and health in moderation.

Her way of getting out from under the submission/rebellion problem was to give herself permission to pursue controlled moderate drinking as a goal. After giving herself this permission, she was successful at achieving and maintaining stable moder-ate drinking. This shift seemed to enable her to identify her own goals and to find motivation and power to exercise her ability to take better care of herself by limiting her drinking. This success supports the understanding of her excessive drinking as reflecting a symbolic rebellion against the inner critic.

References

Alexander, B. K. (1987). The disease and adaptive models of addiction: A framework evaluation. *Journal of Drug Issues*, 17(1): 47–66.

Fenichel, Otto. (1945). Dynamics of addiction. In *The Psycho-analytic Theory of Neurosis*, pp. 375–380. New York: W.W. Norton and Company, Inc.

Freud, S. (1896). Further Remarks on Neuropsychoses of Defense. *The Standard Edition of the Complete Psychological Works of Sigmund Freud*, V-III, p. 170, pp. 162–185. London: The Hogarth Press.

Horn, J. L., Wanberg, K. W., and Foster, F. M. (1987). *Guide to the Alcohol Use Inventory.* Minneapolis: National Computer Systems.

Krystal, Henry (1977). *Self and Object Representations in Alcoholism and Other Drug Dependence: Implications for Therapy in Psychodynamics of Drug Dependence.* Research Monograph 12, pp. 88–100. National Institute of Drug Abuse.

Morganstern, J. and Leeds, J. (1993). Contemporary psychoanalytic theories of substance abuse: A disorder in search of a paradigm. *Psychotherapy,* 30(2), pp. 194–206.

Prochaska, J. O., DiClemente, C. C., and Norcross, J. C. (1992). In search of how people change: Applications to addictive behaviors. *American Psychologist,* 47: 1102–1114.

Sullivan, H. S. (1953). *Conceptions of Modern Psychiatry.* New York: W. W. Norton and Company.

Winnicott, D. W. (1965). *The Maturational Process and the Facilitating Environment.* New York: International Universities Press.

9

The Healing Power of Groups and the Residential Therapeutic Community

Ms. E.: A Study in Success and Mutual Transformation
—Barbara Wallace

Residential treatment has been one of the most recommended modalities for the remediation of substance use disorders since the end of the nineteenth century. Many professionals and laypeople firmly believe that residential treatment is required in most cases of addiction, at least in the initial phases of treatment when the focus is on detoxification and establishing abstinence from drugs and alcohol. This position is described in a paper called "Alcoholism as Chronic Suicide," written by psychoanalyst Karl Meninger in 1938. He says, "Most persons addicted to alcohol are too 'far gone,' too far removed from the reality principle, to be treated . . . under ordinary circumstances. . . . In other words, they must be treated in a specially adapted environment, and for practical purposes this means that they should be confined, and opportunities for alcohol must be removed from availability" (p. 97).

This was a dominant position in the field up until the late 1980s, when financial concerns about the high cost of residential treatment led to extensive reevaluation of its effectiveness. The result of this reevaluation was essentially that residential treatment did not show success rates justifying it as the best available practice for addicted people. These findings led to a renewed interest in outpatient options.

When the intensive outpatient program was born, there was a renewed interest in individual and group therapies practiced in outpatient settings. I believe there are a number of compelling reasons why outpatient treatment is actually more appropriate and effective for most substance users. In short, outpatient treatment affords the client the opportunity to confront challenging situations and associated feelings that are provoked by the environment in which use takes place.

In spite of this, residential treatment remains an important and, in many cases, life-saving option for that group of substance users who, for numerous reasons, have not been able to make effective use of outpatient treatment, self-help support groups, or individual treatment.

The modern era of residential treatment for substance users began in the 1960s with the development of long-term residential therapeutic communities (TC) beginning with and modeled after Synanon. Synanon was the first residential therapeutic community and the model for modern therapeutic communities such as Daytop Village, Phoenix House, and Project Return. The program was founded by Charles Deiderich in the early 1960s to treat heroin addicts who were not accepted at Alcoholics Anonymous meetings at the time. Synanon used intense aggressive encounter groups run by program graduates and strict rules and harsh discipline in an effort to teach residents how to manage their feelings constructively and function drug free in society. Since then, the residential therapeutic community has been one of the most interesting, powerful, and controversial treatment modalities for substance users. Many of those developed in the 1960s still thrive today, including Phoenix House, Daytop Village, Project Return, and Oddessey House.

Therapeutic communities have had a controversial history, in large part because of their reputation for using harsh confrontation and humiliation as part of the therapeutic approach. This was believed to be necessary in an effort to break down the addict's tough self-protective defenses. These defenses are considered forms of protection against the feelings of emotional pain. It is also presumed that these defenses block the participant's ability to take in help from others and to learn other, more effective ways of taking care of themselves.

In part, the very strength of TCs may have contributed to this overly confrontational style. The therapeutic community emerged at a time when there was very little professional treatment available to people with substance use problems. Like Alcoholics Anonymous, it was developed originally on a peer model by ex-addicts. The strength of this is that many users feel less stigmatized and more immediately understood by others who have experienced problems similar to their own. This can go a long way toward creating the sense of safety necessary for change to begin. However, unresolved issues of the ex-user also tend to reestablish themselves, which can confound and cloud the therapeutic process. Many people who develop problems with substances have harsh inner critics. This harsh, punitive conscience or superego is often expressed as a lack of compassion for oneself and a tendency to become angry at oneself when failing to live up to one's own expectations. This can also be turned around toward others who fail to meet expectations. It is likely that an incomplete resolution of the harsh, punitive inner critic in many of the founders of the therapeutic community movement led to the institutionalization of harsh confrontation in its treatment approach.

Confrontation is an intervention in psychotherapy that consists of reflecting something back to someone about himself about which he is unaware. It may be a necessary part of helping people to see themselves more clearly, but it may be very difficult for a person to hear when delivered without empathy. There is no doubt that many therapeutic community participants over the years found this approach helpful toward personal breakthroughs, enabling them to give up this hard shell of self-protective but self-limiting defenses. Many others experienced it as abusive. Some stayed and were hurt by the process; others developed stronger defenses against the attacks and left without their deeper issues being addressed; and others, in acts of self-affirmation, left the TC to protect themselves. The problem was not the approach itself, but that it tended to be applied somewhat indiscriminately without sufficient regard to emotional differences among the diverse group of people with substance use problems.

Over the years, therapeutic communities have matured, generally incorporating a higher level of professionalism into their approach. There is greater attention given to individual differences in participants' needs and emotional vulnerabilities and a better understanding of who is a good candidate for the TC. In the early days of drug treatment, therapeutic communities were the only game in town; this is no longer the case.

In the therapeutic community the participant is removed from his normal routine and placed in a highly structured environment in which almost every aspect of his life is closely regimented and scrutinized by the community. The participant is offered the TC's philosophy of life; a clear set of rules, conditions, and consequences governing daily life; and assigned roles within the community. There is also frequent, intensive group and large community therapy designed to process all the issues that participants must face as they struggle to maintain drug-free status and adapt to life in the community. The TC is designed to be a microcosm of the real world. With the effort at making it successfully in the therapeutic community, comes the possibility of preparation for the real world. This effort is done with a diverse range of support.

Aside from helping the participant to learn to cope effectively without the need for drugs, the therapeutic community also aims to address the variety of different emotional, attitudinal, and personality problems related to drug use. This includes learning to manage feelings; changing problematic attitudes and behaviors, particularly those that interfere with getting one's needs met in relationships; and developing greater ability to tolerate frustration and to control impulses.

Historically, the typical stay in a therapeutic community was eighteen to twenty-four months, with additional involvement afterward as an outpatient. Today, TC treatment is generally much more brief, from three months to a year, although longer-term treatment can still be found. Shorter treatment has become the more popular modality because it is less expensive, more attractive to individuals seeking treatment, and as effective statistically as long-term treatment once had been.

The value of the therapeutic community is grounded in the power of groups and community to heal. Just as our families and communities contributed to our suffering in our formative years by failing to meet our needs, healing groups have the power to repair the damage by offering opportunities for new, positive outcomes as alternatives to the earlier traumatizing ones.

Once the participant has met the community's criteria for success by adapting to daily life and by addressing personal issues related to substance abuse, the participant moves into a phase of treatment designed to facilitate transition back into the outside world.

Therapeutic communities are generally a good option to consider for people whose substance use has become seriously problematic and who are not able to benefit from less intensive, outpatient treatment. Those who benefit most from TCs are frequent substance users with intensive, compulsive, or out-of-control habits developed over such long periods of time that the habits are intertwined into life patterns. People whose substance use and related problems have impaired the foundation of their lives find support that they haven't had in the way of family, friends, employment, housing, or basic life structure.

As the story in this chapter by Barbara Wallace illustrates, many therapeutic community participants are people who have experienced severe trauma either earlier in their lives as children or in the context of more recent substance use. In these cases, the substance use and related activities are often being used to ward off the pain and memories associated with trauma. The safety, structure, and support of a TC may be uniquely able to create the conditions necessary for the user to feel safe enough to begin the arduous, painful process of healing these traumas. This is discussed in more depth in my commentary after Wallace's story.

The story in this chapter illustrates the kind of life-transforming power that the therapeutic community approach can have for people. The case of Ms. E., by Barbara Wallace, shows the contemporary TC at its best. Ms. E. is a woman who had a childhood history of severe sexual and physical abuse before developing a ten-year-long addiction to crack cocaine. Outpatient treatments failed to help her before she was court-mandated to Damon House, a TC in New York City where Dr. Wallace worked as a psychologist. Wallace writes about how she and the TC community used a powerful combination of empathy and confrontation in the therapeutic approach that helped Ms. E. make profound, lasting changes in herself. Ms. E.'s gains included an ability to connect honestly and authentically with others, while healing severe emotional pain that she had been carrying as a result of the traumatic abuse she suffered as a child. These changes enabled her to go on, with Wallace's ongoing therapeutic support, to maintain sobriety from drugs for more than seven years through the writing of this story.

The story describes the power of community-based healing. It is also a vivid illustration of the depth of despair and traumatic suffering that often lies beneath compulsive substance use, as well as the amazing potential for change that can be delivered by the correct therapeutic approach. In my commentary, I explore some of the important ingredients that contributed to success in the case of Ms. E.

The Case of Ms. E.: A Study in Success and Mutual Transformation
by Barbara C. Wallace

INTRODUCTION

How is it that a 30-year-old African-American mother of two adolescent children may stand with pride and claim more than eight years of abstinence from chemicals, having survived the crack cocaine epidemic in New York City? The ingredients of success in the case of Ms. E. include multiple personal variables she brought to her own recovery, therapeutic factors that I contributed as a psychologist, and systemic factors involving her interactions with several New York City institutions. Ms. E.'s personal factors include her fierce determination, perseverance, and survival instincts, in addition to her openness and trust in the therapeutic process.

Quite simply, when it was time to have courage and to open up and trust, she did so. The therapeutic factors that I contributed include my use of trauma resolution and relapse prevention techniques, described elsewhere (Wallace, 1992, 1995, 1996), as they evolved during three years working with women such as Ms. E. in an intense, three-hour weekly group within a residential therapeutic community setting. Systemic factors include the manner in which Ms. E. was forced to interface with the New York City Bureau of Child Welfare and family court, being mandated to attend outpatient and residential therapeutic community treatment, and the actual availability of New York City's treatment community and 12-step group network. Beyond the combination of multiple personal, therapeutic, and systemic factors, I must also recognize intangible factors that played an important role in her success. Synchronicity, or meaningful coincidences, as defined by Carl Jung, and spirituality as infused and articulated throughout New York City's 12-step support network and treatment community, must also be recognized as key ingredients. This complex mixture of ingredients and the process of healing and transformation that they produced in the life of Ms. E. seem to be directly connected with her living the past seven years of her life as a mother abstinent from chemicals of abuse. This mixture of ingredients also transformed me as a clinician, suggesting a process of mutual transformation.

The details of her transformation constitute the main of this story. My transformation, as an African-American woman who had studied Sigmund Freud and Carl Jung, involved discovering how to be a midwife, a practical source of support and assistance in the process of healing the injuries to the soul and the miraculous process of birthing a new self. I individuated into a self that combined my roots in reading Freud and Jung with roots suggesting an African matriarchal tradition of nurturing. This case study provides me with a unique opportunity to tell Ms. E.'s story, having witnessed the miraculous birth of her new drug-free self. It also provides an overview of the therapeutic processes to which Ms. E. was exposed, the manner in which her history unraveled in treatment, the management of her symptoms within a residential therapeutic community, and my continuing relationship with Ms. E. over several years through my private practice and beyond. In the process, discussion will not only cover the combination of multiple ingredients that played a role in her successful maintenance of abstinence during seven years, but also the nature and dimensions of our mutual transformation as client and clinician.

THE THERAPEUTIC PROCESS IN NEW YORK CITY

In 1990, Ms. E.'s grandfather contacted the Bureau of Child Welfare over concerns for her children, a latency-aged son and daughter at that time. Ms. E. had a prior case for suspected physical abuse of her children and was living in a welfare hotel. In this hotel, she was caught in a cycle of smoking crack and having her welfare identification card held by the drug dealer until "check day," permitting her to smoke the duration of the month on "credit;" the dealer knew he would be able to go with Ms. E. on the first of the month and receive the majority of her check as payment for her month-long crack use. With her grandfather initiating a second investigation into Ms. E. for neglect, Ms. E. entered the New York City system's machinery, being sent to outpatient treatment for her crack cocaine dependence. Ms. E. compiled a record of going to fourteen different outpatient clinics without success. Finally, she was mandated to enter a residential therapeutic community for nine months with her children going into the temporary custody of her mother.

Ms. E. entered the residential therapeutic community, Damon House of New York Inc., in December 1990. My employment as a part-time psychological consultant to this facility had begun in January 1990. The executive director was hoping that I could address the histories of sexual and other abuse that overwhelmed the female counselors, many of whom had the same history of sexual abuse. By the time Ms. E. entered treatment in December 1990, the women and I who shared the space of a weekly three-hour women's group pretty much knew what we were doing. Our therapeutic process evolved its unique form over time in collaboration and dialogue with one another (see Wallace, 1992). Ms. E. was mandated to treatment until September 1991, but elected to remain with the TC, until her treatment was terminated by a crisis in the facility. This led to Ms. E.'s sudden discharge in early March 1992. There were accusations made against Ms. E. of having a romantic involvement with a male peer, and there were some tense interactions with another female client in the facility, with whom I worked and about whom I have written in another case study (see Ms. U. in Wallace, 1993). In this way, Ms. E. experienced fifteen months of residential therapeutic community treatment.

Hence, one element of success that emerges very early in this story is the manner in which clients who are mandated to treatment by family court or the criminal justice system quite typically adapt well to residential therapeutic community treatment. The behavioral change process that Ms. E. experienced brought many rewards, and the process of further behavioral change over time becomes continually reinforcing. It is, therefore, not surprising that, when the date toward which Ms. E. had looked forward—the date when she was no longer mandated and could leave treatment—finally arrived in September 1991, she expressed a commitment to continue treatment in the program.

When we think of the crack cocaine epidemic that spanned the mid-1980s to early 1990s, the explosion of children entering foster care is readily recalled. Stories of children who were taken away from clients later placed in abusive situations and termination of parental rights supposedly occurring without proper notification of clients abound a decade after the height of the crack epidemic. However, as strange as it may seem to some, the system's machinery emerges as deserving of recognition for playing a role in Ms. E.'s successful recovery.

MANAGEMENT OF SYMPTOMS IN A THERAPEUTIC COMMUNITY

I'll never forget the first day I met Ms. E. the first day she attended group at Damon House. The room seems very bright in my mind, almost suggestive of a spring day, although it was winter, warmly foreboding of things positive and hopeful. That first day in group Ms. E. was sitting in the circle toward my right at some distance in the large, spacious group room in which we met. She was well groomed and seemed to have a bright disposition, being very ladylike and feminine, but also very strong and hard. This was someone who seemed able to survive in the street. She spoke loudly and emphatically, almost seeming to yell. The details of her speech mattered less than the impulse to broadcast her presence loudly in the group. She also seemed to be giving a message to the other females in the group and in the residence as a whole that with her apparent strength no one should challenge her. She seemed capable of self-defense, as well as a highly effective preemptive strike.

At first, Ms. E. received the typical psychoeducation, often delivered by other females in the group at my prodding, regarding what the group was all about. This covered members all being from dysfunctional families of one kind or another, with members specifying the nature of their past abuse and trauma. Ms. E. was able to loudly join in and speak about some aspects of her own past, but without affect, as she threw out some facts.

THE FIRST INTERPRETATION: STIMULUS FOR TRANSFORMATION

After a full three months in the group and exposure to much psychoeducation on dysfunctional families and trauma, as well as to other group members undergoing a therapeutic process, an interpretation was created and offered just for Ms. E. The first interpretation delivered to Ms. E. focused on what was apparent about her from the very first day in group, given her loud presence and strength. The first interpretation, or piece of information designed to stimulate her under-standing of the self-protective stance she primarily utilized, was as follows: "You seem to be very hard and strong like a rock on the outside, but I wonder what is going on inside." Giving her some time to listen, hear, and reflect on this interpretation, it was followed up with an expansion of the interpretation: "It's almost like you are a rock with loudspeakers. I wonder about the pain that you have inside." Indeed, she seemed to possess 100-watt loudspeakers from which she broad-cast her verbal pronouncements, while she sat like a hard boulder.

On other occasions in the weeks that followed in months four to five in the group, when her self-protective stance was in full operation, a brief codified form of the interpretation was repeated; it was sometimes delivered with humor. This brief codified form of the interpretation follows: "You're being hard like a rock with loudspeakers." Knowing the full interpretation, with time, Ms. E. could somberly acknowledge what I was trying to tell her and would reflect aloud, stating "I have my pain inside," as the group moved on to other issues.

Always respecting a client's use of a self-protective stance, I had to ask myself a question: "Will she get to the point of being able to talk about, feel, and process her pain, unburdening herself in the group?" Not knowing the answer to this question, and at times fatiguing (both she and myself, as well as the other group members) from her overuse of this hard, rock-like, self-protective stance, a codified form of the interpretation also served to impart an implicitly stated message: "Others want to share today, and you do not seem ready to share. We need to move on and allow others who are ready to process their pain to use time in group," acknowledging our large group size of fifteen to twenty-five women. This subtle message permitted us to move on and give attention and time to such group members. But before moving on, we shared a fleeting moment of deep respect for what Ms. E. was accomplishing in yielding to her pain for even a moment and stating that she had her pain. There were many moments when she sat and was able to tolerate brief moments of being deflated, without the inflation and bravado of her main self-protective stance. Meanwhile, when we did move on to allow other members to use the group, she witnessed others role-modeling how to genuinely talk about their feelings and how other group members and I reached out to them and helped them to process their pain.

This first key interpretation in the Spring of 1991 obviously resonated very deeply with Ms. E., as well as with me, personally. The Spring months served, metaphorically, as a time of new growth for Ms. E. and eventually gave way to a kind of bursting forth that is typical of Spring foliage ending up in full bloom. However, in the case of Ms. E., what was to come after these months of growth was full-blown posttraumatic stress disorder in the Summer of 1991. Her posttraumatic stress disorder reflected the reality that she had experienced past trauma wherein she feared for her own death and perceived it as a possibility. It involved symptoms of having nightmares and flashbacks of her trauma, as well as anxiety. It also frequently led her to isolate herself, seemingly unable to feel any tender and loving feelings. She frequently expressed angry outbursts, was very irritable at times, and also appeared quite depressed.

However, regarding this interpretation, I think it generally proved to be a well-timed interpretation of her main self-protective stance in a safe environment of the group and residential therapeutic community, leading to a metaphoric gradual taking away of the protective encasement in which she wrapped herself.

Another key ingredient in her treatment may also include my turning to a seasoned group member, Ms. S., one who had been in the group for one year, and asking her to tell Ms. E. about how we dealt with histories of trauma and valued the goal of healing from past trauma within the group process. Ms. S. described what other members had gone through, including herself, ending, perhaps most importantly, with volunteering the following: "Trust her. Use the group." Ms. S. also experienced this (as she told me later) as me asking her to reach out and be there for Ms. E., making a connection. It was as if I had "gotten them together" or "joined them" as sisters in the house. Amazingly, Ms. S. not only played this first, early role as a conduit for initiating Ms. E. into the process of trusting the therapeutic process in the group, but also played a central role in another brief, synchronistic moment in time, as we shall see later.

Following the gentle invitation and urging of Ms. S., Ms. E. allowed herself to open up to the group process, to trust her sisters in residence, and me. She exchanged the hard, protective shell of her former rock-like existence and accompanying 100-watt loudspeaker system for the safety net created by the women in the group. The safety net upon which she depended also included my consistent empathic support, as well as the structure of the residential therapeutic community. In giving up her rock-like encasement, she entered a pool of pain, perhaps, more a deep and vast lake of pain, discovering that she did not drown in this pain. In addition, in giving up her loudspeaker system, she found her own inner voice, including that of a little girl traumatized and tortured, speaking in clear, resonant tones about her pain and suffering, as well as giving voice to the pain of a little boy who suffered with her, her brother who was now in jail.

However, she also gave voice to what was almost a collective pain, including the pain of other women in the group who perhaps never survived the magnitude of what Ms. E. had known and never had the capacity to stand with strength, as did Ms. E. with her well-rehearsed rock-like self-protective stance. It is as if the part of her personality that had formed and developed around the long-standing use of the self-protective stance of "being a rock with loudspeakers" also served to give her a genuine strength. Indeed, this may be the essence of what it means to be "street" in one's attitude and behavior, recognizing the inherent positive qualities that are key to survival and having adapted to far-from-ideal situations. Her basically strong and intact ego, with its early capacity to carefully observe the adults around her as a child, knowing how to survive for her sake and that of her brother, emerged in the group process and in moments of trauma resolution as capable of excellent self-observation and sound reporting of the images that were coming back as her

main symptoms of posttraumatic stress disorder. Ms.
E. literally spent a couple of months walking around
and working within the therapeutic community with
full-blown posttraumatic stress disorder, successfully
using the three-hour Friday group to process her
recurrent memories, nightmares, and flashbacks of
trauma and torture.

MS. "E." STANDS FOR "EVERYONE"

Ms. E.'s function in group became quite meaningful as
she embraced the treatment process. She became the
prototype for what the essence of trauma resolution
work in groups is all about. For me, this remains a
profound truth, as I both survey all who have passed
through my groups, passed through my private practice, and sat with me in Tavistok groups. Tavistok
groups present a rather unusual model for learning
about group process and involve small and large group
activities in which a consultant will give impersonal
feedback to the group about the group's behavior as a
whole. The impact of what Ms. E. accomplished in her
group work carried over into my own participation in
such groups as a professional. Somewhat playfully, at
a weekend-long Tavistok large group conference in the
Spring of 1993 I interjected what I had learned from
Ms. E. into the group process. I did this because the
conference theme had shifted to the personal histories
of trauma, violence, rapes, and childhood abuse that
seemed to be coming up in multiple group members. I
offered aloud and poetically the following declaration:
"I am a rock with loudspeakers. But, then, I enter a
pool of pain. I discover I can swim, process my pain,
and swim to other side." This declaration had a powerful impact upon others in the large group. So, on
some level, Ms. E.'s transformation and the final full

interpretation of what she had been through impacted me deeply and taught me a great deal personally, also leading me to trigger a process in others.

This African-American female with a second-grade education who suffered unheard-of trauma and torture in Harlem emerges as a heroine of profound proportions if we measure the power of the stance of one who role-models how to fully process one's pain, arriving on the other side with one's voice able to articulate clearly where one has been, while feeling genuine affects. So many of the middle- and upper-class white adults at the Tavistok conference continued to equivocate, intellectualize, rationalize, even in their small group work, and could not enter the pool of pain, nor trade in their loudspeakers for the process of connecting with their inner voice, or the voice of the abused and traumatized inner human being. In my small group work at the conference, a tearful white woman thanked me for providing the stimulus for her to connect with and to begin to process her sexual abuse trauma, even as I largely drew on what I had learned from Ms. E. In this group I processed the pain of being mentored by a professor in graduate school and then suddenly dropped, feeling symbolically raped in public and violently abused. Hence, for a broad range and varied kinds of trauma, Ms. E. stands for "everyone" on several levels, as she role-models having the ability to trust, to open up, and to fully process pain. Whether middle class and white, educated to the level of the doctorate (as were most Tavistok participants), or poor, African-American and with a second-grade education, certain universals of processing pain emerge from this tale of success.

The strength of African sisters who survived the middle passage and the horrors of slavery seems to be the same strength that allowed Ms. E. to enter her pool of pain with a rare courage. That strength also to enter the group each Friday to guide a therapeutic process of trauma resolution that often left me fatigued on Friday nights and flooded with images of the horror that the week's confessions had displayed. I, too, was Ms. E. on many of those evenings. I sometimes struggled to find the ears of friends who had the strength to tolerate hearing what I had heard, even as I had a need to decompress, share, and heal myself for entrance back into the group the following Friday. I had to be strong enough to "hear with empathy" and to return week after week; I did not have to live it, only relive it with the women in a state of empathy. Sitting in a full room with anywhere from fifteen to twenty-five women, where as many as five or eight were simultaneously reentering the pool of pain associated with sexual abuse, physical abuse, parental alcoholism, or domestic violence, seemed to be something about which Freud and Jung did not write. The strength of African ancestors who had survived much more horror seemed to sustain and propel the group process, as I sat as the benign good enough African mother who worked as a midwife to support other colored sisters through the painful birth of a new self.

THE DETAILS OF A PAINFUL CHILDHOOD

Beyond flowery metaphor, concrete details seem essential to convey the nature of the pain that Ms. E. processed in group. Ms. E. described going hungry in a home in which her alcoholic and heroin-addicted parents neglected her. At some point her mother was out of the picture and weekends became a time for torture at the hands of her father. Punishment was being held high in the air and dropped on the floor, with Ms. E. recalling watching this happen to her brother again and again, as well as experiencing it herself. She could describe how her brother's face would be swollen and distorted from being pummeled by her father's hands.

Then there was her torture of being raped and penetrated by her father every weekend as a young child. She recalls his "busting" her open through intercourse and being taken to the emergency room for stitches, as well as the emergency room workers accepting the lies her father rehearsed with her for her to tell. Even more bizarre and unbelievable is how these emergency room workers accepted the recanting of yet more lies when she returned to the same emergency room the following week because her father had busted open her stitches during her subsequent ritual weekend rape.

The meaning and magnitude of the secrets held by child survivors of abuse also resonates loudly from her story. Ms. E. spoke of being a little girl and only telling her secret to another little girl who lived in her neighborhood; both were being sexually abused by their fathers. In a clear voice resonating with second-generation Southern accent and filled with passion, and as a constant stream of tears gently flowed, she stated, "I held her secret, and she held mine." This truth echoed in the group room as all felt her pain and the horror of what she had somehow miraculously survived. Ms. E. went on to tell how one day this little girl was found dead in the alley with her uterus on her chest. The reality of the death her father regularly threatened effectively cemented Ms. E.'s silence, a silence broken for the first time in the sanctity of our group circle of sisters.

Living between weekends of torture, Ms. E. went to school only to get food for her and her brother. She was expelled from the New York City public school system in second grade for stealing money out of her teacher's pocketbook, needing to use this money for food for herself and her brother. Prior to this expulsion, school had held little good for her, besides access to food, given that she was teased by other children for her appearance and grooming, following from the severe neglect she suffered at home.

MS. E. AS A ROLE MODEL OF DEEP PROCESSING OF PAIN

The most severe forms of neglect and physical, sexual, verbal, and emotional abuse, as well as domestic and street violence, seem to have been integral parts of Ms. E.'s lifelong existence. The depth, nature, duration, and range of her trauma seems to have produced a sufficient pool of pain with characteristics that make her an ideal figure with which "everyone" can identify.

Ms. E. fully processed her pain and her tears fell like rain that spring and summer of 1991, as she role-modeled how to fully process the deepest of pain and most horrific memories of trauma. A loving empathy and profound respect for Ms. E. pervaded the room as she shared her story and came to group week after week to further unfold and share her pain and symptoms. This led to a collective, shared process of other women opening up and sharing their pain. What Ms. E. shared in group served to trigger buried memories in other survivors of rape who began to open up and share. For example, one day in late spring 1991, she was sitting in the circle of the group to my left against the wall at a distance from me and spoke of how for the entire past week her stomach (uterus) had been hurting; she merely interjected this in the middle of processing her pain and the sharing of memories. Another woman in group, the same Ms. U. (Wallace, 1993) mentioned previously, began to wriggle in her chair. I asked, "Ms. U., what's coming up in you now? What are you feeling?" Ms. U. spoke, following this encouragement, explaining how she could feel men's hands groping all over her body. Ms. U. had been kidnapped as an adult, placed in a van, and raped by a group of men, as she briefly explained to the group, joining in the process of trauma resolution. It was suddenly time for me to deliver a piece of psychoeducation about how we have body memories, and both women were experiencing memories stored in their bodies.

What was triggered in other women by Ms. E.'s disclosures also led to months of productive work in group for these other women. By going deep into her pool of pain and sitting engaged in deep, full-body sobs as she spoke of what happened to her, other women learned the process of trauma resolution. They followed her lead, also having material that was deeply buried in the unconscious triggered so that this material could rise to the surface of their own inner pools of pain and became available for conscious processing in the bright light of day. At another point in group in the summer of 1991, Ms. E. shared a dream about lying in bed with her father naked; an actual memory delivered to her from her unconscious. A survivor of rape at age 18, Ms. J. asked Ms. E., "Did you like it?" Suddenly it was time to deliver yet more psychoeducation on identifying with the aggressor. When someone is abused, she witnesses the behavior of the aggressor and tends to memorize details of that behavior. Ironically, despite having been traumatized by an aggressor, the individual who has automatically and without conscious awareness identified with her aggressor can later perform a near-perfect imitation of that aggressive act. One who has identified with his aggressor is now able to repeat the behavior now as the aggressor toward an other. It is as if one who has identified with her aggressor goes on to reverse roles and can take on the role of the aggressor putting someone else in the role of the victim. The rapid delivery of this piece of psychoeduction permitted us to avoid a potentially hot and violent conflict in the group. Group members were reminded of elements of Ms. J.'s trauma and came to understand the roots of the question posed by her. Ms. J. had been raped at age 18 at gunpoint by someone who watched her mother leave the apartment, then rang her apartment door bell, and was standing there holding a gun when she opened the door. Later that day at the police station a police sergeant asked her, "Did you like it?" In this manner, Ms. J. was engaged in a role reversal (Wallace, 1996) wherein she was taking on the role of the police sergeant, revealing how she identified with this aggressor, and placing Ms. E. in the role of the victim in which Ms. J. had been that day in the police station. Hence, the material that Ms. E. brought to the group served to trigger in other women memories that they then shared in group, as well as triggering their adaptive coping stances and self-protective stances such as the role reversal Ms. J. demonstrated with her question. This shows the power of Ms. E.'s memories and symptoms to trigger material that was deeply buried in other women in the group. This meant that we often had to engage in brief psychoeducation to explain what was happening to other group members who had been triggered to respond in varied ways. Sometimes we had to simultaneously and/or consecutively address the pain of individual group members, helping them to resolve and work through their traumatic memories and symptoms. For good reason, on many Friday evenings I was flooded with diverse memories of trauma.

Indeed, there was a broad range of trauma covered by Ms. E. over the course of her fifteen months as a group member. Other trauma included witnessing as a child and adolescent extremely severe domestic violence between her mother and her stepfather; violent physical fights arguments with her mother as an adolescent and young adult; assaulting another woman for her mother and going to prison for a year for this; the murder of the father of her first child, her daughter; and a period of homelessness when she was taken advantage of by an older family member who would only offer her money and temporary lodging in exchange for incestuous sex.

BEYOND THE MANDATE: REMAINING IN TREATMENT

Working hard in group and functioning as a role model for trauma resolution work, Ms. E. successfully ended her mandated nine-month period in the therapeutic community in September 1991, stabilizing considerably and having fully processed those traumatic memories that emerged in the spring and summer months of treatment. The fall of 1991 brought with it stability and accomplishment. The judge decreed that in her new drug-free state she could get her children back, assuming that she had a suitable place to live. In these fall months in the residential therapeutic community, Ms. E. dealt with the resulting practical matters in her life. She spoke of realistic concerns about how her mother was taking care of her children and the judge's willingness to give her children back to her. She struggled with fears associated with resuming parenting of her children, and anxieties about living outside the safe confines of the treatment facility.

Given her concerns about how her mother was caring for her children, Ms. E. also had to work to ensure that she never reverted to the violent arguments that had become commonplace with her mother over past years. She did not agree with her mother's parenting techniques, or lack thereof, despairing that her son had likely been beaten to the point that he had blood in his urine. However, she knew she had to control her temper and what she said to her mother regarding her suspicions of beatings. She had learned what had become a mantra for members of the group who typically struggled with regulation of aggressive impulses: "Violence is not an option." Accepting this, she had to walk away from her mother's home on visits to see her children, especially when she felt dissatisfied with their clothing and appearance, even as she struggled with her ambivalence about when to leave the therapeutic community and resume the parenting role herself.

HONORING SUCCESS AT THE 1991 GRADUATION CEREMONY WITH A POETIC ODE

By late fall 1991, as the possibility of her departure to take over custody of her children hung heavy in the air, a Damon House graduation ceremony was scheduled. Having the opportunity to speak at the graduation, which included many women who had been a part of the Friday women's group, I chose to read a poem written to honor Ms. E. and that served as an ideal graduation message for all departing TC members. This poem ended by explaining how Ms. E. stood for "everyone" who both looks forward to and dreads the family reunification goal with their children. The poem was a powerful reminder to all graduates of what they had learned in the "house" in which they had resided and received treatment, and how they, too, should be prepared for all future tests, drawing upon their new body of knowledge and tools gained in treatment.

A series of key questions that I had to ask myself that fall of 1991 were as follows: "Is it appropriate to share this poem (written in a private moment in which I felt deep emotion and was tearful at my computer) with Ms. E., let alone with a public audience? Is it appropriate to raise this client to the level of being symbolic of everyone? Will I overstimulate the client with my own expression of feelings, as conveyed in the poem?" I took some time in making the decision as to whether or not it was appropriate to share this poem with Ms. E., let alone with a large audience at the TC graduation. But as I examined the poem, I analyzed how it served as a vehicle for my expressing genuine and valid perceptions about the therapeutic group process, as well as served to validate what was, indeed, an extraordinary effort to make progress in treatment on the part of Ms. E. The content of this poem follows:

Our Pride and Love for Ms. E.

It is with pride and love that we behold Ms. E., our
    dear friend,
as her time in women's group is about to come to an
    end.
For, according to the judge's dictate,
she and her children will be reunited under a new
    drug-free state.
She is here before us about to take a stand,
embodying all that is the beautiful, drug-free, Black
    woman.
A magnificent love and such depth to her soul
she does emanate in ways both so soft and so bold.
Her hands embrace her sisters with such love,
even when she must confront them with or without
    "kid gloves."
Ms. E. worries if with her children she will again
    resort to abuse
for her whole life experience is a lesson in its
    overuse.
From rape at her father's hand, to a witness of
    physical torture,
from mother's addiction and abandonment to intense
    food hunger.
She went to school just so she and her brother could
    get food,
fearing weekends when there would be no meals and
    nothing good—
just domestic violence, more rapes, and intense fear
that if she told of her secret torture death would
    come near.
How many times can a soul suffer every conceivable
    abuse?

Why does violence as a solution emerge for common
   daily use?
Can a tortured and injured soul hope that she can
   turn her life around?
Can we replace the doomsday prophecy to which
   such souls are bound?
That mental space where low and negative
   expectations are found—
along with scripts for repeating dramas of family
   dysfunction—
we speak of an internalized set of fateful instruction.
Directions for each new generation to feel pain at
   that junction
where we either chose a path of the old, familiar, and
   same;
or chose another path with directions for a new
   transcendent game.
This new game and script of which I speak
pemits free expression of a creativity which we must
   all seek.
This creative energy permits expression of a God
   potential within.
And our place in the kingdom of heaven on earth we
   finally win.
In this state of grace we break cycles of pain with
   ease.
And surrender violence, compulsions, and chemical
   disease.
Ms. E. has sat with us in group and fully processed
   her pain.
She cried so intensely her tears fell like rain.
Her body sobbed and shook with such somber force
that the depths of her pain became for her group a
   great resource.
'Cause her sisters watched and felt this powerful
   healing process.
And her sisters began to sense that in this role of
   witness

they learned about the path to their own healing
inside,
and, though frightened, tried to open themselves up
more wide
so they, too, could cleanse and heal injuries to their
soul
and dream of that wonderful family reunification
goal.
Looking forward to the day when they, too, can
speak with pride
of school, aftercare treatment, and home with
children inside.
Ms. E., it is with love and an outpouring of faith
that we see you off to join your family and start a
drug-free race.
Remember your feelings, inner voice, and gut should
be your guide.
Remember the lessons of the "house" which you
learned here, inside.
Remember how you were strength, direction, and
gentle correction
to your peers with whom you will always have a
connection.
As we witness your climb up a golden set of stairs,
remember any mistakes or errors can always be
repaired.
Just reach out for support and learn how to pass the
next test,
'cause there will always be another one, after just a
brief rest—
opportunities to grow and learn even more
so we can make it to that great shore.
I speak of a place where we will get that ultimate gift
of being rocked in the arms of God and feeling the
ultimate uplift
when reunited with the one who always loved us so
dear,
even when lying raped, battered, and abandoned
with death near.

So, Ms. E., go out into the world replacing new faith
for old fear.
And never forget the magic therapeutic group
process we did share.
But, as we say a soulful goodbye remember one
thing.
Our intense pride and love for you, Ms. E., makes
our hearts sing!
A poem for Ms. E. who is Everyone who both dreams
of and dreads the
reunification goal with their children.

Written by Barbara Wallace 9/28/91

To the extent that so much about Ms. E.'s story
reaches a collective level, I felt comfortable with my
decision to both give Ms. E. a copy of the poem and to
read it aloud at the graduation ceremony. I have never
regretted this decision. Her experiences seemed worthy of an ode as tribute to one African-American female
who had risen to great heights from the day she waited
in an emergency room with her father after being
raped. Her rise was also symbolic of what everyone at
the graduation had accomplished in rising from their
chemical dependency, suggesting the collective impact
of the ode.

The ode has evolved into a tool that is intended for
practical purposes as orientation to entering into the
kind of group process we shared at Damon House. As
a collective ode on the transformation process that
may occur in group, this poem appears in a workbook
as introduction to the therapeutic process (Wallace,
1996). It is suggested that the poem facilitates awareness of the following seven issues that guide group
work:

1) When we have been physically, verbally, or sexually abused, we have to admit our own risk of
   becoming a physical, verbal, or sexual abuser of

others. This may be shocking and may cause us fear;

2) When we have experienced violence and abuse, because of what we have learned, we think that violence and abuse are normal ways of solving problems;

3) Because of our trauma we may have negative thoughts about ourselves and what we can do. Our thoughts are like a doomsday prophecy or negative expectation that we may unconsciously try to meet or fulfill;

4) We have family scripts for repeating dramas of family dysfunction inside of us. We follow these scripts unconsciously. Our children and each family generation that follows can experience the same abuse;

5) We have hope because we can break old patterns, and can create new dramas, new scripts, new behaviors, new thoughts, and new expectations for ourselves;

6) As we create new behaviors and new patterns of relating to our partners and children, and create new patterns of relating to each other in the group, we are moving closer to our highest potential or God potential;

7) We reach our highest potential by following Ms. E.'s example from the poem. We may need to fully process our pain. We may find that by moving through that pain we end up traveling a path that leads to healing.

RECOGNIZING TRANSFORMATION IN CLIENT AND CLINICIAN

Regarding my own personal transformation, my poetry was also serving an important function in my personal life at that time. Writing poetry served as a vehicle for me to allow myself to be a much more integrated human being who could, out of the therapeutic context of the group, process and fully feel the magnitude of the trauma that the women in the group had shared together, as well as my own pain. Just as Ms. E. had role-modeled for us all how to fully feel affects of pain, I allowed myself to express my emotional and intellectual responses to entering into prolonged states of empathy with women in deep pain who had survived trauma. When the ears of friends who could tolerate hearing what I had heard in group failed me, poetry allowed me to heal from the stress of intense trauma resolution work.

My intellect and professional training, with careful inculcating of all the "rules" of ethical conduct, had left me, too, in somewhat of a hard rock-like encasement as I broadcast the right things to say and do as a clinician. It seemed important that my personal transformation came to include evidence of my own emotional softening, as the public sharing of the poem revealed my own experience of deeply felt affect in poetic rhyme, pouring forth perceptions infused with deep feeling. Also, I demonstrated that "I got it" to the extent that I could articulate in poem the experience of abuse and the process of healing.

Parallel to my own transformation, Ms. E.'s transformation beyond the fall 1991 graduation ceremony continued on course. The water of her tears running and flowing against rock served to wear away the hard edges and served to soften her as part of her transformation. Similarly, the tears that regularly fell when I privately composed poetry served to wear away the rock-like encasement of my overdeveloped intellectual self that had memorized the rules of ethical conduct and tenets of Freud and Jung. She was less street and more emotionally available and whole. I was more whole and human and balanced, feeling rooted in the stance of an African matriarch who had nurtured dozens of women and served as the midwife when they gave birth to new selves through the group process. My own group initiation as a midwife seemed to count for something, as my own poetry codified. Indeed, dozens of women had been transformed through the group process. Women who had processed their pain and trauma in group could compare their functioning to upper peers in residence who did not participate in group, feeling free of some of the symptoms they could identify in these peers who were too busy going to school to attend the Friday group sessions. Mouthing the words, "I am so proud of you," I was the earth mother who mirrored with empathy the growth of women who, like Ms. E., had passed through the women's group and been transformed. It was the gleam in my eye, as the symbolic African matriarch, providing reparation for damage done by other caretakers that nurtured a healthy narcissism, pride, self-esteem, and self-love in the women in the group.

By the time Ms. E. marked a year in treatment and moved into preparing for her second spring in treatment in 1992, the calm of new stability in her personality structure reigned. It is not surprising that she was also found to be quite attractive to many men in the facility also in recovery. Ms. E. admitted to having feelings for and talking to one man in particular. I was not surprised that, in addition to having an argument with a female, Ms. U., the accusation of her having a romantic involvement with a male in the facility led to her sudden discharge in March 1992. However, at this point she was free of symptoms that had been successfully managed over the course of fifteen months as a member of a women's group and within the overall structure of the TC.

SYNCHRONICITY: CONTINUING RELATIONSHIP IN MY PRIVATE PRACTICE

One Tuesday during the second week of March in 1992 I held an early afternoon individual psychotherapy session with Ms. S., as she had left Damon House on schedule to live independently as a reentry client. Ms. S. was receiving psychotherapy (at a token, reduced fee) with me in my private practice, as did a handful of women once they were no longer in residence at Damon House. This was the same Ms. S. to whom I had extended the request to explain trauma resolution to Ms. E., even as Ms. S. ended by volunteering the following statement: "Trust her. Use the group." Having moved on to the reentry phase of treatment, Ms. S. still remained connected with her many sisters in the house and informed me that on the previous Friday Ms. U. and Ms. E. had a confrontation and that Ms. E. had been asked to leave treatment. I continued my session with Ms. S. feeling extreme urgency and concern. Immediately after the session ended I called the TC and spoke to a counselor. I inquired about Ms. E. Not having gotten very far into our conversation, we were interrupted and I was placed on hold. The counselor informed me that he had Ms. E. on the other line and she was calling to ask about being able to come pick up her clothing. I asked the counselor to give her my private practice phone number and to tell her I wanted to see her in my private practice. Ms. E. called me and we made an appointment. I sat at my desk shaking my head in amazement at this synchronistic moment in time, an amazing coincidence, saying aloud "This is God." The psychologist Carl Jung has described meaningful coincidences such as this using the term synchronicity. Others might simply acknowledge the spiritual working of a higher power, following 12-step language.

RETURNING HOME TO HARLEM

Upon her sudden discharge, Ms. E. was forced to stay with her father in his small Harlem apartment. The man whom she had described in moments of regression to the nightmarish Harlem apartment of her childhood torture, during the process of trauma resolution, was now a caring and concerned father. He was now sober and drug free, struggling on a meager income and with health problems. Perhaps he was working the fourth step of Alcoholics Anonymous' 12-step program and making amends, or merely was there at the right time in her life to engage in reparative acts. I was impressed with how this man had gone out of his way to get a day bed in his apartment for Ms. E. He was also an important figure in her children's lives, living in the same Harlem neighborhood and frequently giving them money for snacks, clothing, and the neighborhood game room.

As a poor graduate student in the early 1980s living off of $400 a month and paying $200 in rent, I, too, had lived in this same Harlem neighborhood, remaining until 1990. I felt very connected to the images of the either still active, recovering, or relapsing adults in my Harlem community who had been struck down in the prime of their lives by the heroin epidemic of the 1960s and 1970s and wandered the neighborhood as shells of their former selves, struggling with health problems or living on methadone maintenance. I could have easily passed or stood next to her mother in the corner store, or laundered my clothing next to her other family members. When Ms. E. went back to this neighborhood, through ever so clear mental images of this neighborhood, I could visually travel back there with her, seeing in my mind's eye Lenox Avenue and the school and game room her son frequented, or the laundromat where her daughter did the laundry.

As much as members of the 12-step network and recovering treatment community might have told Ms. E. to disconnect from her family, given their either "still active" or intermittent substance use histories, I was amazed at how reconnection with her family occurred in the real world of Harlem. Here, people originally from the South made and kept family connections and bonds despite having shared horrendous trauma. There was much more to her life that reflected these Southern roots than the remnants of a second-generation Southern accent that resonated against the walls of the group therapy room when she declared in group "I held her secret and she held mine." I came to feel gratitude and warmth toward the man I once felt was a beast when he regularly raped and tortured Ms. E. He was doing his best to take care of her. And, strangely, it seemed to be a healing process that he was "there for her" when she needed a place to stay to avoid becoming homeless upon sudden discharge from Damon House.

Her daily round involved walking through this central Harlem community and visiting her mother's house where her children lived, being temporarily in her mother's custody. She would go to see her children after school, witnessing the life they lived with her mother. Again, a strange healing seemed to be occurring, as this mother, now grandmother, was still far from perfect, still being a loud talker and drinker, but one who somehow was "doing for" Ms. E. by taking care of her children, having entered the second year of this arrangement.

THE SEARCH FOR HOUSING FOR HER CHILDREN

Ms. E. soon took up the task of searching for an apartment so that she could regain formal custody of her children. By the late spring and summer of 1992, Ms. E.'s daily round involved walking through this central Harlem community, expanding by bus to search the Bronx also, looking for an apartment that would be suitable for her and her two children. This was a most frustrating search, causing her to enter states of despair and to pray. When she was in pain, hurting, crying, and praying in the middle of the night for a home for herself and her children so that she could regain child custody, one summer night she felt the sensation of arms gently hugging her, embracing her with love and leaving her with a sense of peace and faith. Ms. E. interpreted this as the arms of Jesus. She was not alone. Her higher power or some spiritual force seemed to be present in her life and aware of her need, reassuring her.

As if moved by spirit to help her, older women in her neighborhood became involved in her search for housing. She listened to the bits of wisdom on how to work the system offered by every older Black woman in Harlem who had some piece of advice on how to proceed with social services and welfare to realize her dream. These women could also see in Ms. E. the respectful image of what they all yearned deep in their souls to see—a recovered addict striving to regain child custody. Instead of the prodigal son who returns to be embraced by his father, Ms. E. was like the prodigal daughter who returned to Harlem reborn drug free—a miracle these women could deeply appreciate. The context for their desire to help Ms. E. was a kind of collective yearning in the Harlem community, as it was overrun with skinny crack addicted mothers who were still caught up in active addiction or were "treatment failures." These women who sought to help Ms. E. were the multitude of aunts, sisters, grandmothers, and strangers who "took in" the children of these crack-addicted women via family court and foster care. Ms. E. was, once again, a collective symbol of what these women wished for—the recovery of every crack-addicted mother. She returned to Harlem the way they wished every crack-addicted mother would—abstinent, worthy of the parenting task, and motivated to take back the care of her children. Ms. E. emerged as a symbol of this dream realized.

With fierce determination she pursued her mission to regain child custody, seeking to meet the condition of having adequate housing. Ms. E. came to feel legitimate rage at the system for not sufficiently cooperating with her in this search for housing, as she pounded the pavement. Social services seemed ill-prepared for what was a rarity—a recovering addict working hard to get her children back. They seemed to not know, nor have much experience helping such women, although they were expert in the first stage of the process of taking children away from addicted mothers.

Her connection with the male peer, her boyfriend, now preparing for his own reentry phase and departure from the TC, continued and blossomed. Meals and movies spent with this male also became part of her daily round. His need for housing independent of the residential therapeutic community, as a requirement of his pending graduation from Damon House, coincided with her need for housing suitable for her children. By late summer/early fall, commitment emerged for these two to pool their resources and to get an apartment together, feeling that evidence of his employment together with her benefits would increase the chances of her securing an apartment suitable for her two children to be released into her custody. The coincidence of their need for housing and growing affection for each other seemed highly meaningful, enabling her to realize her dream and secure housing for her children. The wheels were set in motion for family reunification in November 1992.

To underscore the magnitude of her accomplishment, imagine the painful reality pervading this Harlem community. Her children were the only ones in the entire tenement and immediate neighborhood who were going back into the custody of their own biological mother, suggesting the rarity of one winning the battle that Ms. E. could claim as her success. Her children simply did not know any other children in their situation who were leaving it. This alone suggests the nature of the success of Ms. E. However, this success also seemed intimately bound up with evidence of a spiritual influence, whether through synchronicity and meaningful coincidence, or the actions of a higher power that acted in her life with compelling evidence of the spiritual dimensions to which she could even feel a tangible connection, as when embraced by loving arms when in a late-night state of spiritual rapture.

HONORING SUCCESS AT THE 1992 GRADUATION CEREMONY

A question for me as a professional centers on the degree to which I was to allow myself to enter the life of Ms. E. I was also a human being who was capable of appreciating not only the magnitude of her pain when in states of empathy in group and individual sessions, but also the magnitude of her growth. I had been present as a midwife to the birth of her new drug-free self, but I was also able to witness her stages of growth beyond the therapeutic community, as she was a client in my private practice who continued to astound me with her progress in recovery. In appreciation of the magnitude of her growth, forms of recognition seemed appropriate to honor this progress, even if it meant I entered her life outside the confines of the consultation room. It seemed to me that as witness to her overcoming incredible odds in winning back custody of her children that I was in a position to honor her progress and I chose to do so. The fall Damon House (1992) graduation ceremony was to again provide the setting for honoring Ms. E.

Staff discussion over the years about Damon House graduations had centered on how there seemed to be relatively few female graduates each year. Another common theme involved an apparent pattern of discharging more females than males when "undercover" romantic relationships were discovered in treatment. My decision to honor a female who stood as a symbol of being abruptly discharged, but who attained the highest level of success for a mother—regaining child custody—equated with justice in my mind. When the fall 1992 Damon House graduation celebration arrived I chose to give Ms. E. a framed piece of artwork with words I wrote honoring her for regaining child custody earlier that November 1992. As she was in attendance at the graduation ceremony as a guest of her peers, including her boyfriend, I called her up to the podium and gave her this surprise award, reading the citation. Her boyfriend, as a graduate seated up front, was able to closely witness how I honored Ms. E. with this award, as did all in attendance. Ms. E. received a standing ovation.

A FEBRUARY 1993 WEDDING

Yet another occasion arose where I had to decide if I would further expand the boundaries of my relationship with Ms. E. and her boyfriend. In February 1993 I accepted the invitation to her wedding reception, which was held in the basement community room of a Harlem apartment building one block from the brownstone where I had lived for ten years until 1990. I videotaped the reception, providing a copy of the tape as a wedding gift. At the reception I was the African matriarch performing practical tasks; I sliced the cake and passed out plates of cake, as well as stayed late to help clean up the community room. For me this was practical support in action. Just as I entered into states of empathy with her pain, giving what was needed in group, I did what was needed at the reception—slicing cake and cleaning up.

DOING WHAT WAS NEEDED: FAMILY, COUPLES, GROUP, AND CHILD THERAPY

Over the next year (1993 to 1994), my practical support of Ms. E. involved weekly and then twice-monthly sessions as needed, as well as couples sessions, family therapy, and therapy for her son. Ms. E. also participated in a short-term women's group in my private practice. This was a group in which her former Damon House peer, Ms. S., also participated, along with five other females from my private practice. Family therapy helped this new family learn how to communicate, with her son absolutely loving the opportunity to talk about his feelings and opinions. Her daughter refused to say a single word in family sessions, but frequently snuggled up around the arm of her mother. Her son effused warmth and a sharp intelligence, desperately loving his mother, as his frequent touching and long looks of love for her declared. Both children looked exactly like her. Issues of child discipline without resorting to physical hitting, as well as her son's acting out in school, called for my doing whatever was needed, providing appropriate support through varied modalities of treatment. There was a period when she and her son came for therapy, seeing them both together and her son alone, in light of his continued difficulties acting out in school. In these joint and other family sessions she pleaded with her children to avoid her fate and to obtain more than her own second-grade education.

Doing what was needed, this was my community service, providing treatment to Ms. E. and her family for free or nominal cost. Ms. E. also continued to do what was needed. She persevered in using the removal of the things her children liked the most instead of corporal punishment, as well as using time-outs wherein she separated her children in different parts of the house away from the television and radio. She despaired when these tactics did not seem to work and when the strain of child care seemed overwhelming. Yet, she continued to do what she needed to do.

Suggesting her success in doing what was needed to assist her son, Ms. E. was honored at the end of the school year in spring 1993 with a certificate for being an outstanding mother at the school, due to the level of her involvement with her son's school. Sometimes she sat at the back of her son's special education class, trying whatever it took to guarantee he be on his best behavior. He triumphed in graduating from elementary school, something she had never done, and going into junior high school so that he was partially mainstreamed into regular classes, moving out of his primary placement in special education classes. Paralleling her son's progress, her own progress in basic education classes was such that she progressed to a nearly fifth-grade reading and writing level. She was proud to share with me a copy of a one-page story she wrote about her life that was published in her basic education school newsletter. She ended this brief story, which touched upon her painful childhood, recovery from drug addiction, and relationship with her therapist with the following declaration: "I am a miracle."

CONCLUSION

In telling the story of Ms. E. and how we worked together as client and clinician and were mutually transformed, I feel her one-page story ending with "I am a miracle" says best the nature of her success in obtaining a state of stable abstinence. She can claim more than eight years of stable abstinence with no slips or relapses to crack or any other substance of abuse. But, to analyze how she managed to obtain this level of success, it seems important to acknowledge multiple ingredients. The benefits of the Bureau of Child Welfare opening a case for reported neglect of her two children upon the recommendation of her father and the positive outcome following her being mandated to residential therapeutic community treatment for nine months may be cited. In addition, the positive impact of a total of fifteen months in the residential therapeutic community, Damon House Inc. of New York, as well as her participation in a once-a-week three-hour long intensive women's group for trauma resolution has been discussed in detail. My continued contact with Ms. E. in my private practice and work with her, her husband, and children in couples, family, child, and group therapy have also been analyzed as my doing what I felt I needed to do. Beyond this, Ms. E. also participated in 12-step groups and for a short period she was an active member of a women's group at the center where she attended basic education classes. She talked in session, in particular, about women's Narcotics Anonymous meetings in Harlem where she told her story, always sobbing openly and deeply whenever she shared, moving other women to come up to her and hug her, while others were moved to disclose similar stories of their abuse in meetings for the very first time.

However, there are things that Ms. E. did not do that are worth noting. Her attendance in 12-step meetings did not meet over the years the standard of regularity that her husband managed to keep up. But, she was maintaining abstinence and actively involved in her children's lives. She also did not seem to maintain the number of social contacts and alliances with drug-free friends recommended as the ideal for recovery. Her friendships with Damon House female peers such as Ms. S. seemed to dwindle over the years into lack of contact. She also chose to give up the security of her husband's income, electing to separate from him and prove that she could make it on her own. I didn't think this was such a good idea, but she is making it on her own. As she admitted when I last saw her in December 1997, when she was negotiating a crisis precipitated by her son's poor school attendance, "I isolate." But, before we assess the nature of her isolation, her involvement in her children's and extended families' lives must be considered. For, in the very next breath she can describe taking care of one of her sister's children, nearly raising her for her sister, or having another sister temporarily staying with her, as well as visiting her brother in prison. All this suggests how she will likely continue to emerge over the coming years as the family matriarch, the one who can be depended upon for advice, practical support, or mother wisdom. I have reflected to her in sessions how I have witnessed her taking on this role, serving as the family matriarch in many ways for the past several years. As the family matriarch, she simply does what needs to be done.

In addition to a tendency to isolate, sometimes Ms. E. feels depressed. Typically, this depression is related to the frustration of raising her children and observing some of the subtle effects of their disruptive childhoods. She matter-of-factly pays for the insurance that she hopes she will never need; policies that will pay for the burial of her children. Her life includes intimate knowledge of the violence that took away the father of her daughter; she prays this violence will not claim her son. She has spoken of the pain of watching families go around the neighborhood and try to collect money for funerals. This is something she wants to avoid having to do. Ms. E. has hopes and dreams for her son, but wishes he would just go to school every day for now.

Once when I saw her in December 1997, Ms. E. told me about her meetings with the psychologist who had just started treating her son, following her appeals for help. The psychologist told her how smart and perceptive her son was, and how he spoke with certainty that his mother would not relapse from the stress he was causing in her life. In their private session this psychologist continued to explore the theme of her prolonged abstinence, seemingly baffled by the miracle of what he was witnessing. She told her son's psychologist, "I have a therapist I can call when I need to." I trust that she will, and when she does that I will do what I need to: see her for no fee, or a nominal fee, and do what I feel moved to do, perhaps by spirit or a higher power. I last saw Ms. E. in the summer of 1999, and I will continue to see her as needed, doing what I feel moved to do.

On another level, we might conclude that Ms. E. did what was needed in serving as a collective symbol of success, being a miracle, given the nature of her rise from the days of childhood abuse and crack addiction. On many levels, Ms. E. has done what was needed, serving as a prototype for the hard work of working on her trauma and deeply processing pain. She represents "everyone" who has felt the pain of horrendous trauma and needs to enter that pool of pain, trusting in a process that will take them to the other side, healing injuries to the soul and giving birth to a new self. She represents every woman who has ever been sexually abused, raped, and become addicted to drugs, carving out the path on the side of a mountain that others may follow in trying to reach a state of healing and abstinence. Ms. E. symbolizes the will of all of those from dysfunctional families who seek to persevere in breaking the cycle of family dysfunction. She symbolizes the determination of all mothers in Harlem and in every inner city to save their sons from the prison where their uncles sit, or from the grave. Ms. E. embodies the tradition of all women who watch one generation age and who find themselves suddenly serving in the role of family matriarch, bound to a tradition where she will do what she has to do for her extended family. While many wonder how communities such as Harlem will survive the ravages of the crack epidemic of the late 1980s and early 1990s, Ms. E. stands as a collective symbol of hope, again doing what needs to be done in reminding us that healing can occur, new drug-free selves can be created, and miracles do happen.

I codified what I learned at Damon House over three years about the process of working on and resolving trauma in groups, providing a guide for other clinicians (Wallace, 1996). Going on to work at other residential and outpatient chemical dependency treatment programs, I have met many miracles. I have met many in the process of recovering from severe addictions of many kinds. But, I most closely witnessed and observed over eight years the miracle of Ms. E.'s successful recovery from severe crack addiction. In the role as her psychologist, I was also forever transformed in the process. I have been transformed into a clinician who is much more grounded in being an African-American woman who can, in states of prolonged empathy, feel the pain of my sisters and share the burden of their recurrent visions of their traumas, which haunt them as flashbacks and frightening memories. I am free from the confines of what Sigmund Freud and Carl Jung said I should say, do, and think, as transmitted by my own mentors. In the sacred circle of the group, I witnessed the birth of new selves, after months of hard labor in short-term resolution of trauma in group work. I was initiated into the mysteries of being a midwife, following some sacred African tradition. I have fully felt the miracle of the healing of soul injuries. I am honored by the gift of being able to witness such miracles in my lifetime and am grateful to have done what was needed as Ms. E.'s psychologist.

Although I have endeavored to tell her story at some length, simply remember her own words, "I am a miracle."

Commentary by Andrew Tatarsky

Like all the stories in this book, the case of Ms. E. speaks to many of the central issues related to the successful treatment of people with substance use problems. First and foremost, it stands as a testament to the reasons to be hopeful about the possibility of positive change in the most apparently hopeless of situations. Ms. E.'s success suggests that, given the right set of circumstances, almost anything is possible!

Ms. E. was a woman who had been seriously addicted to crack cocaine for many years prior to the successful therapeutic community treatment described in this story. She had become unable to properly care for herself or her two children and had failed in numerous outpatient treatments in the past. She began her treatment this time around not on her own steam but by court mandate and, upon entering treatment, she was angry, disruptive, hostile, "street," and emotionally walled off. In short, like Frankfeldt's client, Donnie (see Chapter 5), she was the kind of drug user many would have given up on as a hopeless case.

Yet, despite this grim picture, Ms. E. goes on not only to make good use of the treatment for dramatic and lasting personal change, but to emerge as a leader to other women in her therapeutic group, to have a powerful transformative impact on her therapist, and to stand as a model for how we might all heal our own personal traumas.

How did something this amazing occur? Does this suggest that all severely compulsive substance users require the support and structure of a residential therapeutic community?

In this case, as Wallace suggests, it seems that Ms. E. had demonstrated her need for residential treatment by her numerous prior failed outpatient treatment attempts. Further, she needed the outside motivating pressure of the court to accept residential treatment in order to regain custody of her children.

We might say that Ms. E. was motivated for treatment by her desire for her children but was not able to mobilize herself without the external support of the court's mandate. In this case it worked, and it seemed to really reflect the fact that Ms. E needed this outside support; her own internal resources were not enough.

How might we understand her need for this kind of intensive treatment? Firstly, her crack use was intense and out of control. Her social supports and life structure had virtually disappeared. She was caught in the classic bind that many people are in when substance use becomes central to their lives. Drug use and associated attitudes and behaviors were both causes of increasing problems in all areas of functioning and primary ways of trying to cope with these problems and self-medicate the difficult feelings connected to them. Giving them up becomes increasingly difficult because it leaves the user flooded by a greater clarity about the current problems facing her and the painful feelings associated with them with few if any resources for dealing with them. If this weren't hard enough, like Ms. E., many users also have to contend with whatever difficult issues might have preceded and possibly contributed to the substance use in the first place, such as Ms. E.'s history of childhood abuse and the reservoir of pain connected to the abuse. No wonder many people find this vicious cycle nearly impossible to break.

Given the right fit with the client's needs, motivation, and appropriate timing, the structure and support of the therapeutic community may create the optimal conditions for enabling the client to give up old dysfunctional ways of coping and become open to learning new, more deeply satisfying solutions. Because drug use and the associated attitudes and behaviors were primary ways of organizing oneself and functioning in the world, giving them up may leave the user temporarily less able to function in many areas. The TC's consistent daily routines, rules, and clear expectations; the reduced life responsibilities of TC living, such as to earn income, pay rent, deal with the difficulties of family relationships, and so on; and the intense relationships with peers and staff that are likely to develop with others whom the client lives with and is in frequent intense therapy with on an almost daily basis create a kind of external "ego" or group mind that the client can rely on while giving up dysfunctional addictive defenses and other ways of organizing herself. This is the "safety net" Wallace speaks of that is there to catch the client when she is ready to fall free of her self-defeating coping mechanisms and symptoms. As this falling free experience occurs, which some call surrendering, it becomes possible to access the previously walled-off, powerful, painful feelings and experiences that can now be "processed," or resolved in new ways. Early losses can now be grieved, frustrated rage can be expressed, and ignored needs can be discovered and brought out of the darkness of shame into the light of current relationships where satisfaction becomes possible. In this circumstance, deep healing and personality change can take place.

This is what Ms. E. achieved and Wallace witnessed. What is also clear from this story is the universality of Ms. E.'s experience. Her experience spoke deeply to Wallace, as well as to a large group of professionals with whom she shared Ms. E.'s healing experience.

Wallace courageously shares with us the personal emotional work that the therapy with Ms. E. forced her to do on herself. This is a universal element of the work that people outside the profession rarely know about and that we rarely see revealed so clearly in therapists' descriptions of their work. Yet it is often the case that our clients force us to address something in ourselves or change in some way in order to be able to help them. If the therapist is not open to being transformed in this way by the process, the therapy is likely to get stalled and lead to a rapid unsatisfactory end. In contrast to many people's fear that their therapists are sitting as unemotional, uninvolved analyzers, it is often precisely the therapist's willingness to be emotionally open to being moved by the process that makes the therapy work for the client.

Closely related to this was Wallace's willingness to do "what was needed" to help Ms. E. For Wallace, this frequently meant breaking many of the rules she had learned in her training and engaging in unorthodox practices. This is one of the important themes that runs through most of the therapies described in this book. In responding to the uniqueness of each client, therapists often find themselves pulled to do what the client seems to need rather than adhere to some orthodoxy. Knowing when and how to do this in the service of the work is the art of being a psychotherapist. These moments of courage and creativity are also often the springboards for the development of new approaches to the work.

I believe that both of these qualities of Wallace's involvement in her work with Ms. E. reflect the real caring that Wallace developed for her. It was out of this caring that Wallace became willing to do what was needed. In doing what was needed in terms of strategies, fees, and so on, Wallace conveyed that she really cared for Ms. E. and sent the powerful message that Ms. E. was a person worth caring for. This was what Ms. E. had never gotten as a child; in fact, she was repeatedly shown that she was not worthy of her parent's care. Ms. E.'s experience of being worthy of Wallace's care seems to have been the kernel of the new self to which the treatment helped give birth, the kernel that sustained Ms. E. in her commitment to drug-free living, her efforts to successfully regain custody of her children, and her desire and ability to go back to school and become economically self-sufficient.

The story of Ms. E. yields another example of the power of the therapeutic relationship to inspire both partners to muster the courage and creativity necessary to bring about amazing positive changes in the life of the one in the role of patient.

References

Wallace, B. C. (1996). *Adult Children of Dysfunctional Families: Prevention, Intervention, and Treatment for Community Mental Health Promotion.* Westport, Conn.: Praeger.

Wallace, B. C. (1995). Women and minorities in treatment. In A. M. Washton (Ed.), *Psychotherapy and Substance Abuse: A Practitioner's Handbook.* New York: Guilford Press.

Wallace, B. C. (1993). Cross-cultural counseling with the chemically dependent: Preparing for service delivery within our culture of violence. *Journal of Psychoactive Drugs*, 24(3): 9–20.

Wallace, B. C. (1992). The therapeutic community as a treatment modality and the role of the professional consultant: Spotlight on Damon House. In B. C. Wallace (Ed.). *The Chemically Dependent: Phases of Treatment and Recovery*. New York: Brunner/Mazel.

10

Harm Reduction Group Therapy

The Sobriety Support Group
        —Jeannie Little

THE BENEFITS OF GROUP THERAPY

Group therapy has been one of the mainstays of traditional substance abuse treatment. While many people
with drug problems can benefit greatly from individual
psychotherapy, as exemplified by most of the psychotherapy
stories in this book, group therapy offers some unique benefits
that individual therapy does not. It should be considered either
as an adjunct to individual psychotherapy or as the primary
modality for those clients who are not able to take advantage of
individual therapy for practical or psychological reasons.

Group therapy offers many of the benefits of therapeutic
communities in a less intensive form. In groups, members have
the opportunity to see their own problems in a more realistic
perspective that helps to lessen the shame, anxiety, and guilt
that often accompany drug problems. They get to see that others
share their problems and that other people with similar problems have been successful at resolving them. These experiences
can inspire hope where there was none and engender the
courage and motivation required to try new solutions. Group
therapy can also be a laboratory for observing which interper-

sonal strategies don't work, for trying out new ways of being with others, and for getting feedback from others that can correct negative distortions about oneself. It is also a place where ideas and strategies for making changes in oneself and in the world can be shared, discussed, and tested. Finally, in contrast to individual therapy, groups also offer members the chance to use their strengths to help other members. So they also have the chance to access and develop their interpersonal strengths as well as working on their difficulties.

BENEFITS AND LIMITATIONS OF
ABSTINENCE-ONLY GROUPS

Since traditional substance abuse treatment has been dominated by the abstinence-only assumption, substance abuse groups have generally been restricted to clients who are committed to achieving abstinence from all mood altering substances. I have run many groups of this sort over the years and have witnessed the power that they can have to support members in doing some things they had been unable to do despite making sincere efforts before joining the group. There seems to be a kind of magic that happens when a group of people get together to pursue the same goals, a magic that inspires and motivates. We see this in sports teams, educational classes, and work groups.

The obvious limitation of these groups is that members unwilling or unable to stop using altogether are not admitted or are asked to leave these groups. They are often seen as "not serious" or "not ready" and a threat to other members who are pursuing abstinence.

This approach does not sufficiently consider that people's motivation to stop is generally mixed and can change for some time while the user is becoming clearer about the nature of her drug use and what goal to pursue for the long term. Often, people enter treatment in a crisis and with strong pressure from others that have caused their motivation to stop using drugs to be high. This can lead people to temporarily push their desire to use or ambivalence about stopping underground only to have it resurface when the crisis has passed. At this point a return of the desire to use or a decision to use may be a signal that the issues the person came to group for help with are now more available to the user. Asking the person to leave group or to push those desires away may be both unrealistic and counter-therapeutic. Just when the real work can begin and the group member has begun to develop supportive relationships that may help the member to make use of the group in addressing the issues that are surfacing, a termination from group can be a lost opportunity or a serious blow to the client's commitment to work on himself.

A requirement that a prospective member stops using to be a part of a group when she hasn't yet resolved her ambivalence about using can lead her to unwittingly push the desire to use underground rendering the issues related to this desire unavailable to the individual and waiting to resurface at a later time. I often saw this happen with clients in the treatment programs I worked for in the past who were mandated to treatment by their jobs in order to keep the job. Like Tom, the client I discussed in Chapter 1, many of these clients were able to comply with the program's abstinence requirement until the job's mandate was satisfied, only to return to using drugs, often with a vengence as if no deeper work had been accomplished. The striking thing was that the clients seemed to be very sincere while they were in the program. It did not seem that they were pretending in treatment but rather that the mandate had sent their desire to use underground and they themselves were surprised at how quickly and intensely it returned when they were no longer under the gun.

Bobby is another client I worked with who exemplefied this. He had come to an intensive outpatient program that I directed at the urging of his father, who discovered Bobby smoking crack. Bobby had smoked marijuana daily for many years until starting to smoke crack about two years before coming to us for help. Over the two years his crack smoking had become a daily habit that was causing serious problems in many areas of his life. Bobby joined a three time weekly group that I ran, quickly stopped using drugs completely and set about getting his life back in order and sorting out the personal issues being expressed by his drug use. After one year in treatment he left the group as a success. Two years later he called me for help in my private practice; he had fallen back into a very similar pattern of using crack and was once again in serious trouble. In our first meeting he told me that he had never really intended to stop "for life" while in the prior treatment program and had actually had a bag of pot in his pocket in his last group, intending to get high after group that day. Since our group had a clear bias toward complete lifelong abstinence and would have regarded any drug use or intention to use as a failure, Bobby did not feel free to bring up his ambivalence about abstinence to work on in group. This may have contributed to his decision not to discuss his intention to return to smoking marijuana, thereby setting him up to return to his former pattern of using because relevant issues were not fully addressed in his treatment.

While I do believe that this limited group should be available to those clients who request it, I do not think it is clinically necessary for many clients and that a harm reduction group with a less restrictive criterion for membership has many advantages for people pursuing a range of different goals regarding their drug use.

HARM REDUCTION GROUPS

Over the last ten years a small number of clinicians in private practice and a few drug and alcohol treatment programs around the country have been offering harm reduction groups for clients with substance use problems. These groups generally challenge the traditional abstinence-only requirement by making the group available to people who are concerned about their drug use and want to reduce the harmfulness of using without necessarily stopping. This enables the group to work together on identifying what is harmful about drug use to each member and what are the most realistic, self-affirming, and healthy goals for each member. Differences between members in their definitions of harmfulness and personal goals regarding drug use can actually help each member in her efforts to clarify this for herself. Rather than trying to "protect" members from others who express the desire or intention to use drugs, the harm reduction group sees this as potentially very useful to members who may feel threatened. The threat can be understood as related to some similar desire being stimulated in the threatened member that needs too be explored and addressed rather than pushed away. Members in these groups are joined together in the goal of supporting each member in achieving what is most important to him. Rather than requiring conformity, these groups honor the uniqueness of each member in a way that ultimately supports the value that each of us has to find what is best for us.

For this chapter I have chosen a story by Jeannie Little, a clinical social worker in San Francisco, who has been a pioneer in applying the harm reduction model to group therapy. Her story is about the development of a harm reduction group that she and another clinician ran with a group of homeless veterens with serious drug use problems alongside severe psychiatric problems. The story demonstrates how this approach was uniquely able to be helpful to a group of people that have not reliably found help anywhere else. The story is also the story of the evolution of the group and how Little came to many of the decisions she did about group structure and norms. She discusses both the rationale for her decisions and gives a detailed description of how to set up a harm reduction group.

The Sobriety Support Group: A Harm Reduction Group for Dually Diagnosed Adults
by Jeannie Little, CSW

Ten people were in attendance: three were abstinent, seven actively using drugs or alcohol. Seven were dually diagnosed (having a co-existing substance use and psychiatric disorder such as depression, schizophrenia, or posttraumatic stress disorder). My co-leader, George Gibbs, and I were facilitating the group. This group session began with a potential conflict. Joseph, who was new to the group, lived in a residential treatment program, and had been in 12-step recovery for ten months, began by talking in an agitated fashion about experiencing high levels of resentment and anger. Because he was transitioning to another phase of his outpatient treatment program, he was to lose his counselor and doctor. As a Vietnam veteran with severe posttraumatic stress disorder (PTSD), he was very untrusting of people's reliability, and this situation was quite traumatic for him. He told us his goal was to develop a spiritual program that, he believed, would keep him calm and help him to avoid negative feelings.

Alberto spoke next. In a long and rambling monologue, he talked about feeling good and ended up telling us that he had had a beer earlier in the morning, which made him feel "very well-balanced." This was an astonishing revelation from Alberto, who had never in four years of attendance spoken of his active alcohol use. The group took this in quietly, most of the members knowing that Alberto, who is psychotic, would interpret any response as criticism. Joseph, who was new to the group, looked astonished and started to challenge Alberto's assumption that alcohol would help him to feel balanced. Alberto rounded on him: "It feels like boot camp in here." He was using a metaphor to object to Joseph's challenge to his perception of his own alcohol use. I explained to Joseph that it is customary in this group to ask permission before commenting on someone's check-in, thus cutting off any opportunity for conflict.

Jose (severe untreated PTSD and advanced alcoholism) talked about feeling compelled to drink following a negative interaction on the bus. He mused for a while about how easily he is prompted into a negative frame of mind. Randy (major depression, extremely isolated, abstinent from heroin and alcohol) wondered about whether he could commit himself to volunteer work and be reliable. His focus was on fear of maintaining stable relationships. Arthur (schizophrenia, daily heavy crack cocaine use) said, "I can't say anything because I am still out there."

Harold (crack cocaine and marijuana use) began by saying that he wanted to "get out of Dodge." At this point, the group leapt into interaction. Harold had spent weeks struggling to figure out how to beat his employer's random drug tests so he could continue to smoke marijuana. He was also trying to maintain relationships with two women and was trying to avoid crack use. Suddenly he was proposing that, if he left San Francisco, he would have an uncomplicated life with no temptation to use crack. The group assumed that something had happened to upset Harold and reacted to his unlikely proposition by advising him that "doing a geographic" would change nothing, advice which Harold welcomed.

Mike had been quiet, and George and I invited him to speak. Mike is a chronic alcoholic with untreated PTSD, depression, and self-defeating personality traits, who has had many unsuccessful attempts to engage in outpatient treatment. He seldom attended the group, and when he did, he never stayed for the full session. On this day, he spoke about a desire to visit his family in June or July. I asked if he thought he should be sober before he went. (I had had contact with his family and knew of their concerns about his heavy drinking.) He said he supposed so. Jon asked, "How much time does it take for you to consider yourself sober?" I said, "That's a good question, June is happening in . . ." "Eight days." (Jose finished my sentence.) Mike said, "Well, perhaps I'll go in July." He and the group laughed uproariously. It seemed like a small interaction, but this kind of humor, especially for Mike, who never attracted positive attention, was important for the group to experience. And for Mike to have a self-revelatory moment in this way was unheard of. He stayed for the full session.

The group was quiet for a moment after this, then spontaneous discussion developed. Harold returned to the subject of leaving town and shared his fantasy that in a new environment he would be able to feel good about himself all the time, which would take him naturally away from using drugs. George said, "You will never feel good about yourself all the time." I connected Harold's fantasy to Joseph's, in which he would develop a spiritual life that would allow him to relinquish his anger, resentment, and pain. The remainder of the session was focused on many personal thoughts and experiences of pain and on the difficulty of learning to tolerate it in ways that were not learned earlier in life. The interaction between experiencing painful life events and emotional states and using drugs and alcohol was at the center of the discussion.

It is important to note that we never returned to Orlando's having had a beer. I was conscious of this omission. He had been uncharacteristically silent. Though it is better not to ignore such revelations, especially from such a committed group member, I made a choice to do just that. The discussion of pain and the need to be soothed was so pertinent to his point, and I could see him making so much eye contact with me, that I refrained from addressing him directly. I chose instead to let the group mood take him in, which it finally did, as indicated by his finally joining the discussion.

This vignette is taken from a session of a drop-in support group that has been running since 1994. I created the group as an alternative treatment for dually diagnosed veterans who were rejected by, or who rejected, other drug and alcohol-focused treatment groups or programs. The Sobriety Support Group, as it is called, uses harm reduction strategies and a drop-in structure to help dually diagnosed clients struggle with their drug and alcohol use. A drop-in group is one that people can attend as and when they wish. There is generally no commitment required for attendance. Harm reduction refers to any interventions with active drug users that serve to reduce the harm caused by drugs and alcohol, without necessarily reducing drug use itself. The harm reduction movement promotes and abides by a set of principles which are embodied in the group (although I had not heard of harm reduction when I started this group.) The most important of these principles are 1) that we should start where the client is and accept anyone who requests treatment without questioning motivation or goals; 2) we should conduct ourselves respectfully with our clients and trust that they are doing what they need to do, even when they use drugs; and 3) we should honor the uniqueness of each person's story and relationship with drugs and alcohol and realize that, in telling one's own story, a person gains wisdom about oneself.

The group is part of an outreach program for homeless veterans associated with the VA Medical Center in San Francisco. It was the first treatment group open to dually diagnosed veterans who are actively using drugs and alcohol and remains the only group whose goal is not necessarily to promote abstinence, despite its somewhat misleading name. I selected the name to highlight the group's primary focus on drug and alcohol use and out of deference to the fact that, realistic or not, most clients, especially those who have been exposed to the VA treatment system, avow a commitment to abstinence since that is the agency's orientation. The name is now part of the history and tradition of the group and has generated interesting discussions about the many meanings of sobriety, such as seriousness and gravity, discussions that have only served to enhance its members' feelings of importance. Clients and clinicians alike seem to ignore the bias inherent in the name.

The goal of the Sobriety Support Group is to create a

nonjudgmental treatment environment that will decrease its member's sense of crisis, enhance each member's sense of competence, encourage self-reflection, explore each person's relationship with drugs and alcohol, create a sense of belonging in people who are often alienated from societal structures, and promote the development of constructive relationships in which each person's intelligence and wisdom are important and useful.

The group became popular very quickly. In the five years that it has met three times a week, approximately 500 veterans have attended the group. Sixty percent of those have attended regularly, using it as their primary treatment for three months to five years. Only 10% have attended just one session. Attendance at each session ranges from 6 to 22, with the norm being 8 to 14 people. The group is heterogeneous, with two significant exceptions: All members are veterans and most are men. Typically, half of those in attendance at any group session cite crack cocaine as their drug of choice, one quarter use primarily alcohol, with the remainder divided between heroin, speed, and marijuana. Most are polysubstance users or abusers. Over half of the members at any group session are dually diagnosed, most commonly with a personality disorder, a psychotic disorder, a mood disorder, and/or posttraumatic stress disorder (PTSD) or other anxiety disorder. The group is also racially and ethnically mixed: Over half are African-American; slightly fewer are European-American; one to three Latinos and one Native American are in attendance at a given session. About half at any one time are homeless. Finally, approximately half of those who attend are committed to abstinence.

THE PROBLEM OF DUAL DIAGNOSIS

In my work as a clinical social worker on a dual diagnosis inpatient unit at the Veterans' Administration in San Francisco, I observed a pattern among certain patients who presented for admission each time they relapsed. These patients' social, psychiatric, and/or medical condition would deteriorate to such a point that it would be difficult to treat them on an outpatient basis, even if they had been eligible for outpatient treatment, which they often were not due to exclusionary diagnostic criteria. They were generally unwilling or unable to be abstinent or had difficulty complying with other programs' expectations and structure. For the same reasons, these were patients who did not join 12-step programs. Most were homeless, economically marginalized, and with minimal social supports. Most lived highly stressful, combative lives with no respite from their hostile environment. No amount of "advice" seemed to impact the "revolving door" nature of their relationship with treatment.

Dually diagnosed persons present unique treatment challenges. The effects of drugs and alcohol can mimic symptoms of psychiatric illness, making accurate diagnosis difficult. Street drugs can interact with psychiatric medications in ways that render them ineffective or unsafe. As a result, psychiatric staff is often reluctant to prescribe medications to active drug users until they are in substance abuse treatment and/or are abstinent from all street drugs.

Traditionally, psychiatric illness and substance use disorders have been treated in separate systems. Usually, one or the other disorder is identified as primary, and the client is directed to the relevant treatment facility. The disorders are treated sequentially, as if they have unrelated symptoms that could—in fact, that must—be treated independently of each other. The result is that clients, who experience the two disorders as interactive and often indistinguishable, are pushed back and forth between two treatment systems, neither of which can accommodate clients who have the other disorder.

Experts in the drug treatment community, many of

whom are themselves in recovery, have deemed the supportive nature of psychiatric treatment insufficient to confront active drug use. This attitude has convinced mental health workers that they are inadequately prepared to treat their clients' drug and alcohol problems and that treatment must be left to drug treatment staff. (Expertise in drug treatment, unlike in other branches of health care, has often been most revered if it comes from personal experience.)

Substance abuse programs have traditionally assisted drug addicts who have "bottomed out," are ready to surrender to a higher power, and are willing to follow the advice of others who have achieved success in abstinence. The style of treatment has been confrontational, sometimes aggressive, with a goal of breaking down the addict's defenses (especially denial) so that further damage can be forestalled and a quicker recovery achieved. This kind of treatment is unsuitable for the mentally ill, whose mental/emotional stability may be too fragile to withstand such treatment; this unsuitability has been used as an argument to exclude mentally ill persons from substance abuse treatment. In addition, use of psychiatric medications has been viewed historically with suspicion, and there are many programs that continue to refuse admittance to persons who are taking prescribed psychotropic medications.

The biggest problem is that of finding any treatment program that accommodates clients who are not committed to abstinence. All substance abuse treatment is predicated on the assumption that the drug or alcohol user is seeking abstinence. Abstinence is a requirement for entry into most programs. Even 12-step groups (e.g., Alcoholics Anonymous and Narcotics Anonymous), which are easily accessible and open to anyone, require only that one have a desire to stop drinking. Substance abuse or dependence seem to be the only diagnostic categories (in the *Diagnostic and Statistical Manual of Mental Disorders*) that require that the sufferer give up his symptoms before being eligible for treatment.

Willingness to be abstinent from alcohol and street drugs is perhaps the most complicated issue for the dually diagnosed person. In addition to causing or exacerbating psychiatric symptoms, drugs and alcohol also provide symptom relief and are thus sometimes used for the purpose of "self-medication." Just a few examples include the blocking out of traumatic memories, the temporary relief from depression, a curbing of irritability or rage, relief from the symptoms of attention deficit disorder, and reduction of symptoms associated with schizophrenia. In addition, many psychiatric medications have undesirable effects, which drugs or alcohol can counteract. Most notable are the blunting and/or agitating effects of antipsychotic medications. Stimulants can restore some sense of normalcy, and alcohol or sedatives calm agitation. Despite the special nature of mental illnesses and their treatments, the social benefits of drugs and alcohol are the same for the mentally ill as for others. These include social lubrication, peer involvement, and stimulation of sexual activity. These benefits may be especially significant for the severely mentally ill, who are often socially isolated because of their psychiatric symptoms.

I believe that just as drug use exists on a continuum from problematic to nonproblematic, so does dual diagnosis. In other words, all people who abuse drugs or alcohol, not just those who have a mental or emotional illness, may be "self-medicating." People who have abused substances or have become drug dependent often describe themselves as having problems with trust, self-esteem, and relationships. Many believe that they are using drugs to cope with pain or suffering, or with some felt imbalance in their emotional state or in their relationship with the world. The difference between the mental suffering of drug abusers and the mentally ill may lie only in degree and in the presence or absence of a formally assigned diagnosis. To the extent that a person experiences psychic pain that demands relief, and chooses to use drugs or alcohol as a means of coping or compensation, that person could be considered to be dually diagnosed.

The main purpose of the Sobriety Support Group is to engage this particularly vulnerable group of people in the process of evaluating their drug and alcohol use and understanding the complex interactions between street drugs, psychiatric illness, and life stress. They need not be committed to, or even interested in, abstinence. To engage these clients requires a low-threshold, or easily accessible, group, a group that can accommodate the chaos and impulsiveness so often prevalent in its members' lives. A drop-in group seemed to come closer to mirroring the pattern of clients' lives than any other structure I could envision.

HARM REDUCTION GROUPS

Groups are therapeutic because of such factors as universalization (seeing that others share the same problem), the instillation of hope (seeing that others can handle similar problems), support and mutual aid, and existential factors (seeing that life isn't fair and that not everything can be explained) (Yalom, 1995). Traditional substance abuse treatment groups tend to emphasize, in fact promote, commonality by insisting on a goal of abstinence as a condition of membership and by assuming that everyone's experience of "addiction" is essentially the same. Addiction is considered a disease that is progressive, incurable, fatal if not treated, and treatable only by abstinence from all mind-altering substances.

Harm reduction theory, on the other hand, assumes that each person's drug use experience is unique. Harm reduction is based on the idea that there is a continuum of drug use from occasional to chaotic, from nonproblematic to very problematic. Each person's experience, and the harm caused by drugs and alcohol, needs to be individually assessed. Likewise, there is a continuum of motivation for change, from those who want to continue using in the way they do now, to those who aren't sure, to those whose goals are clear: They want to use less harmfully, consume less, or discontinue using altogether. In addition, there is a continuum of mental health, from those who have reasonable emotional stability to those who are significantly impaired by severe mental illness. Harm reduction treatment requires exploration into each person's relationship with drug(s), into their ambivalence about drug use (on the one hand, one is aware of the problems drug use is causing, but on the other, one has reasons for continuing to use), and extensive work on the decision-making process. This is a complex task, even in individual work.

How, then, can a number of individuals, each of whom has a unique experience of drugs and alcohol, differing levels of motivation, and divergent goals, be contained and work successfully together in a group? The possibility for conflict is great. Moreover, a drop-in group cannot even guarantee having the same membership from session to session. How can a unified, commonly supported culture develop at all? Strange as it may seem, it is precisely the diversity of experience, motivation, and goals that makes a group like the Sobriety Support Group therapeutic.

Harm reduction groups can foster clarification of each person's own range of possibilities by providing visible evidence of the continuum of drug use, the continuum of motivation and goals, and the continuum of mental health. The only prerequisite for combining people with such diverse lives and goals, and the most highly prized value of the group, is validation and respect for each individual's choices. Diversity is imperative if the group membership is to represent the range of drug-using behaviors and options for change. Such evidence of variety of experience and of point of view helps to break down the belief in an all-or-nothing world where drug use is concerned (i.e., one is either in the throes of "addiction" or one is in "recovery").

Despite the potential for competition and conflict between different points of view, I have found that the group values my embracing of diversity. When I have questioned people who are "in recovery" but who continue to come to this group full of active drug users, each person says the same thing: "I need to remember who I am and where I came from. I want to stay humble. I want to remember what I am capable of. I never want to forget my roots." Likewise, rather than feeling ashamed by their drug use, active users seem to feel stimulated and proud when they see others' lives change. They are not used to viewing drug users—themselves or others—as people capable of successful mastery of difficult challenges. It is not just a theoretical concept that, by embodying the range of personalities and of drug use, a group is therapeutic. It is very meaningful in practice.

GROUP STRUCTURE

I began the group with a number of ideas about structure that were based on my understanding of these complex clients' needs. First and foremost, it is a drop-in group. Members are free to regulate the intensity of their treatment by attending as often or seldom as they need. I like to think of this as "self-dosing." The drop-in structure is my first step toward impressing upon clients that they are in control of their decisions and that they are entrusted with the total responsibility for gauging their need for treatment. A drop-in group is an ideal harm reduction intervention: By its nature, it engages the drug/alcohol user in a freely chosen working partnership. I chose to hold the group three times a week to give as many people as possible the opportunity to attend at least once a week and to give those who could attend more often something to integrate more fully into their lives.

I do not screen members before they join the group. Anyone can attend. Often, I have never seen a new member before his first group. In fact, he might not even have registered at our center or been to the VA before. It is possible to enter the group room without passing the reception desk, so anyone can join the group without having spoken to a staff member. Truly, this is a group with no threshold for entry except the curiosity or courage to enter the room.

The structure is quite simple: The group meets three mornings a week for an hour; it always begins and ends on time; it is co-led by me and another professional staff member; and it is never cancelled. This last point is very important. The more vulnerable the clients, the more they need reliability from group leaders (or any person in a helping capacity) in order to develop trust. As it is not possible to notify all members of a drop-in group of a cancellation, it will quickly destroy trust to have members come for a session that has been cancelled with no notice. This, in turn, will destroy the group.

Each group begins with an introduction by the leader, which is shortened if there are no new members: "Welcome to the Sobriety Support Group. We meet Mondays, Wednesdays, and Fridays from 9:30 to 10:30. The purpose of the group is for people to get together to talk about any issues you are having with drugs and alcohol, with sobriety, or with related life issues. You don't have to be clean and sober to come here. Just be willing to take the issues seriously while you are here. We will introduce ourselves. Then, at some point during the group, whenever you feel comfortable, each person should check in and say how you are doing or what you are thinking about. We will discuss whatever folks want to spend more time on after that."

There are no rules in the Sobriety Support Group. Nor is there any other structure. I have found over the years that the less you structure people's behavior with rules, the less they are needed. The group is guided instead by norms (customs) that have evolved over its life, by the clinical expertise and the sensitivity of its leaders, and by the knowledge and wisdom of its members.

The check-in process often takes the entire group session. Members do not speak in any particular order. If anyone declines to check in, that is accepted without comment, unless there is some cause for concern about that individual (such as uncharacteristic silence or agitation). People check in and talk about whatever is on their mind: how they feel, their recent drug use, what they dreamed last night, what they plan to do this weekend, something that made them angry, ideas stimulated by another person's check-in, and so on. This group is unlike 12-step meetings in that there is much interaction. Discussion about particular members' dilemmas, or about issues that arise, are part of the check-in process. It is also unlike interpersonal group therapy because interaction is not the point of the group, and it is controlled so that individuals can engage in self-exploration. Here it is important to mention a group norm: People must ask permission to respond to another person's check-in. This custom demands respect and allows each member to control the amount of input that he is able to hear. It is this that protects members from conflict over their divergent opinions and goals vis-à-vis drugs and drug use. It protects members developing awareness of their own relationship with drugs from the pressure of having to think in particular ways. Members value both the sanctity of the check-in as their time to speak freely without interruption and the spontaneity of interaction.

GROUP PROCESS

"Process" refers to what happens in a group, both for each individual and among members. There are three important steps to the process of each session of the Sobriety Support Group. The first is that each person has the opportunity, free of interference, to reflect on what he is feeling or thinking. The second is to focus on ambivalence about one's continuing use of drugs and alcohol or about abstinence. The third is for the group to join together in some common feeling or experience.

The most important part of the process is that each member be given time to focus on himself, which leads him to express his thoughts—to think out loud, if you will. It is the process of expressing his thoughts, in a supportive group with no interference or judgment, that enables a person to identify his wishes and clarify his decisions. The rest of the group members, including the leader, must allow each person his time and contain their own reactions. In one session, Eugene commented, "Sometimes I don't know what I think until I get in here and start talking. Then I hear what I am saying and can think about it. I don't come here to listen to anyone else. I come to listen to myself."

Identifying and working with ambivalence is the core work of this group. Indeed, it is the primary focus of clinical harm reduction work. The main task of the Sobriety Support Group is to help people identify their ambivalent feelings about their drug(s) of choice and to feel comfortable expressing these in the group. Everyone who is contemplating any major behavior change experiences mixed feelings about giving up the behavior in question. There are numerous reasons for this. Drug and alcohol use is no different. The destructive nature of many people's use is often not enough to negate the benefits of one's drug of choice, nor the feelings of loss when one gives up one's drug of choice. In contrast to the traditional (disease model) idea that denial of the consequences of drug use is a primary symptom of addiction, it is more likely that a person is aware of, but ambivalent about, doing something to change it. Group members, many of whom have been told in the past that they are in denial because they are resistant to abstinence, need to be educated about the difference between denial and ambivalence.

Learning to express one's ambivalence is equally as challenging as recognizing it. There is a tendency, especially in a group, for people to join together in agreement. Drug and alcohol users are especially prone to band together in group agreement. Despite appearances to the contrary (e.g., displays of aggression while under the influence), they have a tendency to avoid conflict. To reinforce this, group members' prior treatment experience of having to adhere to program dogma and rules breeds superficial compliance, lip service to concepts like denial, and fear of speaking openly.

I am most likely to draw out and highlight ambivalence during the check-in process. I will ask a person who appears to be zealous about abstinence and recovery if there is any part of him that would like to still use or that misses being able to use. This gives permission to group members to recognize their full range of feelings about their drug of choice and to realize, "It doesn't have to be all or nothing. I don't have to go from where I am now to a full commitment to abstinence." Over time, the group becomes increasingly comfortable with people holding various positions along the continuum of drug use and motivation to change, thus giving each individual permission to clearly identify his place there. Once a person's wish to continue using is articulated, the group can get on with the task of helping that person to manage his drug use. For example, a person abusing alcohol might be assisted to cut down on the number of drinks per drinking session or a crack user might learn to limit the amount of money he has access to in order to cut short a crack run. The group helps individuals monitor whether they are meeting their own goals and, given the freedom to explore their relationship with their drug of choice, those goals can change.

After encouraging each individual's self-definition and unique goal setting, the final essential element of the group that makes it attractive to members is that each session has some common experience that binds members together. In some sessions this has been an emotional discussion of a crisis in one member's life, such as the death of a child or a recent trauma. The group gathers respectfully around the individual at such times to share empathy and similar experiences. In other sessions, it is laughter about an interaction in the group or a particularly funny individual entertaining the group that creates the bond. In yet other sessions, the group is struck by an existential issue that provides the basis for an animated discussion on topics ranging from economic deprivation to separation from and responsibility for one's children to the ravages of long-term drug use.

GROUP NORMS

The drop-in structure makes it possible for the group to meet and to function in a manner appropriate to the needs of each member. But it is a group's norms that define its character and make possible its life and work. Group norms are those customary behaviors or commonly understood traditions and ground rules upon which the group leader and its members tacitly or explicitly agree. Group norms, taken collectively, define a group's culture and evolve as the group develops. The fewer rules a group has, and the more it relies on its norms, the healthier it will be. While they are held and maintained by the group as a whole, it is the leader's responsibility to see that they are maintained consistently and that they evolve as needed. Certain norms have developed that both illustrate and support the structure and principles of the Sobriety Support Group and that make possible the work of the group.

Inclusiveness

The Sobriety Support Group is inclusive. Its drop-in structure and absence of screening procedures ensure that anyone may enter the group at any time. The only criterion for membership is a desire to be there at that moment. The inclusiveness of the group was felt and expressed most profoundly in its early days by Antoine, a homeless, schizophrenic heroin and cocaine addict. By his choice, Antoine rarely received treatment for his schizophrenia. He was usually actively delusional, his speech metaphorical and tangential, and he was easily agitated. He joined the group in its first session. His major contribution was to identify the importance of inclusiveness. During one session he described himself lying on a sidewalk "like a piece of garbage with all these nicely dressed people stepping over me, turning up their noses and wishing I didn't exist. Then the police came along and kicked me around and told me I had no right to even be in the gutter." Whether this was entirely accurate is unclear. Antoine's point, as he passionately stated one day, was the following: "Society is like a chain: It is only as strong as its weakest link, and if we don't take care of the weak links, we are doomed."

Because of his unclear speech, agitation, and time-consuming monologues, tolerating Antoine was the group's greatest early challenge. The group could have disintegrated if I had failed to make sense of Antoine's place in it. My job was to listen very carefully to everything he said and not to give way to impatience as he took up large amounts of the group's time to articulate his thoughts. As I modeled for the group respectful attention to its most disturbed member, the group, by allowing me to do so, signified that it could accept anyone. Although people would become impatient with Antoine, and wonder how he was benefiting from the group, they understood that I would treat any of them with the same respect, should they find themselves in his condition. This acceptance of someone whose ability to use the group was unclear, but who simply wanted to be there, became the hallmark of the Sobriety Support Group and was very closely guarded from then on.

Another event that marked the importance of inclusiveness occurred in the second session. Kim, a long-term homeless heroin addict, was persuaded to attend. He had recently begun frequenting our center, parking his shopping carts in the waiting room. Kim had no previous treatment experience. He was passive and unengaged (much later he was diagnosed with depression). During the session, he fell asleep with his head bent awkwardly against a window. Other group members looked questioningly at me. Rather than ask him to wake up and attend to the group, as would happen in a standard substance abuse treatment group, I made him a pillow. The group was shocked. Kim became a regular member until he was admitted to a residential program where he began three years of abstinence, which led to his holding a job and finding a home. He has always gratefully acknowledged the group as the place where he got a foothold in recovery.

My intention from the beginning of the Sobriety Support Group was to create an environment that would be substantially more accepting than other treatment groups or programs, a group that would be able to work with the most complex substance-using clients. Because I was working in a social worker–run outreach center, I had the liberty of developing a very flexible group with no barriers for entry set by the program administration. I had only to challenge the tendency of those clients who had prior experience of substance abuse treatment and who were recovery-oriented to demand a level of motivation for abstinence that was not appropriate for all of the clients I was trying to welcome. On a number of occasions early in the group, I had to challenge the tendency toward rigidity, exclusivity, and confrontation of others' choices vis-à-vis drug use. What amazed me was that it took only eight weeks to transform the culture of questioning and confrontation into one of acceptance, generosity, and curiosity about others' choices. I shouldn't have been surprised; people were hungry for kind, expansive, and nonjudgmental treatment. I had been so accustomed to program staff's intolerance of drug use and of recovery resistance that I assumed I would have to work hard for a long time on partici-pants' similar intolerance. Not so. Group members' apparent intolerance was only superficial and they seemed grateful for a place where they did not need to pretend compliance to any particular program goals. The group helped me to maintain a culture of accep-tance, which continues to this day.

Freedom To Choose

Members can come and go as they please. People attend the group as often or as infrequently as they like. Many people arrive late and leave early. Someone can come three minutes before the end and consider himself to have benefited from the group. If anyone apologizes for being late, I say, "Better late than never." In addition, there can be an enormous amount of movement in and out of the room as people get coffee, go the bathroom, even go out for a cigarette. In leading a group such as this, with such varied membership, one has to expect a wide range of ability to sit in a room with eight to fourteen other people who are talking about highly stimulating or emotional matters. As one member stated, "You never know what is going on with someone. You have to trust that they know what they need and are taking care of it." Another member commented, "The structure must be flexible to make it easy for people to attend no matter what is going on." Although too much movement in and out of the group becomes disruptive, the overriding point is to be as welcoming and permissive as possible and to intervene as little as possible.

People can also attend the group without participating. A necessary component of developing clear ideas about oneself and expressing them verbally is the need also to be silent, to "isolate." Isolation is well understood as an occupational hazard of addictive behavior. Paradoxically, it is also a state that must be protected in order for healing to take place. This leads to my rather unorthodox practice of allowing, even supporting, someone to attend a group and not interact, despite how odd this seems in a group, which is typically an interactive therapeutic format. Thus people who are fearful of contact, or who are habitually unaccustomed to interaction, are able to join a treatment setting where they can take in different ways of looking at things, yet without having to do anything differently themselves. They can relax, which allows for more flexible thinking, and control the pace of change.

The freedom to come and go (or to come and not participate) corresponds to a basic assumption of mine that people are free to choose to use or not use drugs. Likewise, they should feel free to attend treatment as and when they choose. The first principle of social work and of harm reduction, "Start where the client is," is central to my thinking. Because attending the

Sobriety Support Group requires no commitment to a particular behavior or point of view, it is almost as easy to drop in here as it is to go around the corner and buy a rock of crack cocaine. (In fact, it might be easier, and it is certainly cheaper.) I have taken to referring to the drop-in structure and nature of the Sobriety Support Group as self-dosing. Just as people dose themselves with drugs, they can also dose themselves with treatment. Moreover, they get to regulate the dose.

Telling One's Own Story

Each person has the right to tell his own story without comment or interference. Unlike in Alcoholics Anonymous, where stories are also important and where it is assumed that everyone's story is essentially the same, I believe that everyone's story is unique. Telling one's own story is a process of discovery and involves unlocking one's own wisdom about oneself. If one does not discover and tell one's own story, one stands little chance to get healthier, whether or not this includes abstinence from drugs and alcohol. It is the means by which each member conducts his own self-exploration in the group.

Arthur, who in the vignette declined to check in "because I am still out there," normally describes very eloquently his life of daily panhandling and compulsive crack cocaine use. He is a highly successful panhandler and usually is able to raise up to $100 a day, all of which he spends on crack. Arthur is homeless, has schizophrenia for which he is treated sporadically, and takes very poor care of himself. The group listens with a mixture of horror and fascination. He is probably the most compulsive crack user most have known. There is no suggestion that he should stop; everyone understands his search. Instead, they get involved in helping him to identify what he is looking for in crack. People have, however, expressed concern that he is physically frail.

Perhaps as a result of this concern, and with the help of his case manager, he has more recently spent periods of time staying in a hotel, eating, and shower-ing. Arthur demonstrates the importance of giving someone space to describe his experience. He interacts poorly, usually staring at the floor as if he is not hearing anyone, and never speaks unless it is his turn. But when it is his turn, he comes alive, is eloquent, and engages our rapt attention. Because he has the freedom to tell his own story, and because we have interfered only very gently, he stays in the group.

Permission To Give Feedback

If people are to express themselves openly, there must be absolutely no consequences for any point of view or drug-using behavior. At times, the work of the group is to restrain negative, or for that matter positive, reac-tions. The most powerful norm of the group has devel-oped in response to the tension between allowing freedom of expression and curbing members' reactions to particularly stimulating or disturbing information. When the group began, I intervened often to stop challenging responses. Many people who attended the group were familiar with substance abuse programs where the culture was to "pull someone's covers, get in people's faces," and so on. In other words, part of being in a group meant getting feedback. After several weeks in the Sobriety Support Group, members got the idea that this was going to be a very different kind of group.

At the beginning of the second year, Ken, a Vietnam veteran with PTSD, who has schizophrenia and is prone to paranoia, joined the group. He very quickly became involved in altercations and had very little tolerance for feedback from others, no matter how supportive. "I am my own man," he said frequently, while beating his chest. It seemed necessary to reinforce respectful distance between members so that he did not become overwhelmed. It may have been he himself who suggested the following "rule": Anyone who wants to respond to another person must ask permission of the speaker to offer feedback. In this way, a respectful, nonintrusive atmosphere is maintained. A secondary benefit is that the person speaking has the opportunity to develop judgment about how much interaction he wishes to have, thereby developing confidence and skill in managing interpersonal interactions. Most people attending this group have had problems with relationships. Moreover, people with certain mental illnesses, especially schizophrenia, are particularly sensitive to interpersonal contact. Here, they can regulate the distance and the contact they have with others and maximize their comfort in group.

Intoxication In Groups

Intoxication in the group is handled on a case-by-case basis. When a group member arrives obviously intoxicated, the group discusses whether it is comfortable having someone there under the influence. Each person must check in with his own level of comfort or discomfort. In each case (about six occasions in five years), the decision has been made to welcome the intoxicated member if he is able to sit (relatively) quietly and listen. Naturally, it can be disturbing to sit with someone who is high or "tweaking," especially for people trying to be abstinent. But members value the group's inclusiveness enough to tolerate personal discomfort. "You have to assume that a person comes because he needs to be here," the group agreed one day.

Alberto was not the first person to arrive in the group one morning obviously drunk, but he was the most significant. A member since the day the group began, he had become the group's senior member and, because of his unique psychological makeup, served as the bridge between psychotic members and others. His identity is defined by his belief that he is "a social worker, just like you [me]. I help veterans that the VA won't help." No one has ever challenged this belief. He is easily humiliated, and the group intuitively understands this.

Alberto always insisted he was abstinent. His self-respect and his status in the group depended on it. Somewhat psychotic and disorganized, he tended to ramble about seemingly unrelated topics and could not be stopped until he was done, usually not until the group became restless. He provided an invaluable service, however, in his ability to understand people with overt psychosis and brain injuries. He could empathize with whatever they were saying and could interpret for the rest of the group. He was always right. He became the group "translator" and, as such, became an invaluable asset to the group. At the same time, according to the VA's medical and psychiatric staff, he was one of the most frustrating veterans to treat because of numerous vague medical complaints, never substantiated, which took him often to the emergency room, often by ambulance, and cost large amounts of hospital funds in tests that revealed nothing. The group allowed him to show his strengths and to be genuinely appreciated.

Alberto finally told the group that he was drinking by coming to a group drunk after about three-and-a-half years of regular attendance. Not only was he drunk, he was quite obnoxious. We welcomed him and encouraged him to sit quietly. He was unable to do so, so I asked him to leave, prompting an uncharacteristic outpouring of abusive language. This occurred about three times over a period of a year. Several months ago, he began to tell us when he was drinking (see vignette). Then he began to share his concern about drinking. It took that long, three-and-a-half years, for him to believe that he was important enough, valued enough, and would be accepted enough, to trust the group to hear, without judgment, when he needed help.

All of the group norms I have discussed here are based on the principle of respect. I cannot choose, nor do I know, what is best for another person. I may have concerns about people's health or welfare; I may have ideas about how they might act differently to improve their situation. These I can share. But my job as a therapist is to facilitate a therapeutic environment in which a person's drive toward health can be discovered and nurtured. It does not involve prescribing behavior. It was agreed during a group in which this issue was being discussed that "respect runs this group."

GROUP LEADERSHIP

During the same discussion, the issue of leadership came up. The group agreed that leadership is key to the success of the Sobriety Support Group, despite a strong feeling that the group belongs to its members. To members, the most important quality in the leader is the willingness to treat each member with utmost respect for his wisdom and his autonomy. Following are the other important tasks that the leader must attend to in running such a group as this.

Be Reliable

It is the leader's job to maintain a group's basic structure. It should go without saying that the group must always meet and meet on time. No therapy group can survive with unpredictability. It is worth stressing, however, that people as vulnerable as the dually diagnosed homeless, because of the socioeconomic deprivation and marginalization they have suffered, absolutely must have a reliable situation in which to develop the trust that will allow them to undertake therapeutic work. For these reasons, the group is never cancelled (as I explained earlier) and always begins and ends on time.

Minimize Conflict

Society, family, and friends, and his own thoughts ply the drug user with negative messages about himself and his behavior. Typically, self-esteem is low, with shame being one of the most common feelings. This is one reason that disagreement and conflict are so painful; they weaken what little confidence people with substance use problems have to speak their minds. Even a difference of opinion can be perceived as an insult or a challenge, which then arouses defensive anger. One way to stop this happening is to reframe all potentially negative statements. For example, if someone is describing self-destructive or outrageous behavior, and the group begins to react negatively, I might first ask what benefit the person perceives in that behavior. I will say, "Well of course you think/want to. . . . That makes perfect sense, given your experience." They begin to see their own and others' behavior as adaptive and clever coping devices. Pointing out the logic of each person's choices reinforces their strengths. The more confident people feel, the more able they are to think and act flexibly and perhaps consider other choices.

Maintaining basic safety is, of course, the first responsibility of the leader. No one should feel physically or emotionally threatened or abused. No one can work creatively in a dangerous environment. If there is any hint of violence or aggression, the leader should step in to stop it. All members should know that the leader is willing to challenge any threat to their safety. It is particularly important for people whose lives in the streets are often dangerous, and who must be constantly on guard, to be able to relax in a therapeutic environment.

Trust the Group

It is typical of professionals working with substance abusers, whether individually or in group, to be active and directive. In substance abuse work with individuals, the therapist's role is to guide the client through the development of new behaviors until he or she can internalize them. In a group, therapists are active in order to promote certain ideas (such as confrontation of denial) so that the group guides individuals toward the prescribed goal of abstinence.

I have found that, while guidance may be useful, the group really only needs me to be active when it feels unsafe. At these times, members need a mediator to manage or smooth a difference of opinion or a conflict, to reframe a perceived insult, or to soothe someone's anger. I trust that the group will take care of the rest. (They will often take care of these more delicate matters, too!) I trust the group to be sensitive to each member's moods and needs, often more than I. I trust them to fill the space. Given the room, their minds will be free to find what they need to focus on next. For example, in one session with a large number of people with schizophrenia and depression and very little talking, it looked as though the hour was going to be interminable. As I sat quietly, they began to free associate to whatever was said. The discussion that took place rambled over many seemingly unrelated subjects. The feeling at the end of the group was that it was one of the best they had had. They had certainly shared anxieties about subjects that might never have come up in a more controlled (or directed) situation.

Understand resistance

Resistance, in psychotherapeutic language, refers to the tendency of psychotherapy clients to resist the therapeutic process, despite their intention to work with the therapist on their problems. When understood and handled properly, it is the source of the greatest amount of information about a client's vulnerability: The things we resist the most are the things we are most frightened of. These things are useful indications of our most damaged parts. Understanding the sources of our resistance provides the greatest opportunity for therapeutic change. At its simplest, resistance to therapy means resistance to change or to feeling and becoming things that are unknown and therefore frightening. Seen in this light, resistance is adaptive; no organism would willingly choose an unknown existence when its current existence has guaranteed survival so far, albeit with a diminished quality of life.

When applied to drug and alcohol users, resistance refers to "treatment resistance," which sounds like the same thing, but which is put forth by substance abuse treatment staff as a negative assessment of motivation (that often renders a person ineligible for treatment). In fact, drug users resist change for the same reasons as everyone else: Change means an unknown life where survival, either physical or emotional, is not guaranteed. We cannot work successfully with drug and alcohol use problems unless we understand this; if we do not, we just strengthen their resistance or drive it underground and create false compliance with our point of view.

Manage Countertransference

Countertransference refers to any reaction of a therapist to a client, whether that reaction comes from some personal experience of the therapist or is induced by some behavior or characteristic of the client. It is the counterpart of transference, which is the client's perceptions of and reactions to the therapist based on his previous life experiences. The most common countertransference reactions likely to be experienced in a group like the Sobriety Support Group are 1) worry or fear about particularly dangerous or self-destructive client behaviors and 2) frustration at how long it takes for change to happen, at the repetitiveness of the relapse cycle, and at how unreliable these factors make group members. (By relapse, I refer to movement away from any desired change, not just a return to active drug use from abstinence.)

My greatest countertransference struggle was to tolerate people not showing up. I worried that the missing member had felt judged or excluded and I hadn't noticed. Or possibly I had missed the signs that a person was more emotionally fragile and needed more support than I had given. Note the emphasis on my responsibility for members' attendance. As vigorously as I protect people's right to their own choices, including to "dose" themselves with treatment as they wish, I still feel overwhelmed by responsibility for their comfort in treatment. As I have pointed out, I bear much responsibility for the emotional and physical safety of the people in my group, but they are still free to choose their attendance based on their own judgments about what is best for them. I must trust that they are making wise choices. This is my "thing" that I have to guard against: the tendency to feel too responsible for the choices others make.

Despite how difficult it is, the leader must tolerate the possibility that group members may destroy themselves through their drug or alcohol use. We cannot, by our fear of such destruction, become controlling, or even excessively opinionated, else we risk driving people out of treatment altogether. The more we are willing to treat disturbed and high-risk people, the more we must manage our own feelings about their behavior, leaving them free to think about their choices with a minimum of prejudice.

CONCLUSION

The techniques that the Sobriety Support Group employs evolved organically over the years in response to its members. I began the group with a number of assumptions based on years of experience with these clients and based on harm reduction principles: People are free to choose to use or not use drugs. Each individual knows best what he needs. My job is to facilitate the discovery or clarification of that knowledge; the most helpful intervention is one that provides a client an opportunity to clearly evaluate her options. Group is an excellent mode of treatment because of its potential to stimulate thinking, to promote flexibility, and to provide peer support.

Group members are the experts. In contrast to the one-on-one relationship between professional and client in which one is the helper, the other the recipient of help, group members fulfill both functions, thus allowing them to experience their own wisdom and strengths.

Group members continually reminded me of these principles over the years. I had to remain open to criticism and feedback in order to maintain the environment that they needed. I think that members always felt comfortable to challenge me when they felt I was not responsive to them. I did not always enjoy this part of the process, but I believe that this, more than anything else I have described, kept the group thriving.

Leading such a group requires maintaining a sophisticated balance between simplicity and common sense on the one hand and, on the other, a deep understanding of how to contain and transform the potential chaos of a random group of complex individuals who are often in crisis. This means being firmly grounded in a philosophical point of view and clinical practice and being open to create a fresh collaboration with the group in each session. In other words, we must have a good theoretical and practical grasp of the work we are doing and of the people we are trying to help and, at the same time, hold these things loosely enough that the treatment becomes a creation of the clinician and each new client or group.

Commentary by Andrew Tatarsky

Little's story illustrates how the harm reduction approach was able to be helpful to a group of dually diagnosed men that were not able to get help anywhere else because of their initial unwillingness to stop using. Beginning with the most inclusive prerequisite for membership, a "validation and respect for each other's choices," she shows how the group was able to be useful to individuals with a wide range of psychiatric problems and diverse goals regarding substance use. Some achieved complete sobriety with the help of Alcoholics Anonymous; some achieved a moderation of their drug use; and some were in group for years before they felt safe enough to begin to even address their drug use. In contrast to the traditional thinking about the need for sobriety groups that require abstinence, Little makes the case for and then illustrates the value of having a diversity of goals in groups.

Her story shows something that we've seen in many of the other stories in this book: Many people need to take a long time working on personal issues and developing sufficient trust in the therapeutic relationship, in this case to the group, before they can address their drug use directly. Harm reduction groups that accept people where they are and respect their need to go at their own pace allow for this work to go on rather than preventing it, as abstinence-oriented groups may do by discharging clients from group because they haven't progressed quickly enough.

We also saw how, similarly to individual therapies, her group evolved in collaboration with the specific group of people with whom she was working. The structure and norms were consistent with the particular needs and preferences of the group members. In this spirit, harm reduction groups with other client groups may evolve different structures and norms that are more relevant to their needs. For example, in harm reduction groups that I have run with clients with less severe personal problems and greater capacity for trust and commitment, there were expectations that members would come weekly in order to create greater continuity in the group. The key to setting up these groups seems to be that the structure evolves in collaboration with the client members.

Reference

Yalom, Irvin D. (1995). *The Theory and Practice of Group Psychotherapy.* 4th ed. New York: Basic Books.

Harm Reduction Resources

PSYCHOTHERAPY AND COUNSELING SERVICES

Addiction Alternatives
Marc Kern, Ph.D., Executive Director
Los Angeles, California
phone: 310-275-5433
www.AddictionAlternatives.com or
E-mail habitdoc@msn.com

Individual and group therapy using harm reduction psychotherapy, consultation, and training. Moderation Management and Smart Recovery meetings available to the public.

Addiction Treatment Alternatives
423 Gough Street   **445 Bellevue Ave.**
San Francisco, CA 94102   **Oakland, CA 94610**
Patt Denning, Ph.D., Director
phone: 415-252-0669
www.addictiontreatmentalternatives.org

Individual and group therapy using Harm Reduction Psychotherapy, consultation, and training.

Behavior Therapy Associates
3810 Osuna Rd. NE Ste. 1
Albuquerque, NM 87109
Reid Hester, Ph.D., Director
phone: 505-345-6100
fax: 505-342-2454
www.behaviortherapy.com or
E-mail rhester@behaviortherapy.com

Behavior Therapy Associates is an organization of psychologists providing scientifically based treatments to individuals, training and consultation to treatment providers, and clinical research in substance abuse problems. We have developed moderation training software and are currently evaluating the efficacy of a computer based brief motivational intervention, the Drinker's Check-up (DCU). The DCU is designed to help individuals look at their drinking, get objective feedback, and decide whether or not to change.

The Harm Reduction Psychotherapy and Training
  Associates (HRPTA)

Andrew Tatarsky, Ph.D.	**Mark Sehl, Ph.D.**
Co-director	**Co-director**
31 West 11th Street, #6D	**59 West 9th Street**
New York, NY 10011	**New York, NY 10011**
phone: 212-633-8157	**phone: 212-228-3467**

www.harmreductioncounseling.com or
E-mail info@harmreductioncounseling.com.

HRPTA helps potential clients find appropriate therapists who are selected by HRPTA based on their harm reduction approach to psychotherapy and substance use. HRPTA also offers education and training in harm reduction to professionals, paraprofessionals, and community organizations.

The Harm Reduction Therapy Center (HRTC)
Jeannie Little, LCSW, Executive Director
**Patt Denning, Ph.D., Director of Clinical Services and
  Research**
423 Gough Street
San Francisco, CA 94102
phone: 415-863-4282
www.harmreductiontherapy.org

A new, nonprofit agency that will provide low fee individual and group alternative treatments as well as train mental health and chemical dependence professionals in Harm Reduction Psychotherapy. Projected opening: May, 2002. Currently in the fundraising stage of development.

Practical Recovery Services
A. Thomas Horvath, Ph.D., President
8950 Villa La Jolla Drive, Suite 1130
La Jolla, CA 92037-1705
phone: 858-453-4777 (4PRS)
fax: 858-455-0141
www.practicalrecovery.com or
E-mail info@practicalrecovery.com

AA not for you? We offer an alternative to traditional addiction treatment. The core of our program is customized, intensive, individual psychotherapy to address fundamental issues such as motivation, problem-solving, lifestyle balance, identity, self-control, connecting to others, strength in adversity, and goals and meaning in life. Groups available. Family sessions available, in person or by phone. Our addiction services are described in *Sex, Drugs, Gambling, and Chocolate: A Workbook for Overcoming Addictions*, by A. T. Horvath, Ph.D. (outline and Chapter One at www.practicalrecovery.com). Moderation or abstinence plans (your choice). Referral available for the entire range of adjunct services (medical, wholistic health, dietary, spa, exercise, etc.). Clients from out of town stay in hotels and walk/drive to our offices daily. Psychiatric admission or inpatient detoxification is available if needed.

Stanton Peele, Ph.D.
27 West Lake Blvd.
Morristown, NJ 07960
phone: 973-538-0430
E-mail speele@earthlink.net or www.peele.net

Stanton Peele is unique in combining a long career as a harm reduction therapist—he defended controlled-drinking therapy when to do so was to endanger one's career—with a more recent one as an attorney who defends against misdiagnoses of alcoholism and coercion into 12-step programs. The Stanton Peele Addiction website is one of the most invaluable resources available in identifying the problems of traditional therapy for substance abuse, presenting alternative techniques, and guaranteeing the right to choose between them. Stanton lives and works in New Jersey, but also is a member of the New York Bar.

HARM REDUCTION CENTERS

Chicago Recovery Alliance
Dan Bigg
PO Box 368069
Chicago, IL 60636-8069
phone: 773-471-0999
pager: 312-797-2223
www.anypositivechange.org or E-mail cra@mcs.net

Chicago Recovery Alliance operates: 21 sites of Harm Reduction Outreach with syringe exchange, three sites of storefront-based exchange, and five areas of cell phone and pager access to sterile syringes. There is also an overdose management training program to empower drug users, especially opiate injectors to successfully avoid and cope with overdose situations. This program incorporates the medically appropriate use of naloxone as an opiate overdose antidote. We have developed a pictorial guide to safer injection and better vein care for cross-cultural utilization in harm reduction programs around the world. This program addresses specific injection practices which can greatly reduce infections/disease, tissue damage, and scarring. We also conduct educational sessions on various aspects of Harm Reduction for diverse audiences (physicians and addiction treatment staff to drug users and the general public). Conducting and/or cooperating with various research projects studying the effectiveness of Harm Reduction outreach with syringe exchange or utilizing the attractiveness of Harm Reduction outreach to study other drug-related issues. Current or planned research projects include collaboration with the Chemical Dependency Institute of Beth Israel Medical Center, Yale University School of Medicine, Loyola University, and DePaul University.

CRA believes "Recovery is Any Positive Change."

CitiWide Harm Reduction, Inc.
Executive Director: Daliah Heller, MPH
226 East 144th Street, 3rd Floor
Bronx, NY 10451
phone: 718-292-7718
fax: 718-292-0500
E-mail: citiwidehr@aol.com

CitiWide Harm Reduction challenges the stigmatization of drug use, homelessness, and HIV within the larger context of society through tireless advocacy as we build partnership and community among homeless People with AIDS. We are an inclusive, cooperative community committed to innovating quality harm reduction models and proactive strategies that promote awareness, education, acceptance, and self-empowerment.

Home delivery services at Single Room Occupancy (SRO) hotels include: Syringe exchange; Toiletries; First aid supplies; Referrals; HIV primary care; and Transportation to our drop-in center. At our drop-in center, participants are invited to access: Coffee; Couches; Clothing; Comfort; Mental wellness counseling; Case management, referrals, and service coordination; Psychiatric care; Acupuncture; Massage; Educational and cultural

forums; Support groups; More syringe exchange; More transportation; Hot meals; Showers; Peer education and training;
and Advocacy and other volunteer opportunities.

The Lower East Side Harm Reduction Center
Drew Kramer, Executive Director
25 Allen Street
New York, NY
phone: 212-228-7734

Full service harm reduction center offering syringe exchange,
coffee, couches, comfort, mental health counseling, case management, referrals to drug treatment, acupuncture detox, support
groups, peer education and training, advocacy, and volunteer
opportunities.

New York Harm Reduction Educators, Inc.
Vanessa Brown, Deputy Director
903 Dawson Street
Bronx, NY 10459
phone: 718-842-6050
fax: 718-842-7001
www.nyhre.org

Founded in 1990 by AIDS activists and injection drug users as
an underground exchange program, NYHRE is now the largest
harm reduction/syringe exchange program in New York City,
providing services at six street-side service delivery sites in six
zip codes throughout the South Bronx and Harlem. It is one of
the six largest programs in the nation, and the largest docu-
mented program in the nation.

The program provides the following; outreach services, harm
reduction services, supportive services, and stress reduction.
Mental health services provided are; sidewalk psychotherapy,
one-on-one counseling, substance user counseling, and group
psychotherapy.

Positive Health Project, Inc.
Jason Farrel, Executive Director
301 West 37th Street, 2nd Floor
New York, NY 10018
tel: 212-465-8304
fax: 212-465-8306
www.positivehealthproject.org

Founded in 1993, Positive Health Project's (PHP) primary mission is to reduce the spread of HIV and other life-threatening infections by providing a range of health and prevention services to a traditionally underserved population: people who engage in behavior known to cause HIV and other infections, including injection drug use and high-risk sexual behavior. As a harm reduction agency, PHP does not make its services contingent upon abstinence from drugs. Instead, they work with substance users "where they're at" on the continuum of addiction and recovery. PHP links harm reduction, recovery readiness, and relapse prevention into a cohesive, continuous model of service delivery through its redefinition of recovery and its focus on peer-driven support. PHP also advocates for the needs of substance users and for those who are HIV-positive, while providing a safe environment in which to obtain and develop skills in accessing services. Additionally, PHP serves as a bridge to other services, such as detoxification, drug treatment, health care, housing, and education.

St. Ann's Corner of Harm Reduction (SACHR)
Joyce Rivera, Executive Director
Cypress Ave., Bronx, NY 10459
phone: 718-585-5544
fax: 718-585-8314
E-mail sachr@aol.com

SACHR is a culturally diverse, community based outreach agency committed to reducing the spread of HIV among injecting drug users, their partners, and family members. SACHR works to minimize the potential for harm associated with unsafe drug use and unprotected sex. SACHR recognizes that there is a continuum of levels of drug use that lead to a continuum of harm; accordingly we work at developing a continuum of inter-vention levels for both the individual and the community.

SACHR is grass-roots and community based. We're located on Cypress Ave., situated above a group of shops. SACHR has been operational for over eleven years. The program is open Tuesday through Saturday. We provide a range of services within a harm reduction model. Some of the services that are offered are: a community gathering space, prevention case management, bodywork/massages, ear and full-body acupuncture, counsel-ing, homemade lunch, referrals, HIV counseling and testing, showers and hygiene kits, syringe exchange, condoms, dental dams, bleach kits, health and community education workshops. Syringe exchange is conducted both indoors and at outdoor locations. The program is grant-funded and charges no fees to clients. All are eligible to participate. Particular attention is given to the special needs of drug users, the homeless, people living with HIV/AIDS, and sex workers. We welcome diversity.

The Streetwork Project of Safe Horizon
Senior Director: Angela Amel
**Site Director (Midtown): David Nish, Assistant Director
    (Midtown): Ines Robledo**
Site Director (LES): Stacey Rubin.
**545 Eighth Avenue (between 37th and 38th streets),
    22nd Floor**
New York, NY 10018
phone: 212-695-2220
33 Essex Street
New York, NY
phone: 646-602-6404

The Streetwork Project of Safe Horizon was created in 1984 in response to the growing number of homeless and disenfran-chised youth in the Times Square area. We offer the young people we work with respite from hunger, cold, loneliness, and fear, as well as the opportunity to reclaim for themselves a sense of dignity and self-worth.

Streetwork Project is grounded in a Harm Reduction philoso-phy that focuses on building trust and fostering self-esteem, empowering youth to change their high-risk behaviors. Our long-range goal is to help these young people find permanent housing and employment. Last year, 1,302 homeless youth visited the Streetwork Drop-In Center and over 4,000 youth were contacted on their own turf by our outreach workers.

We offer the following services to youth up to age 22: Showers, food, medical and legal services, HIV/AIDS counseling, laundry/ clean clothes, and needle exchange. We also provide individual and group counseling in a nonjudgmental manner. Wellness activities such as meditation, acupuncture, and nutritional counseling are also provided.

MUTUAL HELP SUPPORT GROUP

Moderation Management Network Inc.
C/O HRC
22 West 27th Street
New York, NY 10001
www.moderation.org
phone: 212-871-0974

Moderation Management (MM) is a behavioral change program and national support group network for people who have made the healthy decision to address a drinking problem, and make other positive lifestyle changes. MM empowers individuals to accept personal responsibility for choosing and maintaining their own path, whether moderation or abstinence.

HARM REDUCTION INFORMATION, DRUG POLICY, AND COMMUNITY ORGANIZING

Addictive Behaviors Research Center
University of Washington, Seattle
Alan Marlatt, Ph.D., Director
phone: 206-685-1395

The University of Washington, Department of Psychology, established the Addictive Behaviors Research Center in 1981. Our primary mission is to provide research, training, and evaluation in the development and dissemination of interventions to prevent and treat addictive behaviors. In pursuing this mission, we are guided by the following principles:

- Our approach reflects a commitment to evidence-based practices designed to reduce harm and promote health.
- We recognize the commonalities among addictive behaviors as well as the diversity of individuals who engage in these behaviors.
- We are dedicated to increasing our awareness and sensitivity toward sociocultural issues and to bridging boundaries that traditionally separate the university from the surrounding community.

Will send selection of articles on harm reduction.

Harm Reduction Coalition

New York Office:	**Oakland Office:**
Allan Clear, Executive Director	**Maria Chavez-King, Regional Director**
22 West 27th Street, 5th floor	**3223 Lakeshore Avenue**
New York, NY 10001	**Oakland, CA 94610**
Phone: 212-213-6376	**Phone: 510-444-6969**
Fax: 212-213-6582	**Fax: 510-444-6977**
E-mail: clear@ harmreduction.org	**E-mail: chavez-king@ harmreduction.org**

http://www.harmreduction.org/

The Harm Reduction Coalition (HRC), a national organization promoting strategies for reducing the harm related to drug use and sexual behavior. HRC began in 1993 in Oakland, California as a working group of leading syringe exchange providers and advocates from around the country seeking to define the principles and newly emerging methods for working with the drug-using members of their communities. In 1994, the Working Group was incorporated in California as a 501(c)(3) nonprofit organization under the name Harm Reduction Coalition. Along with its Bay Area office, HRC opened a New York City office in 1995.

HRC is committed to reducing drug-related harm among individuals and communities by promoting regional and national harm reduction education and community organizing. HRC fosters alternative models to conventional health and human services and drug treatment, challenges traditional client/provider relationships, and provides resources and support to health professionals and drug users in their communities to address drug-related harm. HRC believes in every individual's right to health and well-being as well as in their competency to protect and help themselves, their loved ones, and their communities.

HRC promoted change through the following national programs:

(1) The Harm Reduction Training Institute—In 1993, with seed money from the Open Society Institute, HRC created the only national harm reduction training curriculum. Since then, it has offered hundreds of courses and in-service trainings in 20 states.

(2) Community Organizing—HRC provides unique resources and technical support to organizations and regional coalitions seeking to support community health and well-being through harm reduction.

(3) Bilingual Educational Publications—HRC creates, designs, publishes, and disseminates state-of-the-art information on harm reduction, as well as current information on regional and national activities, in our brochures, manuals, and newsletters, and on our website. These publications are also available in Spanish.

(4) Regional and National Conferences—HRC hosts the only national conference on harm reduction. HRC's third national conference, "Communities Respond to Drug Related Harm: AIDS, Hepatitis, Prison, Overdose and Beyond," was held in Miami, October 22–25, 2000. Attended by over one thousand, this was the largest-ever single gathering of harm reduction advocates, and offered over 200 presen-

tations by speakers from the United States, Canada, South America, Asia, Africa, and Europe. In the last four years, HRC has also hosted eleven regional conferences, held in San Francisco, New York, Denver, Atlanta, Seattle, Green Bay, and Chicago.

Lindesmith—Drug Policy Foundation

Ethan Nadelman, Executive Director	Glenn Backes Director, Health and Harm Reduction
925 Ninth Avenue	1225 Eighth Avenue,
New York, NY 10019	Suite 570
phone: 212-548-0695	Sacramento, CA 95814
	phone: 916-444-3751

www.drugpolicy.org or E-mail nyc@drugpolicy.org.

Lindesmith—Drug Policy Foundation is an activist thinktank working in the United States and abroad to advance drug policy reform through public education, public servant education, research, publishing, conferences, trainings, and media awareness. Lindesmith-DPF is working with other organizations toward a public policy regarding drugs based on harm reduction, a policy that seeks to reduce the negative consequences associated with drug use and drug prohibition.

Just Say "No More Drug War!" Join TLC-DPF Today.

PROFESSIONAL ASSOCIATION

Mental Health Professionals in Harm Reduction
Andrew Tatarsky, Ph.D., Chairperson
c/o Harm Reduction Coalition
22 West 27th Street
New York, NY 10001
phone: 212-633-8157
E-mail: Atatarsky@aol.com

An organization of case managers, front-line workers, counselors, and other mental health and substance use professionals committed to articulating and promoting the clinical application of harm reduction. Since 1995, through regular meetings, workshops, and conferences, we have provided a forum for this discussion and peer supervision and support for the clinical harm reduction work.

Index

model for treatment,
234–237
successes, 245–247
transition from alcohol to
relationships, 249–252
control and, 226
drug use and, 225
false self and, 221–222
harm reduction psycho-
therapy, 227–230
inner needs, disconnection
from, 222–223
rebellion, 223–225
reinforcement of inner voice,
226–227
revenge of inner voice,
225–226
split inner experience, 223
Cultural factors, cognitive-
behavioral therapy (CBT),
81, 88–89, 94
Cunningham, J. A., 96

Damon House, 267, 270.
See also Residential
therapeutic community
Davidson, R., 83
Davis, J. M., 92
Dayton, G., 12, 75
Daytop Village, 263
Deiderich, C., 263
Denial, of meaning, complexity
and, 136–137
Denning, P., 11, 14, 23, 111,
230
DiClemente, C. C., 109, 112,
243
Disease model. *See* Addiction-
as-disease model

Ditman, K. S., 17
Dual diagnosis, problem of,
group therapy, 319–323.
See also Group therapy
Dunbar, G., 83

Eisler, K. R., 54
Ellis, A., 73
Engagement/assessment
phase. *See* Assessment/
engagement phase
Epstein, J., 18

False self, critical inner voice
and, 221–222
Feedback, group therapy
norms, 336–337
Fenichel, O., 223–224
Foster, F. M., 238
Frankfeldt, V., 13, 139, 156,
157, 158, 305
Freedom of choice, group
therapy norms, 333–335
Freud, A., 57
Freud, S., 51, 52, 163, 187, 200,
227, 268, 269, 278

Gibbs, G., 315
Goals, harm reduction model,
25–26
Goal setting
case example, 38–40
treatment, 27–28
Goodness of fit, 106–135
case example, 114–135
commentary on, 132–135
presentation, 114–132
components in, 109–110

termination decision,
283–284
transformations, 290–292
experience of, 264–267
historical perspective,
262–264
Resistance, group therapy
leadership, 342
Rightness of fit. *See* Goodness
of fit
Rollnick, S., 109, 161, 243
Rosenberg, H., 85
Rotgers, F., 12, 75, 88
Rothschild, D., 23

Sanchez-Craig, M., 89
Sehl, M., 11, 59–70
Self-care, trauma, 186
Self-esteem, trauma, 185–186
Self-medication hypothesis, 2,
165–166
Self-observation strategy,
engagement/assessment
phase, 27
Self-selection hypothesis,
coping, 165
Seltzer, M. L., 84
Skinner, B. F., 73
Skinner, W., 96
Sobell, L. C., 83, 96
Sobell, M. B., 83, 96
Sobriety Support Group. *See*
Group therapy
Split inner experience, critical
inner voice, 223
Spotnitz, H., 140
Stern, D., 158
Story telling, group therapy
norms, 335–336
Straussner, S. L. A., 151

Substance Abuse and Mental
Health Services Adminis-
tration (SAMHSA), 16, 17,
18
Success rates. *See also* Outcomes; Treatment
abstinence-oriented
programs, 6, 16–17,
234–235
goodness of fit, 107–108
Sullivan, H. S., 222
Superego. *See* Critical inner
voice
Symptom management,
residential therapeutic
community, 271–272
Synanon, 263

Tapert, S. F., 22
Tatarsky, A., 23
Tavistok groups, 276
Therapeutic community. *See*
Residential therapeutic
community
Therapeutic relationship. *See*
Goodness of fit
Toneatto, T., 96
Thoreson, R., 49
Trauma, 182–220. *See also*
Vulnerability
case example, 190–219
commentary on, 216–219
presentation, 190–216
change and, 187–189
childhood relationships,
183–184
experience of, 184–186
past/present interrelationship,
189–190

About the Editor

Andrew Tatarsky, Ph.D., holds a doctorate in clinical psychology from the City University of New York. He has a private practice in New York City specializing in harm reduction psychotherapy with drug and alcohol users and he is co-director, with Dr. Mark Sehl, of the Harm Reduction Psychotherapy and Training Associates, a treatment and training organization. His perspective on the treatment of substance use problems has evolved over twenty years of experience working in the area as psychotherapist, supervisor, program director, teacher, and public speaker. Dr. Tatarsky has presented widely in the area of substance use and harm reduction. He has taught at The New School University, The City University of New York, and the Alcoholism Council of New York. He has directed outpatient substance use treatment programs at the Washton Institute on Addictions, the University of Medicine and Dentistry of New Jersey, the DiMele Center for Psychotherapy and Counseling, and the Division of Drug Abuse Research and Treatment of the New York Medical College. He is a founding member and past president of the Addiction Division of the New York State Psychological Association and chairperson of Mental Health Professionals in Harm Reduction, a professional training and support group. His publications include: "An integrative approach to harm reduction psychology: A case of problem drinking second to depression." In *Session: Psychotherapy in Practice,* 4: 9–24 (1998); "Harm reduction in clinical practice with active substance users." *The Addictions Newsletter*, the American Psychologist Association, issue 50, 5 (3): 4–5 (Summer 1998); and "Harm reduction psychotherapy with active substance users." *Harm Reduction Communication,* 6: 33–37 (Spring 1998). E-mail: Atatarsky@aol.com